THE SCIENTIFIC AND CONCEPTUAL BASIS OF INCAPACITY BENEFITS

Gordon Waddell CBE, DSc, MD, FRCS
& Mansel Aylward CB, MD, FFPM, FFOM, FRCP

*UnumProvident Centre for Psychosocial and
Disability Research, Cardiff University.*

CARDIFF
UNIVERSITY

PRIFYSGOL
CAERDYƊ

London: TSO

TSO

Published by TSO (The Stationery Office) and available from:

Online
www.tsoshop.co.uk

Mail, Telephone, Fax & E-mail
TSO
PO Box 29, Norwich, NR3 1GN
Telephone orders/General enquiries: 0870 600 5522
Fax orders: 0870 600 5533
E-mail: book.orders@tso.co.uk
Textphone 0870 240 3701

TSO Shops
123 Kingsway, London, WC2B 6PQ
020 7242 6393 Fax 020 7242 6394
68-69 Bull Street, Birmingham B4 6AD
0121 236 9696 Fax 0121 236 9699
9-21 Princess Street, Manchester M60 8AS
0161 834 7201 Fax 0161 833 0634
16 Arthur Street, Belfast BT1 4GD
028 9023 8451 Fax 028 9023 5401
18-19 High Street, Cardiff CF10 1PT
029 2039 5548 Fax 029 2038 4347
71 Lothian Road, Edinburgh EH3 9AZ
0870 606 5566 Fax 0870 606 5588

TSO Accredited Agents
(see Yellow Pages)

and through good booksellers

© Gordon Waddell 2005

Applications for reproduction should be made in writing to The Stationery Office Limited, St Crispins, Duke Street, Norwich NR3 1PD.

The information contained in this publication is believed to be correct at the time of manufacture. Whilst care has been taken to ensure that the information is accurate, the publisher can accept no responsibility for any errors or omissions or for changes to the details given.

A CIP catalogue record for this book is available from the British Library.

A Library of Congress CIP catalogue record has been applied for.

First published 2005
ISBN 0 11 703584 X

Printed in the United Kingdom by The Stationery Office

Contents

Acknowledgements

Many people have helped to develop the thinking presented in this monograph, directly and indirectly, knowingly and unknowingly. We would like to acknowledge the contributions of Linda Bates, Norma Bennie, Kim Burton, Rod Clark, Mike Daly, Peter Dewis, Katie Fawkner-Corbett, Bill Gunnyeon, Peter Halligan, Marilyn Howard, Jos Joures, Richard Kitchen, Chris Main, Nick Niven-Jenkins, Philip Sawney, Kate Stanley, Ben Stayte, Isobel Stephen, Patricia Thornton, Alan Tyler, Derick Wade, David Wainwright, Tracy Webb, Simon Wessely, Peter White, David Wright and Peter Wright. Many will recognise their ideas, but they bear no responsibility for the use we have made of them or the conclusions we have drawn. We thank the UK Department for Work and Pensions and Analytical Services Division staff for the DWP administrative data. We are particularly grateful to Peter Dewis, Marilyn Howard, Philip Sawney and David Wainwright for reviewing a complete final draft.

Declaration of interest

Mansel Aylward was Chief Medical Adviser, a full-time employee and established Senior Civil Servant in the UK Department for Work and Pensions, till May 2005. Gordon Waddell is an independent consultant whose work on this monograph was partly supported by a grant from the Corporate Medical Group, Department for Work and Pensions.

Executive Summary

The number of people on long-term 'incapacity' benefits in Britain has more than trebled since 1979, despite gradual improvement in objective measures of health. In the past few years the Incapacity Benefit caseload has stabilised but it remains persistently high. Yet many IB recipients are not completely incapable of work, many want to work, and all should have the opportunity to work. Thus, IB reform is a matter of social justice as well as of expenditure.

The aims of this monograph are:

- To develop a theoretical and conceptual framework for incapacity benefits for people of working age;

- To analyse the development and trends of UK incapacity benefits from 1948 to date, in light of these principles;

- To provide a scientific evidence-base for IB reform to meet today's challenges and needs.

This review demonstrates that there is a very broad evidence-base and a compelling theoretical argument for IB reform. Whatever the future direction of reform, it should take account of these basic concepts and principles, though its impact will also depend critically on how the principles are implemented and delivered in practice.

IB covers diverse groups of people, with different kinds of problems, in very different circumstances. Any reform must provide fairly and equitably for all of these people, taking particular care not to disadvantage those who are already among the most disadvantaged members of society.

Basic concepts of sickness and disability are often confused and obscure the welfare debate. Rational policy and legislation depend on clear definitions and precise usage:

Disease is objective, medically diagnosed, pathology.

Impairment is significant, demonstrable, deviation or loss of body structure or function.

Symptoms are bothersome bodily or mental sensations.

Illness is the subjective feeling of being unwell.

Disability is limitation of activities and restriction of participation.

Sickness is a social status granted to the ill person by society.

Incapacity is inability to work associated with sickness or disability.

However, the correlation between them is poor:

- The main problem in current trends is 'longer-term sickness' (>50% of IB recipients regard themselves as sick rather than disabled).

- Sickness and disability do not necessarily mean incapacity for work (50% of 'disabled' people are working).

There is a tension between the traditional sick role which is about the right *not* to work and the modern disability role which is about the *right to work*. Sickness and disability benefits are based on citizenship - a social contract between individuals, employers and Government, with a balance of rights and responsibilities on all sides. There is a pressing need for a new and more explicit welfare contract, more appropriate to today's problems, in which rights and responsibilities are clearly defined.

About two-thirds of IB recipients now have less severe 'common health problems': mild/moderate mental health, musculoskeletal and cardio-respiratory conditions. Many of these conditions should be manageable and long-term incapacity is not inevitable. *Provided* these people are given the right support, many of them should be able to (return to) work. These conditions are very different from the severe medical conditions and permanent impairments for which sickness and disability benefits were originally designed, which are still the public image of 'disability' and which are used as examples in welfare debates.

Many factors influence whether or not a health condition leads to incapacity for work. Health usually comes high on the list. But incapacity associated with common health problems is not a direct consequence of the health condition alone: it depends on interactions between health-related, personal *and* social factors. The less severe and more subjective the health condition, the more important the role of personal factors (motivation and effort, attitudes and beliefs, behaviour, functioning and participation). That does not mean these people are all 'malingerers': all the available evidence is that outright fraud accounts for <1% of incapacity and disability benefits. But it is appropriate to question whether all IB recipients are equally incapacitated for work and to suggest that claimants must bear some responsibility for managing their own health, rehabilitation and return to work.

There are also close links between poor health, disability, social and regional disadvantage, unemployment and poverty. Many IB recipients have multiple disadvantages and face multiple barriers in returning to work: age (half are aged > 50 years), poor work history (1/3rd of new recipients have already been out of work for > 2 years), low skills (40% have no qualifications, 15% have basic skills problems), high local unemployment rates and employer discrimination. Even if the health condition itself is not totally incapacitating, it is confounded by these other disadvantages. Uncertainty is a key issue: about whether they will be fit to work regularly, about the risk of losing benefits or getting back on to benefits if the need arises, and about the financial consequences of coming off benefits.

'Incapacity' benefits contain a fundamental paradox: claimants must demonstrate their *in*capacity for work to establish and maintain entitlement to benefits, but obtaining/returning to work depends on their *capacity* for work. Too often, long-term 'incapacity' wrote people off, created negative expectations and welfare dependency, and trapped people on benefits till retirement age.

Historically, social security in UK was about passive benefits and failed to provide any active support into work. To achieve political consensus, gain the essential cooperation of all the key stakeholders, and deliver real and lasting change, benefit reform should be led by more active support into work, tailored to suit individual needs and designed to help overcome the health-related, personal and social barriers to work. Three key elements underpin IB reform:

• Better clinical and occupational management (particularly of common health problems).

• Re-structuring and re-naming the benefit to 'unbundle' sickness, disability and incapacity for work.

• A much stronger focus on providing opportunities, a new system of support (*Pathways*), and incentives to promote 'work for those who can'.

That positive lead should provide the moral and political justification for a more fundamental debate about 'incapacity', which could potentially have much greater impact on benefit trends than any direct effect of Pathways.

The PCA is often described as the 'Gateway' to IB, but there are actually two gateways to incapacity:

• The primary social gateway to sickness

• The formal DWP gateway to longer-term benefits.

Initial entry to sickness depends on decisions by the individual, the GP and the employer. These early stages are vital, because the evidence shows that the optimum window of opportunity for effective rehabilitation and reintegration is between about 1-6 months off work. DWP has no direct involvement in the primary gateway but can influence the other players.

The DWP 'Gateway' to benefits is based on four principles:

• The DWP Gateway is the only entry to longer-term benefits and no claimant should receive these benefits without passing this gateway.

- The DWP Gateway should be under the sole control of DWP.

- Decisions should be evidence-based, robust and resistant to drift.

- Award of 'incapacity' benefits should be clearly linked to remaining capacities, rehabilitation and support into work.

A fundamental difficulty in the present IB regime and a key question for future policy is the extent to which entitlement and assessment are based on objective evidence of recognisable medical conditions and impairment vs. claimants' self-report of subjective symptoms and limitations. The threshold for incapacity is when sickness or disability makes it 'unreasonable' to expect the claimant to attempt or make efforts to (return to) work. In many common health problems this is ultimately a social rather than a medical judgment.

DWP cannot do this alone. Benefit trends represent the sum of millions of individual decisions and behaviours, by sick and disabled people, their GPs and employers, and DWP staff. Real and lasting reversal of current trends depends on getting enough of these people to change what they do. That will only happen if there is a fundamental shift in the culture of health and work, sickness and 'incapacity', and that in turn depends on getting all of these key stakeholders on side. Crucially, that depends on the reforms being perceived as positive and in everyone's best interests, and avoiding antagonistic approaches and confrontation.

IB reform should reflect and will depend on that cultural change, and form part of the change, rather than expecting it to be the sole or even the primary driver of change. But the situation is eminently changeable and could potentially deliver huge gains for society, employers, DWP, the NHS and, most important, for sick and disabled people themselves and their families. The challenge of changing the culture of sickness, disability and incapacity should not be underestimated, but neither should the prize. The vision is an active benefit system that provides sick and disabled people with the help they need to fulfil their potential and participate in society as fully as possible. Reducing long-term worklessness is one of the most potent interventions to improve physical and mental health, and to address social disadvantage and poverty. That is not just about social security benefits and expenditure: it is about citizenship, social justice and fairness.

These are some of the issues that IB reform must take into account, though detailed consideration of how to operationalise them will only be possible once key policy decisions have been made about the structure of any new benefit.

Key Points

1. On balance, the evidence shows that work is good for physical and mental health and well-being, while there is strong evidence that worklessness is harmful to physical and mental health.

2. The IB caseload has more than trebled since 1979, but it has stabilized in the last few years at about 2.6 million (7.6% of the working age population). Inflow has fallen from 1 million to about 700,000 per annum since 1995; outflow has also fallen but duration on benefits has increased.

3. After 1 year on IB, the balance of probabilities is that recipients will remain on IB till they reach retirement age.

4. IB covers diverse groups of people, with different kinds of problems, in different situations. More than half regard themselves as 'sick' rather than 'disabled'.

5. Severe medical conditions (e.g. blindness, neurological disease, psychoses) now account for <25% of the IB caseload. Most IB recipients have less severe 'common health problems': 42% mental health conditions; 21% musculoskeletal conditions; 11% cardio-respiratory conditions.

6. These conditions should be manageable and long-term incapacity is not inevitable.

7. While accepting these people have health conditions that may cause some limitations, many IB recipients are not completely incapable of all work.

8. 90% of IB claimants initially expect to return to work. A million IB recipients still say they want to work.

9. Many factors influence whether or not a health condition leads to incapacity for work. Incapacity associated with common health problems depends on interactions between health-related, personal and social factors. Personal factors (motivation and effort, attitudes and beliefs, behaviour, functioning and participation) play a central role, particularly in less severe and subjective conditions.

10. Many IB recipients also have multiple disadvantages and barriers to work: age (half are aged > 50 years), poor work history (1/3rd of new recipients have already been out of work for >2 years), low skills (40% have no qualifications, 15% have basic skills problems), high local unemployment rates (ten-fold local variation in numbers on IB) and employer discrimination.

11. Basic IB rates are only £57-76 per week, but total disability and incapacity payments average about £6,500 per annum, not allowing for Housing Benefit and other sources of income. However, there is wide variation: many IB recipients receive much more generous benefits than commonly believed, but an important minority still live in poverty.

12. Only about 1.5% of current IB expenditure is spent on helping IB recipients into work, compared with 27% for JSA.

13. Rehabilitation and support into work interventions for common health problems must address all of the health-related, personal and social barriers to (return to) work. Pathways delivers this with a combination of NHS 'condition management programmes' and 'employment support' from Jobcentre Plus Personal Advisers.

14. The optimum window of opportunity for effective intervention is between about 1-6+ months off work.

15. Preliminary results of the *Pathways* pilots show an 8-10% increase in the IB outflow rate. On a national basis, Pathways might help up to 100,000 people into work each year, but there are widely varying estimates of the likely impact on the long-term caseload.

16. Up to 1 million IB recipients could potentially (return to) work, *provided* they were given the right opportunities, support and incentives.

1 INTRODUCTION

Cooperation and mutual support in adversity are among the earliest and most fundamental hallmarks of human society. The concept of 'the common weal'[1] embodies a sense of values and social responsibility and willingness to help others that determines the kind of civilised society we want to live in[2] .

Social security systems for sickness and disability date from the social, industrial and medical revolutions of the 19th century and the need to provide for industrial injuries. About that time, it was also recognised that economic inactivity and poverty are often not personal failures but may be the result of complex economic and social factors beyond the control of the individual[3]. Only the state can provide ultimate cover for the traditional risks of occupational injury, sickness, old age and unemployment[4], particularly for the more disadvantaged members of society who do not have the resources to provide that cover for themselves. This is not entirely altruistic: social insurance not only protects individual workers but also supports the economic, social and political stability of society. Since World War II, the original concept of social *insurance* has evolved into a broader concept of social *security*, and the focus has shifted from the industrial worker to the citizen *per se* (Marshall 1950, Council of Europe 1996, 2003a, Palme 2003, Euzeby 2004). This is now a matter of basic human, political and social rights (United Nations 1948), but with rights come costs and responsibilities.

From the first civil attempts to address poverty, account was taken of the individual's condition, including health and disability (Vives 1526, Sigerist 1929). Since that time all welfare systems have made special arrangements for sick and disabled people. The generally accepted rationale (Mackay & Rowlingson 1999) is because:

- Sick and disabled people are regarded as 'deserving' because their situation is not due to any fault of their own[5] – though we need to come back to the question of personal responsibility.

- The assumptions that sickness or disability automatically mean incapacity for work and that disability status is permanent[6] - even though we will show these assumptions are untrue.

- People with long-term sickness or disability are often at risk of poverty because of loss of income and additional costs – which certainly can be true.

There is broad socio-political consensus - among the electorate (those who stand to benefit at present and the rest who may need to in future), MPs of all parties, and the House of Lords - on the need to provide for sick and disabled people. There may be debate about how, to what extent and on what conditions, but there has been no serious question about the principle. All surveys show high and well-maintained levels of public support, even if there are concerns about the costs and the need to direct support to those who 'really' need it, and acceptance of the need for reform (Stafford 1998, Williams *et al* 1999, OECD 2003). However, that immediately raises practical questions about how to define and identify which individuals should receive that support.

This review considers 'incapacity' benefits for people who are unable to work because of sickness or disability. It starts from the premise that there will continue to be some specific form of income replacement, because inability to earn causes some of the greatest financial, social and human impact of sickness and disability[7]. There are other options for benefit reform[8], but consideration of these would open a much broader debate. The primary focus of this review is on Incapacity Benefit (now including Severe Disablement Allowance) and its possible replacement, but Statutory Sick Pay, disability premiums, and the disability element of Working Tax Credit are also included where appropriate. The generic term 'incapacity benefits' is used to include all of these financial benefits. The term 'IB' is used specifically when discussing claimants or recipients of the current Incapacity Benefit.

Any review of incapacity must logically also consider support into work arrangements. The Government's philosophy of 'work for those who can, security for those who cannot' (HM Government 1998a) reflects two broad policy goals (OECD 2003):

- Social protection: to provide adequate income support for people whose capacity for work is limited by sickness or disability (benefit transfer programmes - passive policies).

- Social integration: to provide realistic opportunities and support for sick and disabled people who are able to work; to enable disabled people to participate as fully as possible in society (employment and integration measures - active policies).

Social protection and social integration policies complement each other, but there is some inevitable tension between them (Reno *et al* 1997). They have different historical origins, aim to solve different problems, are based on different philosophical approaches, and in a sense offer alternative solutions[9]. To resolve that tension, these two approaches should be integrated as effectively as possible, so that financial support is balanced with more active support into work, tailored to suit individual needs.

Incapacity benefits are only one part of social policy for sickness and disability, and any IB reform must be planned within that broader context. Sickness raises all the issues of health policy and clinical management (Dept of Health 2004a). Disability raises all the issues of human rights and social inclusion (Oliver & Barnes 1998, Drake 1999). Both are intertwined with employment and anti-poverty policies and targets (Strategy Unit 2005) and employers have a critical role to play (HSE 2000, 2004, DWP 2003a &b, 2004). Pragmatic limitations place these areas beyond the scope of this review except in so far as they impinge directly on incapacity benefits and support into work. Nevertheless, they are fundamental to this analysis, which will try to incorporate their philosophies as far as possible. More specifically, incapacity benefits are only one of the social security benefits for sick and disabled people. However, Disability Living Allowance and Industrial Injury Disablement Benefit are each the subject of separate DWP reviews, so they are excluded from the present review except where directly relevant.

Over the past 50 years, there have been profound economic, social, cultural and political changes in society (Box 1), to which social security systems must adapt. So welfare reform is not new and every generation must make choices (Blair 1999, 2004). The expansion of social security has placed enormous financial strain on the system, and the ultimate questions have always been what the taxpayer is prepared to pay for[10], and how to make best, fairest and most efficient use of finite resources. The issues remain: what support to provide, how to direct it to those in need, how to pay for it, and how to balance the needs and desires of individuals and society. The challenge of welfare reform is how best to reconcile these choices in today's and tomorrow's circumstances. Periodically, it is necessary to return to first principles and revisit

---

Box 1: Social changes since 1948.

- Economic prosperity and rising material standards of living
- Labour market changes and patterns of work (globalisation, greater flexibility & mobility, more part-time and fixed contract working, lower job security)
- Overall higher levels of economic activity, but also higher levels of (male) unemployment (since the 1980s)
- The role of women and family structures (in particular the number of women working, gender equality issues and lone parent families)
- Increasing female participation in the labour market, but an increasing minority of men detached from the labour market
- Patterns of retirement (increased life expectancy, increased availability of employment pensions, trends to early retirement, working fewer years but living longer in retirement)
- Attitudes to work, sickness, disability and social security benefits
- Emphasis on human (including disability) rights (not always matched by responsibilities)
- Individual liberty and rising expectations
- Disenchantment with state and professional 'authority'

---

the questions: What do we want the welfare system to achieve? Are we achieving it? How do we need to modify policy and practice to better achieve what we want?

Surprisingly, given the importance of social security for sickness and disability and the scale of the expenditure, welfare philosophy in UK (from Tawney, Beveridge, Marshall and Titmuss to Lilley and Field) has paid little attention to this area. For the past few decades in Britain, disabled people, their organisations and academic writing on disability have concentrated on the struggle for disability rights and social inclusion. In welfare debates, the disability lobby[11] has usually pursued its vested interest in a weaker Gateway to benefits and higher benefit levels. More generally, many of the stakeholders and large parts of the literature seem to accept symptoms and limitations at face value and take it for granted that they justify incapacity and hence benefits[12]. Welfare debate has often been a subsidiary part of the economic debate, rather than based on social or moral grounds. Most benefit reforms in this area have been pragmatic, with little attempt to understand the health-related problems, attitudes and behaviour of incapacity benefit claimants, except in the most simplistic, judgemental sense. Overall, there has been little consideration of the scientific and conceptual basis. To fill that gap, the aims of this review are:

- To develop a theoretical and conceptual framework for incapacity benefits for people of working age[13];

- To analyse the development and trends of UK incapacity benefits from 1948 to date, in light of these principles;

- To provide a scientific evidence base for IB reform, to meet today's challenges and needs.

This is a scientific perspective, with its strengths and limitations. That is only one element of the welfare debate, but a strong scientific evidence base is an essential prerequisite for IB reform.

2 WORK AND WELFARE

2.1 Work and worklessness

Work is a major part of life[14]: it provides the income and goods to sustain life, independence and security; a structure for how we spend our lives; and the social contact, relationships and status that help to define the individual and his or her role in society. Participation in work is the main route to social inclusion and integration in today's society, providing dignity and the opportunity to contribute to society. Sickness and disability are among the main threats to a full and happy life, and incapacity for work is their most significant impact on the individual, his or her family, employers, the economy and society. Job retention, return to work and reintegration are therefore the most relevant and important (albeit not the only) goals and outcome measures of health care, rehabilitation and the social security system, across the range of conditions that cause incapacity[15].

On balance, the evidence shows that work is good for physical and mental health and well-being, while there is strong evidence that worklessness is harmful to physical and mental health (Acheson 1998; Royal College of Psychiatrists 2002; ONS 2000, 2003, Ritchie *et al* 2005, Mclean *et al* 2005, Bartley *et al* 2005) (Boxes 2 & 3).

Box 2: The benefits of work and harm of worklessness.	
Work is beneficial for people with sickness or disability, in terms of:	**Long-term worklessness leads to:**
Symptom management	Loss of fitness
Recovery & rehabilitation	Physical & mental deterioration
Self-esteem and confidence	Poor physical and mental health
Social identity & role	Psychological distress & depression
'Normalisation' of activities & participation	Loss of work-related attitudes & habits
Improved social functioning	Increased suicide and mortality rates
Quality of life	Poverty
Social inclusion	Social exclusion

Box 3: Long-term worklessness is one of the greatest known risks to public health:

- The risk is equivalent to smoking 10 packs of cigarettes per day (Ross 1995).
- Young men who have been out of work for 6 months have a 40X increased risk of suicide (S Wessely, personal communication).
- That is a greater risk to health and life expectancy than many 'killer diseases'
- It is a greater risk than the most dangerous jobs in building sites or the North Sea.

The major qualification to that analysis is the strong association between worklessness, social disadvantage, deprived areas and poverty. To understand poor health and worklessness, it is necessary to look at individuals in the broader context of the communities and areas in which they live (Ritchie *et al* 2005).

There are several common but erroneous beliefs about work and health that are sometimes reinforced by poor medical advice (Waddell & Burton 2004a):

- Anyone who has an illness should not work

- Anyone who has a disability cannot work

- Workers who become ill should stay off work

- Workers on sickness absence should not return to work until they are completely recovered.

Too often, work is seen as the problem, rather than the goal or part of the solution, and usually that preconception is wrong. Because of historical emphasis on the prevention of occupational injury and disease, it is often assumed that work is a potential 'risk' to health - but for most common health problems the evidence shows that work is actually good for health. The second assumption is that rest from work is part of treatment – but modern approaches to the management of most common health problems emphasise the importance of continuing ordinary activities as normally as possible and early return to work. Return to work reduces rather than increases the risk of recurrent or persistent trouble. The third assumption is that it is not possible or advisable to return to work until symptoms are completely 'cured' (i.e. 100% recovered) – but modern clinical and occupational management emphasise that return to work as early as possible is an essential part of treatment for many health problems, even with some persistent symptoms. Thus, work is not only the goal and outcome of treatment: work itself is therapeutic, aids recovery and is the best form of rehabilitation (Waddell & Burton 2004b).

Two-three million disabled people already work and another million economically inactive people with health problems say they would like to work[16]. [This figure of 'a million people on IB want to work' is very useful politically and for presentational purposes, but it is questionable if it provides a realistic basis for policy planning. There appears to be a large element of social desirability – 'of course, I would *like* to work' – because it is immediately qualified – 'but of course I *can't* (at least at present) because I am too ill/sick/disabled'. Only about 3-6% of long-term IB recipients are actually taking any active steps to seek work.] The right to full participation in society and to work is enshrined in the UN Declaration of Human Rights (United Nations 1948). There is a strong social consensus that sees employment as a desirable form of social participation for all adults, and that is applicable to sick and disabled people as much as to everyone else (Council of Europe 1996, 2003a & b). At the same time, there are social barriers that tend to exclude sick and disabled people – particularly those with mental illness - from all aspects of life, including work (Social Exclusion Unit 2004, Layard 2005, Strategy Unit 2005).

Thus, work is generally good for physical and mental health *provided* - and these are major provisos:

- Jobs are available

- Physical and psychosocial conditions are satisfactory and provide a decent 'human' quality of work

- Work provides adequate financial reward and security[17].

Conversely, the ill effects of worklessness also depend on the social and economic qualities of 'worklessness' (as discussed in the next two sections).

2.2 Social disadvantage and exclusion

To a large extent, social disadvantage is a matter of (relative) poverty, but it is more than that – it involves loss of social roles and reduced participation in all aspects of life, which amounts to a reduced form of citizenship (Peace 2001, Howard 2004a).

Social disadvantage is closely linked to worklessness and low income but also involves broader issues of human capital and social exclusion. From one perspective, individual 'human capital' includes family background; education; training and skills; competitiveness in the labour market; the balance between personal capabilities and the physical and psychological demands of work; control and support; financial and social status and security; life-style and behaviour that may affect health and working capacity (Ashworth *et al* 2001). From a different perspective, this is social exclusion and marginalisation, which includes limited access to education and training, work and income; poorer labour market opportunities including availability, quality, pay levels and security of employment; material and attitudinal barriers to participation; discrimination, labelling and stigma (Oliver & Barnes 1998, Social Exclusion Unit 2004, Strategy Unit 2005). From both perspectives, sick and disabled people are particularly vulnerable.

Social disadvantage and exclusion have powerful negative effects on physical and mental health. There is marked variation in self-rated health (Doran *et al* 2004) and self-reported limiting long-standing illness (General Health Surveys) across social class. Sickness absence, long-term incapacity and disability pensions all show strong links to (lower) social class (Upmark *et al* 2001). This is not just a question of absolute destitution, and it does not only affect a separate category of 'the disadvantaged' or 'the excluded'. Rather, there is a strong social gradient in physical and mental health, health-related quality of life and mortality across the entire social spectrum, with no sharp cut-off (Acheson 1998, Marmot 2004). Nor is this just a question of occupational exposure, education or income, but about more fundamental matters of social status, associated levels of control, support and security in life, and the direct and indirect biopsychosocial effects of social stratification.

Social status not only influences the chances of developing health problems, but also their impact. For more socially and economically advantaged people, there may often be a greater element of personal choice and control, and they are likely to have more opportunities and resources to support this choice. In the socially, educationally and occupationally disadvantaged, it may be more a matter of labour market forces over which they have no control (Rupp & Stapleton 1995, 1998). To put it simply, some people are less able to compete effectively in the labour market, due to a combination of their health condition, lowered levels of human capital, multiple disadvantages and the social barriers they face. They may then have limited job opportunities and no financial alternative but to make the best use of the available social security options. These people are the first to suffer and the last to benefit from falls and rises in the labour market. Whether or not their health condition is incapacitating in itself, they are more likely to become and remain recipients of sickness and disability benefits.

So it is not surprising that sickness and disability are among the most powerful causes of poverty. Disabled people have lower levels of education, employment and income (Harris *et al* 1971, Grewal *et al* 2002, OECD 2003, CPAG 2004). Thus, there are strong reciprocal links between sickness and disability, economic inactivity and poverty. The combination is particularly destructive to the lives of individuals and their families, and may impose burdens that are simply too crushing to overcome (Welsh Office 1997, Elwan 1999).

2.2.1 Welfare classes

This led Hill (1990) to suggest that there are different 'social welfare classes'.

People in the first class are in relatively well paid and secure employment, and they do not depend on the social security system, even though they pay contributions and draw benefits when entitled to do so. Their jobs are generally less physically demanding, healthier and more accommodating when they are ill. During sickness absence they receive full or partial salary, and when they retire (whether at retirement age or earlier on health grounds) they have more or less generous occupational pensions. Periods out of work are relatively uncommon and short-lived (although this is less true now than previously) and usually cushioned by generous redundancy and early retirement provisions. Some women in this class, however, may be dependent on their male partner's entitlement and vulnerable to marital breakdown.

Second is the traditional 'working class' for whom the social security system was originally designed and for whom it still has considerable validity. When sick they receive some form of sick pay and then incapacity benefits can provide a reasonable income even for long-term incapacity, *provided they have built up sufficient entitlement*. When they retire they receive a state pension, possibly with some employment-related supplement. However, women in this class may be much less adequately covered, particularly if they are in part-time or low paid jobs, and longer-term sickness or unemployment may 'demote' both men and women to the third class.

Nevertheless, the combination of social security and some employment-related entitlement provides reasonably well for many members of this class.

The third class comprises the socially disadvantaged, with low education and skills, poor and low-paid employment records, limited financial and social resources, and more illness. During sickness absence, they get the minimum Statutory Sick Pay and their employment is likely to be terminated. They may not have built up full entitlement to social insurance benefits. When they are sick or unemployed, it is more likely to be prolonged. When they retire, they receive the basic state retirement pension or less if their employment record is poor. Social insurance fails for people in this class and many are dependent on the means-tested 'safety net' to stave off poverty, both when they are out of work and sometimes even in work. People in the third class face many barriers to social participation and work that trap them there.

There is particular social divergence among workers in their 50s, in whom attitudes to work and (early) retirement vary with gender, income and employment status (Hayden *et al* 1999, Scales & Scase 2000, Humphrey *et al* 2002, Hirsch 2003, Moss & Arrowsmith 2003, Faculty of Occupational Medicine 2004). Older workers have become socially polarised according to type of employment, occupational pensions, marital status and financial commitments such as children and mortgages. Many from professional and managerial occupations have expectations of early retirement as a matter of choice based on access to an occupational or private pension income. If blue-collar workers do retire early it is more likely to be involuntary and more likely to be associated with ill health. Non-working professionals are more likely to be financially comfortable, while many former blue-collar workers are more likely to be finding things quite or very difficult. Professionals are then more likely to be happy, have reduced stress and improved health compared with when they were working, and have longer, healthier lives in retirement. It is blue-collar workers for whom moving out of work is more likely to lead to unhappiness, deteriorating health and all the ill effects of worklessness.

The key conclusion of this section is that any benefit reform must provide fairly and equitably for people in widely divergent circumstances, and take particular care not to further disadvantage those benefit recipients who are already among the most disadvantaged members of society (Rawls 1999, White 2004b).

2.3 Support into work

Many disabled people do work and many more want to work. The medical evidence is that many people on 'incapacity' benefits with longer-term sickness still have capacity for (some) work despite their health condition. Work has health-related, personal and social advantages over worklessness. Incapacity benefits have many financial and other disadvantages (which will be analysed in detail later) compared with the financial and other advantages of earned income.

On average, disabled people in work earn 80-90% as much as non-disabled workers, while disabled people who do not work earn less than half that amount (OECD 2003, DRC 2004a). For all these reasons, work is the best exit from incapacity benefits and, in that sense, 'work is the best form of welfare' (Mead 1997a, Field 1998, King *et al* 1999). The major provisos are:

- for those who can. This must not become an excuse for forcing people who cannot reasonably be expected to work off benefits.

- That suitable work and opportunities are available in the (local?) labour market.

- That adequate and effective support into work is provided.

Most people - including disabled people (Oliver & Barnes 1998, DRC 2004b, Howard 2004a) and IB recipients (Goldstone & Douglas 2003) - agree that whenever possible productive employment is preferable for sick and disabled people, their families and society at large, rather than relying on financial benefits as an incomplete replacement for income. Even when sick or disabled people cannot be fully self-supporting, everyone may gain by enabling them to make some contribution. There is strong public support for encouraging benefit claimants back to work, when this is feasible (Williams *et al* 1999, Saunders 2002). However, most of the evidence is about the unemployed while public opinion is more ambiguous about sick or disabled benefit recipients. Moreover, the preference is for an approach that encourages and helps people to work rather than compels them to do so. Many benefit recipients agree but point out that the onus is on society to make decent, adequately paid jobs available, and that the process and implementation of any 'encouragement' must be fair and reasonable and allow for individual circumstances (Dwyer 2000, DRC 2004c).

Thus, support is not just for those who cannot work, and not just about benefits. Whenever possible, the best support is that which helps people to enter, remain in, or return to work. That is the most beneficial and cost-effective use of social security resources. However, that must never jeopardise the primary purpose and objective of social security - to make sure that those who are too sick or disabled to work receive adequate financial security.

3 ILLNESS, DISABILITY AND (IN)CAPACITY FOR WORK

3.1 Definitions

Words like 'ill', 'sick' and 'disabled' are often used loosely as if they are inter-changeable, reflecting lack of clear thinking about fundamental concepts (Mechanic 1968, Nagi 1969, Susser 1990, Twaddle & Nordenfeldt 1994, Boyd 2000, Hofmann 2002). This has often obscured the welfare debate, where the development of rational policy and legislation depend on clear definitions and precise usage (Box 4).

Box 4: The distinction between key terms.

Disease is objective, medically diagnosed, pathology.

Impairment is significant, demonstrable, deviation or loss of body structure or function.

Symptoms are bothersome bodily or mental sensations.

Illness is the subjective feeling of being unwell.

Disability is limitation of activities and restriction of participation.

Sickness is a social status accorded to the ill person by society.

Incapacity is inability to work associated with sickness or disability.

These terms and definitions are as neutral as possible and try as far as possible to avoid assumptions or implications about causality. However, it is important to note this is not a linear causal chain. These are different elements of the human predicament that underlies incapacity, and the social security dilemma often lies in discrepancies between the elements.

Symptoms are subjective bodily or mental sensations that reach awareness and are 'bothersome' or 'of concern to that person', e.g. feeling aches and pains, tired, breathless, anxious or depressed. Many symptoms are normal, part of life and related to activities of daily living; some represent the clinical presentation of disease; most relevant to the present debate are those that fall outwith the range of what is usually accepted as 'normal' but are not associated with any identifiable disease (Ursin 1997, Deyo *et al* 1998).

Illness or *ill health* is when a health condition impacts on well-being or quality of life. The World Health Organisation idealistically defines health as 'a state of complete physical, mental and social well-being and not merely the absence of disease or infirmity' (WHO 1948). More recently, WHO has stated that 'health or state of health can only be defined in terms of an individual and that person's goals and expectations' (WHO 2004) and that the 'ultimate outcome' of health is well-being and quality of life (WHO 2003). By implication, ill health is anything that falls short of health[18]. More prosaically, illness is 'the innately human experience of symptoms and suffering' (Kleinman 1988) or, more simply, 'the subjective feeling of being unwell' (Finkelstein & French 1993). Central to all of these definitions is that illness is an internal, personal experience.

Sickness or, more precisely, *the sick role* is a social status accorded to the ill person by society, with exemption from (some) normal social roles and carrying specific rights and responsibilities; i.e. sickness is an external, social phenomenon involving interactions between the individual, other people and society (Sigerist 1929, Parsons 1951, Mechanic 1968).

Disability is limitation of activities and restriction of participation in life situations, in people with physical and/or mental condition(s) or impairment(s) (WHO 2001).

Incapacity for work is reduced capacity, functioning and performance in work associated with sickness or disability (and it is difficult to distinguish capacity and performance).

These should all be distinguished from:

Disease is a disorder of structure or function of the human organism that deviates from the biological norm, and is associated with mobilisation of the organism's defences and coping mechanisms[19]. It includes biochemical, physiological or anatomical abnormalities, which can result from congenital, traumatic, infective, inflammatory, degenerative or other pathological processes. The key features are that it is objective, at an organic level, in the individual, and a matter of medical diagnosis (WHO 1980, Boyd 2000). Note that disease may or may not lead to physical or mental impairment, and does not necessarily cause symptoms, illness, disability or incapacity[20].

Impairment: there are several similar definitions of impairment as 'any loss or abnormality of psychological, physiological or anatomical structure or function' (WHO 1980), 'a loss, loss of use, or derangement of any body part, organ system or organ function' (AMA 2000) or 'problems in body function or structure such as a significant deviation or loss' (WHO 2001). The disability movement have proposed a somewhat comparable definition: 'lacking all or part of a limb, or having a defective limb, organism or mechanism of the body' (UPIAS 1976). Central to all of these definitions, impairment is a matter of objective evidence: 'detectable - - - by direct observation or by inference from observation' (WHO 2001). The US Social Security Administration operationalises this as 'demonstrable by medically acceptable, clinical and laboratory diagnostic techniques' (SSA 2001), i.e. it is usually a matter of medical evidence. Impairment should be demonstrable on assessment of the individual claimant, rather than based on theory and general scientific evidence (Waddell 2004a). Note that impairment is not the same as the underlying disease, but is the manifestation(s) of that disease (WHO 2001). The DWP term *loss of faculty* is for all practical purposes equivalent to impairment.

Mental impairment [21] is more difficult because symptoms, limitations, clinical assessment and diagnosis in mental illness are largely subjective. Many methods that purport to assess psychiatric impairment are in fact measures of functional limitation (i.e. disability) or heavily influenced by current psychological distress, or use a circular argument from self-reported limitations to assumed underlying impairment (Mendelson 2004). Medical examiners are also influenced by service traditions, economics, bureaucratic exigency, politics and societal prejudice (Biklen 1988). To fit the basic definition of impairment, Mendelson (2004) suggests that mental impairment should refer specifically and solely to abnormalities of mental function that can be demonstrated, assessed, evaluated and measured by an objective observer on mental state examination. It is particularly important to distinguish such observed impairments from claimants' subjective descriptions of symptoms and limitations. The *Clinical Guidelines to the Rating of Psychiatric Impairment* (Epstein *et al* 1998), which are based on the 2nd edition of the AMA *Guides* and currently in use in the State of Victoria, Australia, provide the clearest and most detailed description of mental impairments:

1   Intelligence: the level of cognitive (intellectual) function, including global orientation (in time, place and person), fund of general information, capacity for abstract thinking, memory functions and aspects of the use of language.

2   Thinking: formal thought disorder involving thought processes (loosening of associations, interpenetration, metonymy, thought blocking), abnormalities of thought content (delusions, overvalued ideas) and abnormalities of the stream of thought (e.g. pressure of speech with flight of ideas, or slowed thinking due to psychomotor retardation).

3   Perception: hallucinations and illusions.

4   Judgment: the ability to evaluate various situations and information and reach an effective conclusion, which may affect the individual's capacity to perform complex tasks or make autonomous decisions, or lead to socially inappropriate behaviour.

5   Mood: the affective state ranging from severe depression to euphoria, emotional lability or anxiety.

6   Behaviour: disruptive or aggressive behaviour, obsessive-compulsive behaviour, posturing or stereotyped movements.

Strictly speaking, mental impairment should not be considered 'permanent' until:

a   the patient has received a full course of optimal medical treatment (in the case of psychiatric illness commonly over 1-2 years) by a recognised medical specialist,

b   the point of 'maximum medical improvement' has been reached and, in the physician's best clinical judgment, the impairment is static or well-stabilised (AMA 2000, Coetzer 2001, P White personal communication).

Distinguishing the two concepts of impairment and disability is fundamental to defining entitlement and to assessment of incapacity (Aylward & Sawney 1999). Impairment is a medical definition, which provides the most objective measure of a health condition, but does not provide much information about the experience of the individual. Disability is a social definition, which focuses on the individual's experience and functioning, and is not just a health condition. The International Classification of Functioning, Disability and Health (ICF) does not define disability *per se*, but describes it as 'an umbrella term for impairments, activity limitations and participation restrictions' (WHO 2001). It defines activity as 'the execution of a task or action by an individual'; activity limitations are 'difficulties an individual may have in executing activities'. Participation is 'involvement in a life situation'; participation restrictions are 'problems an individual may experience in involvement in life situations'. The key point here is that impairment and disability must be distinguished. It is not that one is 'right' or the other 'wrong': these are equally valid but very different perspectives, and each has its strengths and weaknesses.

ICF illustrates the difficulty of defining the complex phenomenon of 'disability'[22], which remains the subject of heated debate (Nagi 1969, Oliver & Barnes 1998, Grundy *et al* 1999, Bajekal *et al* 2004, Marin 2003, Tibble 2004). ICF tried to stay neutral about the extent to which limitations and restrictions are 'caused' by the impairment, the social environment or interactions between them (Ustun *et al* 1998, Bury 2000), even if there is argument about how far it succeeded (Pfeiffer 1998, 2000, Hurst 2000). Against that broad conceptual background, legislative and operational definitions of disability may logically and reasonably vary to identify different groups of people, with differing disabilities, for different purposes (Bolderson et al 2002, Council of Europe 2003b, Howard 2004b). Arguably, these definitions should be as consistent as possible. However, words and 'models' crystallise and then constrain thinking and communication – and conflicts arise when they are based on differing assumptions or are designed to suit different political purposes.

Professional and official definitions of disability are traditionally based on a 'medical model', in which disability is assumed to be a (more or less) direct consequence of impairment. The original World Health Organisation definition (WHO 1980) of disability was 'any restriction or lack (resulting from an impairment) of ability to perform an activity in the manner or within the range considered normal for a human being'[23]. The current 5th Edition of the US Guides to the Evaluation of Permanent Impairment (AMA 2000) still gives a similar definition of disability: 'an alteration of an individual's capacity to meet personal, social or occupational demands because of an impairment'. Thus, de Jong (1999) operationalised incapacity as: 'the inability to meet the demands of work, due to functional limitations, caused by impairment'. Critics argue, rightly, that medical model is too simplistic, over-emphasises impairment and incorrectly assumes a direct causal link from impairment to disability. It fails to take sufficient account of the personal and social dimensions of disability[24].

Disability activists and academics in the 1970s and 80s (UPIAS 1976, Finkelstein 1980, Oliver 1983, 1990, Barnes 1991) therefore proposed an alternative 'social model of disability'. This essentially argues that the participation of disabled people in society is not restricted by their impairment *per se* but is imposed by the way society is organized for able-bodied living. They strongly oppose the medical model and demand 'a switch away from focusing on the physical limitations of particular individuals to the way the physical and social environments impose limitations on certain groups or categories of people' (Oliver, 1983). This is a political model[25] that focuses on social environments, barriers and cultures that exclude or disadvantage people labelled as disabled, and has been used by the disability movement in their fight for disability rights and social change (Barnes 1991, Swain *et al* 1993, Drake 1999, Woodhams & Corby 2003, Barnes & Mercer 2004a)[26]. It produces a very different definition of disability[27] (Strategy Unit 2005) as:

- *disadvantage* experienced by an individual ...

- .. resulting from *barriers* to independent living or educational, employment or other opportunities...

- .... that impact on people with *impairments* and/or ill health[28].

The social model is now widely accepted as the conceptual basis for social inclusion and anti-discrimination policies, even if it is sometimes difficult to operationalise and legislative definitions tend to revert to a medical model[29] (Donoghue 2003). Crucial to the present analysis, however, the social model does not and need not deny the reality of impairment and the functional limitations it may impose[30] (French 1993, Barnes & Mercer 1995, Oliver 1995, 2004). The social model and this definition still recognise impairment as the necessary substrate on which barriers and discrimination act[31]. Arguably, the social model, like the medical model, also fails to take sufficient account of the personal dimension of disability (Waddell & Burton 2004b).

To confound these divergent views, disability rights and social security benefits have been the responsibility at certain times of different Government departments or divisions. This has led to separate legislation, administrative mechanisms and case law, with little or no cross-reference. Disability activists and academics have also failed to resolve, and often simply ignored, the ambiguities and tensions between these two areas (Donoghue 2003, Barnes & Mercer 2004a & b). However, each area must be considered on its own merits. For citizenship rights, the boundaries are broad and it may even be argued that to mainstream disabled people, 'disability' should not be a separate category at all (Zola 1989, WHO 2001). In anti-discrimination legislation, the focus is on the act of discrimination. Social inclusion policy is directed at the systemic social barriers to participation. In all of these areas, the nature or severity of the individual's impairment is not the issue. The goal is to increase inclusion and in terms of citizenship and social justice inclusion errors are acceptable to minimise exclusion errors. Social security benefits, however, are by their nature directed to individuals and there must be a balance between providing individual support and controlling access. The boundary and operationalisation are then critical, and the policy goal is to minimise both inclusion and exclusion errors.

Sickness and disability are essentially, conceptually linked to the individual's physical or mental condition: that is what distinguishes sickness and disability from unemployment or other forms of social disadvantage. The logical basis and *sine qua non* of individual entitlement to sickness and disability benefits is the individual's physical and/or mental (health) condition. This principle is absolutely fundamental. Although disability activists and academics have argued strongly against the medical model in the benefit system (Oliver & Barnes 1998, Donoghue 2003), it is difficult to see how individual entitlement to social security benefits can be defined or assessed purely in terms of social barriers. Social security benefits are paid to individuals, so must be based upon an individual approach. Individual entitlement to wage replacement benefits must be defined and assessed in terms of the individual's incapacity for work (Berthoud 1998, Bickenbach *et al* 1999). The real crux of the argument about how to define and assess disability and incapacity is how far this should be based on objective measures, i.e. medical diagnosis or impairment, or on subjective self-reports of illness and limitations.

Although the social model is directed primarily to addressing systemic social barriers, its philosophy can also be applied to support into work at an individual level. Support tailored to meet individual needs must address individual circumstances, and one part of this should be to address the specific social and occupational barriers faced by the individual. Accommodations and adjustments must be specific to individual impairments and needs.

This approach is consistent with past and current policy and legislation. The concept of 'loss of faculty'[32] (i.e. medical diagnosis of impairment) underpinned War Disablement Pension and Industrial Injury Disablement Benefit, which are the only disability related benefits that have survived with little change for more than half a century without the caseloads escalating out of control[33]. The earliest legislative definition of a disabled person was in the Disabled Persons (Employment) Act 1944: 'a person who, on account of injury, disease or congenital deformity, is substantially handicapped in obtaining or keeping employment, or in undertaking work on his own account of a kind which, apart from that injury, disease or deformity would be suited to his age, experience and qualifications'. The Disability Discrimination Act 1995 defined a disabled person as anyone with 'a physical or mental impairment which has a substantial and long-term adverse effect on his ability to carry out normal day-to-day activities'[34]. One of the key principles of Incapacity Benefit was the definition and assessment of '*medical* incapacity' to direct benefits to those people whose incapacity was due solely to their medical condition. There was considerable opposition to this at the time from disability groups and medical bodies, but maintaining that principle was fundamental to restructuring the benefit and the new test of incapacity.

The definition of disability and particularly any focus on impairment, e.g. for (any element of) any new benefit, are likely to remain areas of contention with the disability lobby and political opponents of reform[35]. Nevertheless, this is a key element to any restructuring and winning this debate is vital to effective reform. The strength of the argument is that impairment has a clear and logical scientific basis, can be operationalised robustly and is in line with public perceptions. The weakness of the argument is that the extent to which someone with an impairment is disabled or incapacitated also depends on personal and social factors.

There are further conceptual difficulties to defining *incapacity for work* associated with sickness or disability (Stanley & Maxwell 2004). Entitlement to benefits requires a cut-off[36], but in reality there is a continuum with no sharp boundary between capacity and incapacity. Health conditions and capacities change over time. There is a conceptual difference between those who 'can't work' because of their physical or mental condition and those who 'can't get a job' because of their physical or mental condition, but in practice there may be much overlap. Personal factors, the social context and the impact of the social security system itself on human behaviour ('moral hazard') may be excluded from legislative and administrative definitions, but their importance cannot be denied. The limitation of any assessment is that it ultimately provides information about performance: it can never be an objective measure of what the claimant is *able* to do or *should be able* to do. As an over-simplification, capacity may be limited by physiology, but performance is limited by psychology: what the claimant does or does not do will always depend on effort and motivation (Nordenfeldt 2003, Waddell 2004a). The age-old dilemma sometimes remains of how to distinguish those who can't work from those who won't (Mayhew 1861-62).

Figure 1. The limited correlation between impairment, symptoms and disability (based on representative data from back pain in Waddell 2004b).

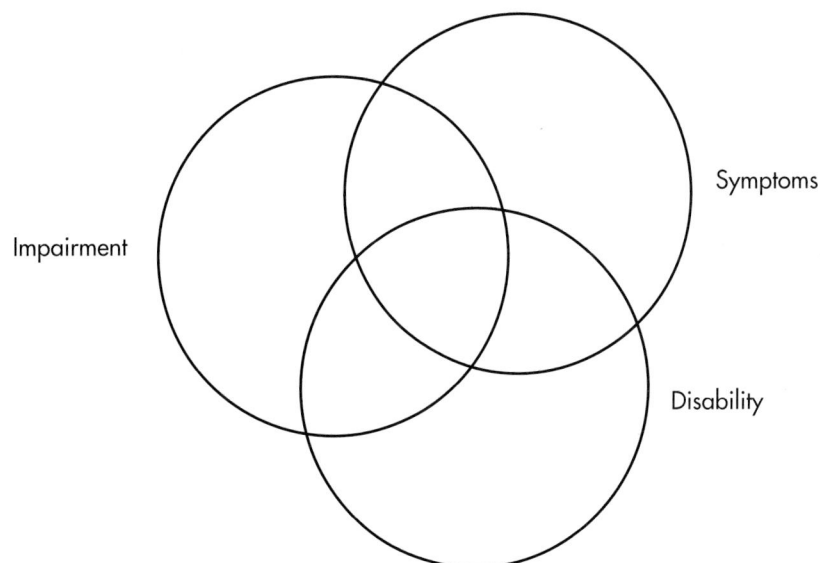

Figure 2. The limited correlation between illness, disability, and (in)capacity for work (based on data in Chap 3.2).

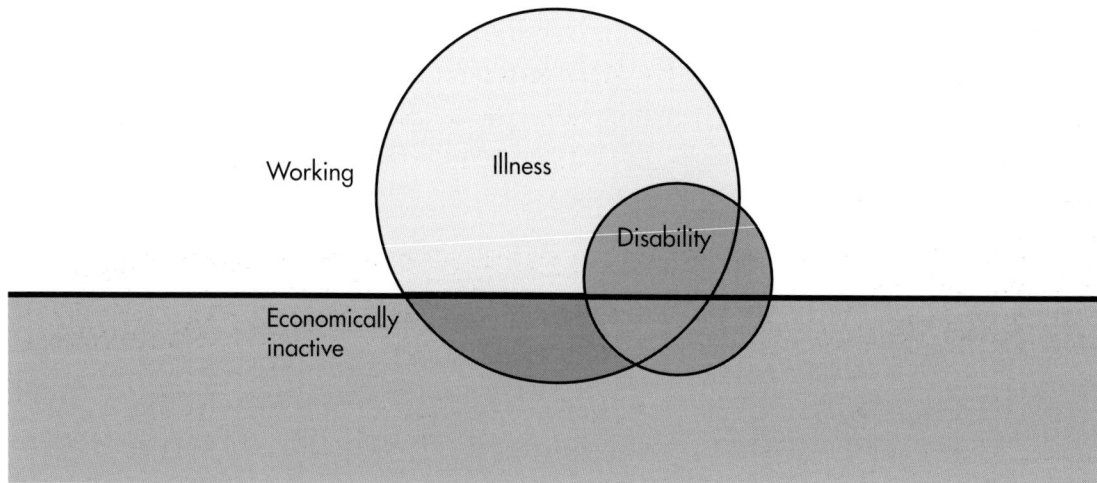

The practical problem in defining entitlement and for assessment is the limited correlation between symptoms, impairment and disability (Fig 1) and between illness, disability and incapacity for work (Fig 2). For catastrophic injuries or severe medical conditions, severe impairment correlates reasonably well with incapacity. For less severe health problems, illness, sickness, and incapacity are clearly related, but the link between them and to physical or mental disease is much weaker than often assumed. Discordance between these elements creates difficulties for assessing incapacity (Box 5).

Box 5: Discrepancies between disease, illness and sickness.
You can have:

- Symptoms without disease, illness or disability (e.g. most people)

- Disease without impairment, symptoms or disability (e.g. early cancer)

- Impairment without illness or disability (e.g. a below knee amputation with a good artificial leg)

- Illness or disability without incapacity for work (e.g. many disabled and non-disabled people)

- Incapacity without disease or impairment (e.g. many IB recipients).

Jumping ahead to set the scene, one of the main social security problems today is the number of people whose incapacity is based on feeling ill (and therefore limited in their activities), claiming the sick role, legitimised by sick certification, often in the absence of commensurate disease or impairment.

3.2 The epidemiology of sickness and disability

There are medical statistics for severe medical conditions (WHO 2000), but there are no good statistics for the population prevalence of 'illness'. The problem is that non-specific physical and mental symptoms are very common in the general population (Ursin 1997, 2004)(Table 1). Most of these symptoms are part of everyday life and experience, and although they correlate with psychological distress (Haug *et al* 2004) there is no clear cut-off for when they amount to illness. Up to three-quarters of these symptoms are not due to any identifiable disease or recognisable medical condition (Kroenke & Mangelsdorff 1989, Carson *et al* 2000a & b, 2003, Nimuan *et al* 2001, Haug *et al* 2004).

Table 1: Prevalence of symptoms in adults of working age in the past month (Based on data from Eriksen *et al* 1998)[37]				
	Any complaints		**Substantial complaints**	
	Men	**Women**	**Men**	**Women**
Tiredness	46%	56%	17%	26%
Worry	38%	39%	13%	15%
Depressed	22%	28%	5%	10%
Headache	37%	51%	4%	9%
Neck pain	27%	41%	9%	17%
Arm/shoulder pain	28%	38%	12%	17%
Low back pain	32%	37%	13%	16%
Foot pain	16%	19%	6%	9%

75% of people reported at least one symptom.

More than half reported two or more symptoms

There is comparable difficulty assessing the extent of 'disability' (LFS Spring 2004, OECD 2003, Bajekal *et al* 2004, Tibble 2004, DRC 2004a):

- Depending on how the question is worded, 5.4 - 6.9 million people of working age in UK report some form of 'limiting long-standing illness' or 'long-term disability' that 'limits daily activities or work'[38]. About one third of them describe this as 'severe'.

- This number has increased from 6.0 million in spring 1998 to 6.8 million in spring 2004.

- The prevalence increases with age: from 10% of those aged 16-24 years, to 34% of those aged between 50 and state retirement age[39].

- There is strong regional variation in the prevalence, from 16% in London and the South-East to 25% in deprived areas such as the North-East and Wales.

- However, about half of these people do not regard themselves as 'disabled' (Grewal *et al* 2002).

- Moreover, about half of these people are working (including 25% of those who say their limitations are severe[40]). Overall, this has increased from 43% in spring 1998 to 50% in spring 2004. Employment rates vary greatly with the type of condition: mental health conditions are lowest (20%) while musculo-skeletal conditions are about average (48%).

The fundamental conceptual and methodological limitation is that these figures are based on *self-reports* of people's own subjective *perceptions* of their overall health and activity limitations, with no external check on their validity. This approach acknowledges that individuals experience and assess health differently, and may provide the best measure of that personal impact. The problem is that self-reports are open to positive or negative bias. It is not clear how people interpret or decide to answer such questions, and their responses are sensitive to the exact wording and presentation of the questions (Bajekal *et al* 2004). Studies of disabled and non-disabled people have highlighted the complex and sometimes conflicting ways in which people define themselves as 'disabled' or not (Grewal *et al* 2002). There is marked cross-cultural variation: on average, 5% of European adults say they are disabled, but this ranges from 1% in Italy to 11% in Finland[41] (MISSOC 2001). Even after allowing for the link between health, social disadvantage and regional deprivation, self-reports of limiting long-term illness and permanent sickness are about 20% higher in areas of high unemployment (Haynes *et al* 1997). This may be poorer self-perception of health associated with social deprivation, or people living in areas where it is difficult to get a job may be more likely to declare themselves ill. Conversely, some claimants, particularly those with mental health problems, may have difficulty providing accurate information because of their health condition, be poor self-advocates, or may under-estimate or under-state their problems, perhaps through shame or fear of stigmatisation (Schneider *et al* 2003). There is no clear evidence on the relative frequency of over- or under-reporting: disability groups argue these figures are an under-estimate; benefit trends suggest they may be an over-estimate compared with historically accepted levels. Whichever, because of the fundamental nature of self-reports they should not be accepted uncritically as objective measures of health or disability (Haynes *et al* 1997).

These figures on disability have other weaknesses. First, they include a wide range of limitations, of which only a proportion is 'severe' (Grundy *et al* 1999). For example, it is questionable how many of these people would meet the criteria of disability for the Disability Discrimination Act 1995 if they reached a Tribunal, or the criteria of incapacity if subjected to the PCA. They certainly do not all correspond to the public image of 'disabled people'. Second, and crucial to the present analysis, the global questions used in these surveys cover both 'illness' and 'disability' and do not provide any separate estimate of 'sickness' or 'disability'[42].

Table 2 shows the main health conditions associated with disability and sickness absence.

Table 2 Health conditions, disability and sickness absence (collected data - Waddell & Burton 2004b).

	People with self-reported ong-term disability	General Practitioner sick certification	Self-reported days of sickness absence due to work-related ill health	Early retirement on health grounds *
Mental health conditions	11%	40%	32%	20-50%
Musculoskeletal conditions	34%	23%	49%	15-50%
Cardio-respiratory conditions	24%	10%	–	c 10-15%

* Major variation in different occupations and organisations.

Table 3 shows a similar pattern for people receiving IB:

- 42% have **mental health conditions**. The large majority have problems like depressive symptoms, anxiety, stress or other 'neuroses', with only a small number having serious psychiatric illnesses such as schizophrenia;

- 21% have **musculoskeletal conditions**. The large majority have non-specific back/leg/neck/arm pain, rather than serious disease such as advanced rheumatoid arthritis;

- 11% have **circulatory or respiratory conditions** such as high blood pressure, angina or chronic bronchitis, with only a small number having heart or lung disease that is severely and permanently limiting.

Table 3 Inflow and stock of IB recipients by diagnostic category (DWP administrative data, February 2004).

Diagnostic category *	Inflow	Stock of recipients
Mental health conditions	33%	42%
Musculoskeletal conditions	16%	21%
Cardio-respiratory conditions	8%	11%
Other conditions	43%	26%

* These are broad medical diagnostic categories, based on sick certification, with all its limitations.

It is important to re-emphasise that 'incapacity benefits' cover a wide spectrum of recipients. Disability varies greatly in nature and severity and many disabled people are working. For most people (e.g. with injury or illness), sickness absence is short-term in the expectation of return to work in due course. At the other extreme, some people have severe medical conditions that are permanently incapacitating (e.g. tetraplegia, advanced neurological conditions, severe learning disabilities). But three-quarters of people of working age on long-term Incapacity Benefit (IB) now have less severe health problems (e.g. 'stress', back pain or chronic respiratory symptoms).

The key conclusions of this section (Strategy Unit 2005) are that:

- IB recipients include extremely diverse groups of people with different kinds of problems in different situations.

- Sickness is not the same as disability, and both vary greatly in nature and severity.

- Disability does not equal incapacity for work: many disabled people do work, many more want to work, and they all have the right to work[43] (United Nations 1948, 1975, Disability Discrimination Act 1995).

3.3 The nature of health conditions associated with incapacity

Social security systems were originally designed for people with severe medical conditions that have objective evidence of disease and permanent physical or mental impairments (e.g. blindness, paralysis, schizophrenia). That is still the stereotype of disability and the example used in most welfare debates. [Though there is lack of public awareness that many such conditions qualify automatically for IB and are exempt from assessment under the Personal Capability Assessment[44].] However, such severe conditions now account for less than a quarter of IB recipients, and they are not becoming any more prevalent (DWP Administrative data).

Some three-quarters of people with long-term incapacity now have less severe health conditions, the most common of which are mental health and musculoskeletal conditions (Table 3). These do not fit the traditional image of severe medical conditions. They have been described and are referred to here as *common health problems* (Waddell & Burton 2004b).

These common health problems may be 'less severe' in a medical sense but that is not to suggest they are less important: they are very real, cause considerable suffering, fully justify health care and may cause temporary restrictions. So attempts to argue about the reality or validity of the individual's subjective experience are illogical, futile and likely to be counter-productive. (Leaving aside, of course, the issue of conscious deception or fraud). Nevertheless, they are 'common health problems' in that they are similar in nature and sometimes even in degree to those experienced by most (working) people (Table 1). Diagnosis is often non-specific and based mainly on the patient's self-report of symptoms and limitations. These conditions are 'characterised more by symptoms and distress than by consistently demonstrable tissue abnormality' (Barsky & Borus 1999) and have been described as 'subjective health complaints' to emphasise their symptomatic nature (Ursin 1997) or as 'medically unexplained symptoms'[45] to emphasise the limited evidence of objective disease or impairment (Burton 2003, Page & Wessely 2003). They have also been described as 'vague' or 'unclear' – not the illness, but the cause and the solution, usually because of their biopsychosocial complexity – and this is reflected in diagnosis and management[46].

Most important, while fully accepting the reality of the symptoms, common health problems are insufficient to explain long-term incapacity:

- Many of these people do not have any absolute physical or mental incapacity for most ordinary activities and most jobs in modern society.

- Most acute episodes settle quite quickly (at least enough to return to most normal activities, even if with some persistent or recurrent symptoms)

- Most people with these conditions remain at work, and the large majority of those who do take sickness absence return to work quite quickly (even if still with some symptoms)

- There is usually little evidence of disease, permanent damage or impairment

- Overall, only about 1% of episodes of sickness absence in workers go on to long-term incapacity[47].

These are essentially whole people with manageable health problems: given proper support, recovery is normally to be expected and long-term incapacity is not inevitable.

The dichotomy between 'severe medical conditions' and 'common health problems' is an over-simplification, with obvious difficulties in drawing the boundary between them and in defining severity. Rather, this is a spectrum with a variable balance between pathology and symptoms and much of the present argument applies across the whole range of health conditions. Nevertheless, there is a qualitative difference as well as a difference in degree between the two ends of the spectrum, e.g. between schizophrenia vs. subjective reports of work-related 'stress' that do not meet the criteria of any specific psychiatric diagnosis (Wessely 2004). Disability and incapacity are *not* all or nothing, and the problem is where across this spectrum to set the threshold or cut-off for 'incapacity'. Originally, in the 20th century, only severe medical conditions were considered for social support. By the early 19th century, in sickness claims under the National Insurance Act: 'In a very large class of cases, the causes of incapacity present subjective symptoms only - - . In these cases the doctor has to rely almost entirely on the statements made by the patient - -' (Schuster 1914). Today, the pendulum has swung towards greater acceptance of self-reported health problems. Without prejudging where any cut-off should be, it may be useful to consider how public perceptions of disability, the nature of disability and medical certification influence the threshold.

Box 6: The nature of health problems associated with incapacity.

- 15-20% Severe medical conditions with severe and demonstrable disease or impairment.
- 10-15% Pathology that provides a sound basis for functional limitations.
- 65-75% Limited or inconsistent pathological basis for incapacity.

3.4 Perceptions of disability

The dominant public images of 'disabled people' include people who are blind or in wheelchairs. The most common perception is that they have severe medical conditions, and this is associated with widely held beliefs about the nature of disability (Grewal *et al* 2002):

- It relates to physical impairment

- Is visible to others

- Means reduced levels of physical or mental ability

- Leads to incapacity for work and dependence

- Is a permanent, unchanging state.

Health professionals (Deal 2003) and employers (Stuart *et al* 2002) have similar perceptions. Disabled people share many of these views, though they also acknowledge a wider range of 'invisible' disabilities such as diabetes or mental illness (Grewal *et al* 2002). Although the disability movement argues strongly that disabled people have a common group identity, there is some evidence that disabled people themselves recognise a 'hierarchy of impairments' (Deal 2003). Most relevant to the present analysis, however, is the traditional assumption that disability automatically means (permanent) incapacity for work, and that disabled people therefore have one of the most secure claims on social security benefits (Reno *et al* 1997). It should be obvious by now that popular stereotype is quite out of touch with IB reality.

Illness is perceived differently to disability because it can recover or be cured, which should correspond to many common health problems. Thus, incapacity associated with these problems may be more accurately described as 'longer-term sickness' rather than 'disability'. That indeed reflects IB recipients' own view: 90% of new claimants initially expect to return to work in due course (Green et al 2000). Even among a sample of recipients of long-term disability benefits[48], 27% still regarded themselves as 'ill' and only 57% as disabled[49] (Rowlingson & Berthoud 1996). Even among people classified as 'disabled', Grewal *et al* (2002) found the most common reason given for not working was 'temporarily or long-term sick' (60%).

When it comes to subjective health complaints, however, both doctors and the public have conceptual difficulties about illness, incapacity and sick certification. When presented with these kinds of clinical vignettes, doctors' decisions on sick certification appear more or less random. When questioned, doctors and the general public are reluctant to accept psychological and social problems as the basis for sick certification[50].

3.5 The multifactorial nature of (in)capacity

Saying that many IB recipients are not completely incapacitated but are still capable of some work does not mean these people are all malingerers or scroungers. [Detailed references to the evidence for the following statements are given in the endnote[51].]

- Virtually all have a genuine health condition or impairment that causes some limitations. All the evidence is that true malingering (feigning an injury or illness that does not exist) is extremely rare and recorded benefit fraud is <1%.

- Virtually all say that illness or disability affects their ability to work, and about three-quarters say it is the main reason they are not working or seeking work. However, less than a quarter say they cannot do any work at all.

- About two-thirds say they have been advised by their doctors that they *should* not work. Health care can sometimes become a barrier rather than the solution to (return to) work.

- 90% of new IB claimants initially expect to return to work, and one third to half of all IB recipients still want to work.

- More than half have personal circumstances and commitments that make work more difficult, e.g. child care responsibilities or caring for someone with an illness or disability.

- Many IB recipients face multiple disadvantages and barriers to (return to) work that are significant and additive:

  - age (half are aged >50 years)

  - poor work history (1/3rd have already been out of work for >2 years when they start IB)

  - low skills (40% have no qualifications, 15% have basic skills problems)

- The longer someone is out of work the more distant they become from the labour market and the lower their chances of getting back into work. 75% of current recipients have been on IB > 2 years.

- There may be lack of suitable jobs in the local labour market. There is a major problem of regional deprivation, with ten-fold variation in IB rates between the best and worst local authority areas.

- Employer discrimination is still a major barrier, especially for people with mental health conditions.

- Uncertainty is a key issue: about whether they will be fit to work regularly, about the risk of losing benefits or getting back on to benefits if the need arises, and about the financial consequences of coming off benefits. This is partly due to lack of information about and understanding of the benefits system.

- The IB regime itself 'labels' people as incapable of work, becomes a barrier to work, and reinforces other barriers.

- 95% of IB recipients face at least one and 60% face three or more barriers to (return to) work, in addition to their health condition.

Nevertheless, none of that should deflect attention from the central role of free will, motivation and effort (Leonard *et al* 1995, Halligan *et al* 2003, Aylward 2003, Green 2003).

There is extensive scientific and epidemiological evidence that incapacity does not depend solely on the individual's health condition or impairment (Swain *et al* 1993, Waddell *et al* 2002). Disability and incapacity depend on interactions between the person with a health condition or impairment *and* their environment (Glouberman 2001, Howard 2003), between biology *and* culture (Morris 1998), and this interaction is always mediated by the mind (Wainwright & Calnan 2002). That is all particularly true for incapacity associated with less severe, common health problems.

Understanding and management of incapacity must therefore take account of all the health-related, personal and social factors that influence functioning and participation (Engel 1997, WHO 2001, Waddell 2002)[52]. There is extensive clinical evidence that psychological and social factors play a central role in functional capacity and the development of long-term incapacity (Main & Spanswick 2000, Linton 2002, Gatchel & Turk 2002, Geisser *et al* 2003, Waddell *et al* 2003). They influence sickness absence (Briner 1996, Luz & Green 1997, Alexanderson & Norlund 2004), rehabilitation (BSRM 2004, Waddell & Burton 2004b), return to work (Krause *et al* 2001) and long-term incapacity (Waddell *et al* 2003). They are particularly important in less severe and more subjective health conditions.

Personal characteristics include age, gender, family and social background, education, training and skills, work experience and work history.

*Internal **psychological factors*** concern how people think and feel:

a   the personal experience of illness and disability influences daily living, social relationships, and people's sense of self and identity (Finkelstein & French 1993, Barnes & Mercer 1995, Reeve 2004);

b   perceptions and expectations;

c   attitudes and beliefs, emotions, mood, psychological distress and coping strategies;

d   (dis)incentives, motivation and effort;

e   uncertainty.

Social factors in the broadest sense concern external influences or interactions with other people and society (Waddell & Waddell 2000):

a   the culture that surrounds health, sickness, disability and work;

b   labour market forces;

c   social and occupational barriers;

d   discrimination, social disadvantage and social exclusion;

e   financial (dis)incentives.

The relative importance of these factors may vary in different individuals and settings and over time.

From one perspective, sickness, disability and incapacity associated with common health problems can then be viewed as 'illness behaviour' (Box 7).

> **Box 7: Illness behaviour includes all the things that ill people say and do that express and communicate their feelings of being unwell[53].**
>
> - Illness behaviour depends, first and foremost, on the severity of symptoms, e.g. intensity of pain (Fishbain *et al* 2003) – the more ill you are, the more ill you are likely to behave. But illness behaviour does not only depend on the underlying health condition (Figure 1). Different people with similar illnesses may or may not be incapacitated (Table 1).
> - Illness behaviour also depends on individual attitudes and beliefs, emotions, distress, and how the individual copes (Main & Spanswick 2000); and on motivation and effort (Halligan *et al* 2003, Green 2003).
> - Illness behaviour also depends on the social context and culture in which it occurs (Waddell & Waddell 2000).
>
> Illness behaviour depends on all of these factors and the interactions between them (WHO 2001, Waddell 2002, Howard 2003).

This is sometimes taken to imply that a) ill people cannot help how they react to pain or other symptoms, b) psychological factors are outwith conscious control, c) most illness behaviour is involuntary, and d) psychosocial factors are so powerful that the ill person cannot exercise any conscious control. That *is* true of a small minority of patients seen in specialist clinical settings, but it is not true of the large majority of IB claimants who do not have any such severe psychological disturbance (Aylward 2003). Most IB claimants have a genuine health condition, and many genuinely believe they cannot or should not work. These beliefs are often reinforced by medical advice (Anema *et al* 2002), by employers who will not permit return to work until symptoms are 'cured' (James *et al* 2002), or by the current culture that surrounds sickness and incapacity. Such perceptions and expectations have a powerful influence on behaviour, but they are not irresistible.

It is also often assumed that disability is a permanent status, but for many people disability is a dynamic process over time (Burchardt 2000a & b, Jenkins & Rigg 2004). Self-perceptions of 'work-limiting health conditions' fluctuate over time, and individuals move between being disabled and not being disabled, and between working and varying degrees of (in)capacity. Longitudinal studies show that 0.3% of employees commence Statutory Sick Pay or Incapacity Benefit each three months: about a quarter leave employment almost immediately and nearly half by 9-12 months (Burchardt 2003a). Over half of those who develop limiting conditions as adults have spells lasting less than two years, though most of those who remain limited for more than four years then remain disabled long-term (Burchardt 2000a). Intermittent patterns of disability are common, particularly in mental illness. Disability policy must be flexible enough to accommodate fluctuating health conditions and these different 'disability trajectories', which may require different support into work strategies and interventions. In general, however, these findings strongly support efforts to reintegrate 'disabled' people.

Most important, though many sick and disabled people and many health professionals seem to be unaware of this, the longer someone is out of work the more distant they get from the labour market and the lower their chances of returning to work (Frank *et al* 1996, 1998, Waddell & Burton 2004b). The 12 month point appears critical: after 1 year on IB the balance of probabilities is that recipients will remain on IB till they reach retirement age. Of those who do leave IB within 1 year, about half return to working 16+ hours per week; of those who leave after more than two years, only one third return to working 16+ hours per week (DWP administrative data). This is partly a 'selection effect' - people with good prospects of recovering health and/or returning to work exit early, leaving behind people with poor prospects. But there is also a 'duration effect' – the chance of any individual leaving declines the longer he or she remains on benefits. There is strong evidence that health deteriorates, psychosocial problems become worse and more complex (Main & Spanswick 2000), expectations of return to work deteriorate (Rowlingson & Berthoud 1996, Woodward *et al* 2003) and the obstacles to recovery, rehabilitation and return to work increase over time (Waddell & Burton 2004b, Watson & Patel 2004). Debate continues on the relative importance of selection and duration effects on exit from IB (Berthoud 2004, Wells 2004). There appears little doubt that both are significant, but duration effects appear more important: even recipients with 'good' characteristics who do not manage to exit quickly find it much more difficult to get back to work.

3.5.2 Obstacles to coming off benefits and (returning to) work

Crucially, all of these health-related, personal and social factors can also act as obstacles or barriers[54] to recovery and (return to) work (Box 8) (Burton & Main 2000, Main & Burton 2000,

Waddell & Burton 2004b). Obstacles are not located in the person or the environment alone: they commonly result from complex and ill-defined interactions between the individual with a health condition or impairment and their social context, compounded by increasing time and distance from the labour market (Howard 2003). In common health problems, many of the obstacles are at least partly a matter of *perceptions*– by the individual, the family, health professionals, co-workers and employer. Perceptions drive behaviour, and behaviour can influence perceptions: interactions between the players may mutually reinforce or conflict with each other.

> **Box 8: Obstacles to recovery and barriers to (return to) work (Waddell & Burton 2004b, Watson & Patel 2004)**
>
> • Physical and/or mental condition, impairment and any functional limitations they impose.
>
> • Personal characteristics.
>
> • Psychological factors.
>
> • Perceptions and concerns[55] about one's health condition, about work, about the relationship between them, and about 'workability' - the ability to cope with and sustain work (Tuomi *et al* 1997, 1998) - are likely to form more specific obstacles to (return to) work (Woodward *et al* 2003).
>
> • Benefit traps and uncertainty about coming off benefits.
>
> • Social and occupational barriers.
>
> • Discrimination, social disadvantage and exclusion.
>
> • Time and distance from the labour market.
>
> Health-related and psychological obstacles are most important for clinical recovery, but psychosocial and occupational barriers are more important for (return to) work.

Uncertainty seems to be a fundamental obstacle to coming off benefits and returning to work: uncertainty about ability to cope with and sustain work because of one's health condition ('workability' - Tuomi *et al* 1997, 1998), about the risk of losing benefits or getting back on to benefits if the need arises, about the financial hiatus between stopping benefits and receiving first wages, about financial differentials between benefits and wages, and due to lack of information and understanding of the benefits and tax credits systems (Gardiner 1997, Corden & Sainsbury 2001). Some people may be overwhelmed by their situation, feel unable to cope or to control their fate, and give up efforts to escape. This is partly a matter of perceptions and partly the realities of the system, but it makes claimants who are already in a precarious situation very risk aversive. This may be a particular problem for claimants with mental health conditions (Seebohm & Scott 2004).

Social barriers are also critical and may be much more important than the health condition itself, as emphasised by the social model (Oliver & Barnes 1998). The disability movement has focused on systemic social change, but individual sick and disabled people face specific social and occupational barriers to work that can also be addressed in that individual's own circumstances:

a   the balance between impairment and any associated functional limitations vs. physical and mental demands of work

b   many are further disadvantaged in employment because of age, low skills and distance from the labour market

c   access and transport

d   lack of suitable jobs

e   labour market forces: unemployment and regional deprivation

f   employer discrimination

g   lack of appropriate accommodations and adjustments.

Effective rehabilitation and support into work should address *all* of the health-related, personal and social barriers to work (Waddell & Burton 2004b). Coming off benefits and returning to work are not simply matters of health or health care alone: return to work is a social process that depends on the workplace and the employer (NIDMAR 2000, OECD 2003, James *et al* 2003). That demands much closer integration of health care, rehabilitation and support into work (Waddell & Burton 2004b, DWP 2004, 2005). However, disabled people's organisations point out that health care and employers sometimes create rather than overcome barriers (Sirvasta & Chamberlain 2005):

- The NHS often has a negative impact on (return to) work, with delays in consultation, investigation and treatment, lack of rehabilitation services, and lack of appreciation of work-related issues.

- Employers often have negative attitudes to sickness and disability, and are unresponsive to the needs of workers.

That demands a fundamental shift in the whole culture of clinical and occupational management, particularly for common health problems (Waddell & Burton 2004b).

3.6 Citizenship, rights and responsibilities

Recognition of the complex factors influencing incapacity must not obscure free will and personal responsibility for one's actions.

From another perspective, functioning and (in)capacity are matters of performance (Fordyce 1995). There is wide consensus that performance[56], rehabilitation and return to work depend on motivation and effort (Waddell & Burton 2004b). Motive is 'what induces a person to act in a particular way, e.g. desire, fear, circumstance' (Concise Oxford Dictionary), but motivation also raises issues about personal choice of goals, drive and effort, efficacy and success in achieving these goals[57] (Leonard *et al* 1995). Sickness and disability may interfere with the pursuit of life goals[58] and motivation to (return to) work depends on concurrence between the goals of clinical and occupational management and individual life goals (Sivaraman Nair 2003). Many health-related, personal, occupational and cultural factors influence the decisions that sick and disabled people make about work. Health-related issues are usually central (Arthur *et al* 1999, Grewal *et al* 2002, Woodward *et al* 2003, Alcock *et al* 2003). But efforts to return to work also depend on whether the individual wants to work, what kind of work they want, if they think they could get such work, and if they think they could manage that work (Berglind & Gerner 2002). Work-related goals are modified by personal and psychological factors, labour market forces, economic and other (dis)incentives, and social barriers (Waddell *et al* 2002). However, even after allowing for all that, various studies suggest that 20-30% of compensation claimants demonstrate some degree of 'lack of effort' or 'exaggeration' of their symptoms and disability (Halligan *et al* 2003, Green 2003). Whatever the difficulties of definition or assessment (Waddell 2004a), issues of (under)-motivation and (lack of) effort are fundamental to performance.

The benefit system must recognise and allow for human nature[59] (Field 1996, 1997, 1998). It is natural to look after one's own self-interest (Mill 1859): there is nothing wrong with that, and it should not be misinterpreted as selfishness or greed. There is extensive evidence that benefit claimants respond to financial incentives (Loeser *et al* 1995, Waddell *et al* 2002). Policy-makers often fashion policies based on assumptions that the people affected by their policies will be motivated and behave in certain ways (Le Grand 1997, 2003). Often, they assume that claimants act like the hypothetical 'economic man' who pursues his self-interest by actions based on the balance of incentives and risks[60], so they argue that reform is mainly a matter of providing the right incentives and controls. Economic incentives are certainly important, but they are only one part of the story and empirical evidence suggests that the strength of their effect is weaker than many policy-makers assume[61] (Loeser *et al* 1995, Gardiner 1997, Waddell & Norlund 2000, Halpern *et al* 2004). Moreover, human behaviour does not always follow principles of economic rationality (Bane & Ellwood 1994, Piachaud 1997). Behaviour may be rational but value other goals higher than economic self-interest. Claimants often lack adequate information and must make decisions in the face of considerable uncertainty. So choices are influenced by 'psychological discounting', immediate gains count for more than future gains (even if the latter would be greater), losses can have a more impact than comparable gains, and 'peak' experiences may have disproportionate impact compared with more constant experience. Choices are strongly influenced by social and cultural pressures. Thus, behaviour is often 'irrational' and includes what economists might regard as 'mistakes'. Tastes and preferences (to use economic terms) may be inconsistent, vary over time, and reflect culture, morality and social acceptability. Welfare policy must allow for the richness of human behaviour, for human failings and individual choice (Mead 1997a & b, Duncan & Edwards 1998, Nye 1998, Jones & Cullis 2000, Pfau-Effinger 2005) and for the complexity of changing behaviour (Halpern *et al* 2004).

But, ultimately, none of this absolves the individual from responsibility for his or her actions. Whatever the philosophical debate about the extent of free will[62] (Dennett 2003), the law takes a pragmatic approach to 'intent' (Gordon 1978, 2000) - acting intentionally, actions with a particular intent or purpose[63]. Individual liberty and responsibility for one's actions are taken to be the norm unless there is strong evidence to the contrary: 'for normally there is a presumption that if a person does something, he does it intentionally' (Gordon 1978). People act consciously, with awareness of what they are doing and of the likely consequences (i.e. not accidentally, or in ignorance). Social policy, like the law, must be based on the presumption that claimants have personal responsibility for their behaviour.

In the particular context of sickness and disability, claimants may face considerable constraints on their behaviour. Some severe medical conditions and severe impairments may impose functional limitations that are too severe to overcome, whatever reason, character and strength of will may say. Sick and disabled people may face considerable social barriers and disadvantages. But the less severe the impairment, the greater the importance of personal and psychological factors, and the greater the degree of choice and personal responsibility. For all the qualifications, most IB claimants retain personal responsibility for their actions. Very few have a severe mental illness or disorder that absolves them from responsibility. Most claimants are answerable to whether it would be 'unreasonable to expect (me) to seek or be available for work'. Or, even accepting that they do have a genuine health problem, can they still reasonably be expected to do some work? Rational, free individuals bear ultimate responsibility for their actions and must answer to these questions.

Social security benefits are based on an implicit social contract. Contracts by their nature are between two (or more) parties who enter into the contract freely, and include obligations and conditions on both (all) sides. This is not some abstract philosophical contract (Locke 1690, Hume 1748, Rousseau 1762), but a very real legislative and economic contract between the citizen and the welfare state today. Or, more accurately, between the citizen claimant and the citizen taxpayers, with Government acting as the intermediary. Employers also bear social responsibilities. However, such agreements between the individual and the state often fall far short of a 'legal contract', and may be better understood in the looser sense of a 'compact' – a mutual bargain or agreement (Halpern *et al* 2004). The inequity is that Government is bound to them as a legal contract but it now seems to be much less binding on individual recipients.

Society is based on mutual support for mutual advantage, which depends on the principle of 'fair reciprocity' (White 2000, 2003, Howard 2004a). Each citizen has an obligation to make reasonable contribution to society according to his or her abilities, in return for the advantages received. The original welfare state was grounded on principles of solidarity, universalism and social rights, but also assumed that each individual would be fair and judicious in claiming their rights according to their needs (Cox 1998). That was an optimistic view of human nature, in a time when standards of conduct and civic virtue were inculcated by family, church and the education system. But as these institutions have weakened, individual liberty increased and moral standards loosened[64], perverse interactions between the welfare state and human nature have encouraged claimants to pursue their self-interest and exploit the welfare system, while shirking their social obligations. The result is that social rights are now claimed on the basis of availability and entitlement, often regardless of need. However, under the principles of social justice and fairness, the state has the reciprocal right to expect and even demand that individuals must make their reasonable contribution in return. In this situation, the welfare system itself may help establish and reinforce the social contract of citizenship, its rights and responsibilities, and even standards of moral conduct. There is then a pressing need for a new and more explicit welfare contract in which rights and responsibilities are clearly defined; in which each citizen is granted a stake in welfare but clear obligations and responsibilities are demanded in return (Blair 1995, 2004, Einerhand & Nekkers 2004, Halpern *et al* 2004).

Since the 1990s, several linked themes have emerged in debates about British citizenship in general and welfare policy in particular:

- The post-WWII concept of citizenship as a matter of 'rights' (Marshall 1950, Titmuss 1956, Abel-Smith & Titmuss 1987) was too one-sided.

- There is a finite limit to the welfare benefits society can afford

- Benefit rights must therefore be balanced by specific social obligations: 'the rights we enjoy, the duties we owe' (Blair 1995)[65].

- This produces the 'principle of conditionality' (Deacon 1994): i.e. entitlement to certain, publicly provided, welfare benefits should be dependent on the recipient agreeing to meet certain social responsibilities or patterns of behaviour.

Government policy and welfare reform is now based upon such a vision of citizenship (HM Government 1998a): 'at the heart of the modern welfare state will be a new contract between the citizen and the government, based on rights and responsibilities'[66].

There is broad public support for the need to balance rights and responsibilities (Stafford 1998, Williams *et al* 1999) and a general trend to demand greater personal responsibility (British Surveys of Social Attitudes, Halpern *et al* 2004). As might be expected, benefit recipients are more divided on this issue (Dwyer 2002). Although this is commonly applied to other social security areas, it is equally relevant to sickness and disability benefits (Duckworth 2001, OECD 2003, Oliver 2004). 'Full and equal citizenship requires (disabled) individuals ultimately to carry the same responsibilities (and rights) as others - - - ' – accepting that these rights and responsibilities may need to be modified to suit their circumstances and balanced by support to enable them to be met (Howard 2004a)[67].

3.7 The sick role

The sick role is a social status accorded to the ill person by society: the individual assumes the sick role; other people judge whether that is appropriate and reasonable. From a sociological perspective, Parsons (1951) defined sickness as exemption from normal social roles because of illness, and first considered the rights and obligations of the sick role (Box 9):

Box 9: the original description of the sick role (Parsons 1951).

Rights:

- absolved from responsibility for sickness i.e. is the subject of a disease process largely beyond his or her control

- exempt from normal social role responsibilities, relative to the nature and severity of the illness*

- entitled to special attention and support i.e. to be taken care of.

  * And this depends on 'legitimisation' by others, often by a doctor.

Conditional on:

- accepting that to be sick is undesirable, and that it would be a good thing to get well as expeditiously as possible

- accepting an obligation to seek professional help and to cooperate in the process of getting well.

The sick role embodies society's attempt to control sickness, and to support and encourage return to 'well' behaviour, which leads to issues of legitimisation, conditionality, motivation and (dis)-incentives.

This remains the classic formulation of the sick role, which has stood the test of time despite many criticisms (Twaddle 1972, Gallacher 1976, Arluke *et al* 1979, Barnes & Mercer 1995). It is questionable if there is a universal role applicable to all sick people, and (some of) the rights and privileges of the sick role may be denied or only partially granted. It is most appropriate to acute physical illness: it is harder to apply to mental health conditions and the very notion of chronic illness runs contrary to its temporary status. It is a theoretical analysis from a societal and medical perspective, which pays little attention to the individual's subjective experience of symptoms or illness, and may not reflect individual or lay thinking or expectations about sickness. For the present analysis, however, its major limitations are that it is firmly rooted in a medical model of illness and is designed primarily as a social framework for health care. It assumes that medical treatment is the solution, providing cure as the means of exit from the sick role[68]. Crucially, it is often inferred that sickness absence is justified until this is achieved. Many patients and IB recipients (and health professionals) still think about sickness in this way. Unfortunately, this approach is quite inappropriate and positively harmful for many common health problems that do not have any good medical answer, and which are often persistent, recurrent or fluctuating[69]. The traditional sick role can then become a trap, in which the patient continues (futile) attempts to find a medical solution and remains passively in the sick role awaiting 'cure', even when there is no medical reason for permanent incapacity.

More fundamentally, Parson's sick role was based on his analysis of cultural values in western society (Shilling 2002). Christian ethics emphasized the 'gift of life' bestowed on human beings in return for which they owed their labour to build the 'kingdom of god on earth', which underpinned the protestant work ethic[70]. Sickness interfered with this, so there was a moral duty to attempt to recover, return to work and contribute to society. Yet religious and cultural values, and concepts of illness and sickness have changed since the 1950s in a way that has upset the delicate balance of rights and responsibilities. The implicit social contract that the sick role is all about getting better seems to have broken down, and instead the sick role is often assumed to confer a 'right' to (long-term) incapacity (Wainwright 2004).

The rights and obligations of the sick role then need to be revised for the common health problems that cause much sickness absence and incapacity today (Box 10).

Box 10: The sick role: a social contract between the worker and society.	
The sick worker	**Society**
Rights:	*Support policies:*
Absolved from responsibility for symptoms and impairment (but carries some responsibility for management of symptoms, illness & sickness).	Society has the right to judge if the sick person is meeting the obligations and responsibilities of the sick role.
Health care to alleviate symptoms.	Provide health care.
Modify normal social duties and responsibilities to a degree appropriate to the nature, severity and duration of illness (which may or may not mean incapacity for work and sickness absence).	Provide income replacement appropriate to the nature, severity and duration of sickness and incapacity.
If sickness absence is justified, the sick person has a right to sick pay and sickness benefits.	Society, as the provider of support, has the right to judge what is appropriate and to set entitlement.

Box 10: The sick role: a social contract between the worker and society (continued).	
The sick worker	**Society**
Obligations:	*Integration policies:*
Recognise that symptoms, feeling unwell, sickness and incapacity are not the same.	Labour market policies.
	'Health at work' policies
Share responsibility for managing health condition, recovery and rehabilitation.	Clinical and occupational management.
Recognise that the sick role is temporary, in the expectation of recovery.	Rehabilitation and support into work interventions.
Crucial to the contract with society, return to work when reasonably possible, even if still with some symptoms.	Address obstacles/barriers to return to work.
	Provide appropriate incentives and rewards for work.

This modified sick role focuses on social functioning rather than health care. It is appropriate for common health problems, mental health conditions, and for persistent and recurrent problems. This role is not static but dynamic and changes over time, with scope for the sick person to play an active role in self-care, adapting, coping and rehabilitation.

The sick role and the disability role initially appear to have much in common, but there is a fundamental ambivalence between them, which reflects the tension between social protection and social inclusion policies. To put it simply, the traditional sick role is about the right *not* to work; the modern disability role is about the right *to work* (Box 11). There is also a temporal dimension: it is desirable to do as much as possible to prevent people *becoming* disabled by chronic sickness (especially unnecessarily); but people who *are* disabled must not be stigmatised or discriminated against. This ambivalence has been confounded by changed expectations about disabled people working (Priestley 2000).

This disability role represents a fundamental shift from the historical role of loss, dependency, exclusion and care (i.e. a long-term sick role) to the modern concept of full citizenship, inclusion and fulfilling potential (Oliver & Barnes 1998, DRC 2004c, Howard 2004a). The social model shifted the focus from medical management of the individual's impairment to society enabling participation. Both the sick role and the disability role now shift the focus from 'health' and health care, to social functioning, support and participation.

The sick role and the disability role should also be distinguished from the patient role. It is often forgotten that most people deal with most common health problems themselves most of the time without seeking health care or entering the sick role. Conversely, seeking health care and becoming a patient does not and should not *necessarily* mean entering the sick role. The sick

Box 11: The disability role: a social contract between the citizen and society.

The disabled person	Society
Rights:	*Integration policies:*
Absolved from responsibility for physical and/or mental condition and impairment.	Promote social inclusion, provide access and prevent discrimination, taking into account the needs and aspirations of disabled people themselves.
Continued health care (if appropriate).	
Equal right to social inclusion and to fulfil individual potential in as full and normal a life as possible.	Labour market and 'health at work' policies
	Education, training and support into work.
If incapacitated for work, the disabled person has a basic human right to financial & other support.	Address obstacles to (return to) work.
	Provide positive incentives and rewards for work.
Obligations:	*Support policies:*
Recognise that impairment, disability and incapacity for work are not the same.	Health care (if appropriate).
Raise level of function and participation to the extent physical and/or mental condition permits and, given adequate opportunity and help, cooperate with attempts to achieve this.	Income support appropriate to the nature and severity of incapacity.
	Additional financial support for the extra costs of disability.
	Support into work interventions.
Crucially to the contract with society and citizenship, this includes the obligation to productive work if reasonably possible.	Society has the right to judge what support is appropriate and to define entitlement.

role does not *necessarily* mean sickness absence: many 'ill' people modify some parts of their life but still go to work; even at work many 'ill' people manage to modify their work without requiring sickness absence. Even when sickness absence is necessary, the sick role is generally a temporary role that receives active health care, rehabilitation and support interventions, in the expectation of recovery and return to work. The sick role is not generally considered nor generally leads to a permanent disability role. The disability role does not *necessarily* imply continued sickness nor continued health care. Neither the sick role nor the disability role *necessarily* implies incapacity for work.

Central to the sick role is the concept of social control and legitimisation - the social process of 'proving' sickness and entitlement to the benefits of the sick role (Telles & Pollack 1981, Glenton 2003). Subjective feelings of illness must be communicated to other people: physical symptoms are more likely to be accepted as a 'proper' and legitimate basis for sickness; psychological and emotional symptoms and symptoms related to social functioning (e.g. irritability, lack of energy, fatigue) are more likely to be questioned (Prior & Wood 2003). Initially, legitimisation usually occurs within the family and workplace, but then generally requires professional corroboration to be accepted by the employer, insurer or social security system. When it goes wrong, the process of legitimisation may lead to incorrectly 'labelling' people sick. Ill-founded diagnoses and continued health care may reinforce the sick role and perceptions of incapacity. Conversely, the process may lead to conflict, stigma and distress when the reality of feelings is questioned, the ill person is 'blamed' for their condition, or the sick role denied.

From its origins, welfare has struggled with the concept of 'deserving' vs. 'undeserving' claimants (Hadler 1995). Whatever the moral debate, however, legislation about entitlement and individual decisions to award or withhold benefits have always effectively required such judgments. Moreover, public opinion has little difficulty with this concept (Weiner 1993, Stafford 1998, Williams *et al* 1999). 'Deserving' claimants are seen as those who are 'genuine' and whose need for support is due to no fault of their own; while 'undeserving' claimants are seen as those who abuse the system and/or are not trying their best to get off benefits. However, most public judgments are again about the poor, the unemployed and lone parents, rather than the sick and disabled. Benefit recipients are more reluctant to make such a distinction, regard the majority of claims as 'genuine', and certainly assume that *they* fall into the deserving group (Dwyer 2000, 2002).

This returns to the issue of personal responsibility. Generally, as described by Parsons, the sick role absolves the individual from responsibility for disease[71], but 'illness' and 'sickness' are different and more difficult issues. There have been radical shifts in social attitudes to sickness and disability since Parsons' time, reflected in the range of health conditions that cause incapacity. Socially, there is a wider underlying theme of 'medicalising' problems in (working) life (Box 12), which has led to an increasing social acceptability of sickness and disability and a reduction in personal responsibility for health, sickness and getting well. However, although such 'cultural change' is unquestionably important, it is only one part of the story. Wainwright (personal communication) suggests that it may have weakened social defences against entering the sick role, rather than providing a positive push into it. Marked regional variations in IB claims shows that structural factors are also important (though there may be regional variations in culture also).

The key conclusions of this section are:

- The sick role and the disability role are not the same.

- Both sickness and disability are social roles that carry rights and responsibilities.

Box 12: 'Medicalisation' of modern life (Foucault 1975, Morris 1998, Berthoud 1998, Noah 1999, Wainwright & Calnan 2002, Aylward 2003, Wainwright 2004, Wade & Halligan 2004).

- More open acknowledgement and expression of feelings, greater sensitivity to physical and emotional needs and vulnerabilities and potential 'harm' – by the individual - and acceptable to others and society

- Expansion of diagnostic categories to include phenomena that were previously considered normal aspects of everyday life and corrosion of observable pathology as the basis of diagnosis

- A 'victim' culture that attributes 'blame' and expects redress

- Institutionalisation of 'the therapeutic state' that expects a professional solution to all life's problems

- Diagnostic labelling (sometimes with little organic basis) legitimising sickness and disability. Traditionally, clinical diagnosis was primarily for the purpose of patient care and treatment. When diagnosis is influenced or driven by non-clinical ends (e.g. to claim benefits), that raises questions about its legitimacy and consequences.

- Any illness provided with a (medically validated) diagnostic label is widely assumed to have a defined pathological basis, to be demonstrable independently of the symptoms, to require 'treatment', and to justify incapacity.

- Increasing numbers of people labelled or labelling themselves as ill and entering the sick role with all the social and economic consequences that follow

- At the same time, there is a general discontent with authority, medical and allied professions.

However, that is not irreversible, as demonstrated by some 'de-medicalisation' of back pain in the UK (Waddell *et al* 2002). A recent study in the Netherlands (Cardol *et al* 2005) has also shown patients' attitudes shifting away from consulting their GP for minor ailments, following information campaigns and policy strategies that actively discourage such consultations.

3.8 Sick certification

Sick certification gives the sick person formal and legal rights in the sick role, most importantly for sickness absence from work. UK workers may self-certify for the first 7 days of sickness absence, which has administrative and resource advantages, but is open to the potential error and bias of subjective assessment and self-report of health problems[72]. It also leads to less external control during the vital early stages of sickness. A doctor's (usually a GP's) certificate is required for periods of more than 7 days.

Advice on Fitness for Work is an integral part of clinical management[73], but GPs also have a contractual obligation to provide medical certificates for social security purposes, i.e. for Statutory Sick Pay (SSP) from employers[74] and for DWP benefits (NHS 2004). When writing a sick certificate, doctors have a professional duty to the patient and also a social duty to society to provide factual medical evidence and impartial judgments. DWP provides official guidance to doctors on certification practice (CMG 2004a), based on the Social Security (Medical Evidence) Regulations 1976 (as amended). Specifically, the doctor should establish a diagnosis, assess reduction in functional ability and relate this to (in)capacity for work (Alexanderson & Norlund 2004). The doctor's judgment of (in)capacity is meant to be solely about the patient's medical condition and the functional limitations or restrictions that result from it, in relation to the type of tasks they actually perform at work[75] (CMG 2004a). However, the subtlety of this logic escapes most GPs and patients. In practice, this 'advice' is taken by patients as 'official' permission to take time off work and subsequently used as the basis for benefit claims. Moreover, the doctor's primary professional responsibility in the clinical situation is to the patient and to promote his or her best interests. There is an unavoidable ethical conflict between patient care, patient advocacy and gate-keeping roles (Toon 1992), which different doctors resolve by a) a hard-line assessment of incapacity based on objective diagnosis, b) attempting to take a biopsychosocial approach that considers the person, their health problem and their social context, c) 'it's not my job', or d) confused (de Bont 2005, Brage 2005).

The less common ground for sick certification is if work might be 'prejudicial to the patient's health'. Many doctors still appear to have concerns about work being generally harmful to physical or mental health and recovery. About two-thirds of recent IB claimants say they have been advised by their doctors that they *should* not work (Meager *et al* 1998, Woodward *et al* 2003, Goldestone & Douglas 2003)[76], even though most of the scientific evidence suggests the opposite except in very specific circumstances[77]. DWP has always taken a more stringent view about possible 'harm' and in practice has limited this to conditions where work may result in 'a substantial risk to the mental or physical health' of the patient or others[78].

Dealing with sickness absence is a daily issue for GPs and the average GP issues 10-15 sick certificates per week. GPs generally understand the 'rules' for sick certification, even if they are less clear about their exact role in the benefits system. But, in practice, doctors follow both formal and informal 'rules' (de Boer *et al* 2004, de Bont 2005). Most GPs consider that sickness absence is almost always 'genuine' (Mowlam & Lewis 2005), while public perceptions are that a medical certificate proves IB claimants are genuine and therefore deserving (Stafford 1998, Williams *et al* 1999). DWP Personal Advisers also generally accept and are very reluctant to challenge GP fitness for work advice and sick certificates (Legard 2002, Goldstone & Douglas 2003).

The reality of sick certification is much less clear-cut, particularly for common health problems where GPs have greatest difficult (Ritchie *et al* 1993, Hiscock & Ritchie 2001, Sawney 2002,

Soderberg & Alexanderson 2003, Alexanderson & Norlund 2004, Mowlam & Lewis 2005). Obtaining a sick certificate is often initiated by the patient, it is a matter of negotiation between doctor and patient, and doctors often base their decisions largely on the patient's own perceptions and desires. In practice, doctors' judgments of patients' capacity for work and decisions about certification are not restricted to the medical condition but are influenced by many complex factors. The patient's medical condition and its impact on employment potential are always high on the list. But they are almost immediately linked to a whole range of non-medical factors, including the patient's age, gender, attitude and motivation to work, potential for rehabilitation or training, prospects of actually getting or going back to work, and the socio-economic consequences of being refused a certificate. To confound that, most GPs have limited understanding of or expertise in disability assessment, their patients' work or occupational health issues. Judgments are particularly difficult for lengthier sickness absence associated with mental health conditions, predominantly subjective complaints and chronic conditions with a fluctuating course. That is why legislative change alone may have little or no effect on certification practice[79] (Englund *et al* 2000, Arrelov *et al* 2003).

These difficulties have most serious consequences in common health problems where there is little evidence of identifiable disease, because the whole focus of 'certification' is about providing a medical diagnosis. Any illness provided with a diagnostic label is then assumed (by the patient, other people, health professionals, employers and society) to be due to defined pathology, which provides 'proof' of the condition independent of the symptoms, means that it should be 'treatable', and justifies entry to the sick role until it is 'cured'. These labels and the associated perceptions become very difficult to challenge (Cedraschi *et al* 1998, Bogduk 2000, Goldstone & Douglas 2003). The problem is that doctors and patients are often unaware of, and fail to consider, the effects of sick certification and extended periods of sickness absence (Beaumont 2003a; Beaumont 2003b). Sick certificates initially issued for acute illness may label people sick and disabled, legitimise and reinforce the sick role, and promote illness behaviour, adaptation to invalidity and long-term incapacity (Anema *et al* 2002). Thus, long-term sick certification for common health problems without any clear medical basis may have catastrophic social consequences for the patient, including loss of employment and long-term incapacity.

Qualitative studies over the past 10 years[80] show the main stakeholders have conflicting views on sick certification[81]:

The views of **GPs** are diverse and complex, but many GPs:

- Do not regard advice on work as a 'core service' to their patients (they see this as largely an issue for the individual and his or her employer), though some do regard it as a key part of good clinical management.

Feel no obligation to employers. See the patient's entitlement to state benefits as a matter for DWP and the Government.

- Lack training, awareness, understanding and even interest in their patients' work situation, occupational health, the social security system and their role within it. GPs lack expertise in disability assessment. More specifically, they find it difficult to judge how far any incapacity is due to the health condition rather than to other non-medical factors.

- Have poor understanding and general dislike of benefit-related paperwork

- Have difficulties with the time required and some practical aspects of certification. (Though that is probably mainly related only to more detailed DWP forms.)

- Are unhappy with the role of 'gatekeeper' to state incapacity benefits. (See below.)

- Show wide variation in certification practice, diagnoses specified and period of sickness absence advised[82]. Up to 20% of GPs do not provide satisfactory certification and a few do not comply with their terms of service.

- Have low expectations of long-term IB recipients ever re-entering the labour market, and do not see it as their job to support this.

Patients generally:

- Want timely access to medical advice on fitness for work that preferably fits their own perceptions of their health condition and associated limitations and restrictions.

- Want independent advice from a source they can trust. They often feel that GPs are 'on my side' while they are distrustful of the motives of Government and DWP (whom they perceive as simply trying to save money), employers and occupational health advisers (whom they perceive as being on the employer's side).

- Believe they need sick certificates to prove they are totally incapacitated in order to get sick pay or social security benefits.

The majority of *employers* have negative views[83]. They consider that:

- Doctors, particularly GPs, lack interest and understanding of occupational health issues.

- Doctors often see work as harmful to health and see employers as 'the enemy'.

- Doctors sign people off work too easily and use patient advocacy as an excuse for acceding to patients' demands.

- They are generally disappointed with NHS input to sickness absence management and rehabilitation[84].

Similarly, ***occupational health physicians*** regard passive management by treating physicians and passive attitudes of patients as obstacles to return to work (Anema *et al* 2002).

These differing views reflect underlying ethical questions (Toon 1992, Hussey *et al* 2003, Mowlam & Lewis 2005). There is little argument about the need to provide factual medical evidence as the basis for a patient's claim for financial benefits, provided personal medical information is kept secure and confidential[85]. The problem lies more with 'impartial judgments' about functional limitations and incapacity, where the doctor's primary professional duty to the individual patient conflicts with a more abstract social duty in sick certification. The GP's contract is with DH/NHS (NHS 2004), while sick certification is on behalf of DWP. There is conflict between the GP's patient advocate vs. gatekeeper roles, which may be confounded by confusion between the patient's short-term and long-term interests. Over recent years, the doctor-patient relationship has changed with loss of professional authority and GPs moving to the role of health adviser and advocate, making it more difficult for them to act also as gatekeepers to benefits. Doctors want to avoid confrontation with their patients to avoid jeopardising the doctor-patient relationship that is essential to clinical management.

It is then not surprising that the majority of GPs are at best ambivalent about sick certification (generally believing their role should be reduced) and at worst actively hostile. Sick certification has been a matter of medico-political dispute between the British Medical Association and Government for many years, with the BMA campaigning to end or at least reduce GP involvement. GPs accept that Government needs to control benefits and, if anything, believe it should do more rather than less: it is just that they do not want to be the ones to do it. The trouble is, given GPs' central role in clinical management and their general professional expertise and status, no one has come up with any realistic alternative.

4 DEVELOPMENT AND TRENDS OF UK SICKNESS AND DISABILITY BENEFITS FROM 1948

4.1 Overview

Each day in the UK, nearly 1 million people (3% of workers) are on sickness absence from work (CBI 2003, 2004, CIPD 2004)[86]. Most return to work quite quickly – with a median of about three days - but the problem of long-term incapacity is much more serious. Each week 17,000 people reach their sixth week of sickness absence and 3,000 of them will then remain off work for 6 months and move to IB. Altogether, just over 3 million people of working age are on some kind of longer-term disability and incapacity benefit[87]: that is more than 8% of the UK population of working age. About one-quarter of men and one-fifth of women retire prematurely on grounds of ill health (Humphrey *et al* 2002).

Because of the way it has evolved, the present system of disability and incapacity benefits is complex, involving a number of different benefits for different people in different circumstances based on different principles (Lonsdale & Aylward 1996, Berthoud 1998). These benefits broadly provide income replacement for people who are incapable of work, help meet the extra costs of disability, compensate people for injuries and diseases incurred in the course of their employment, and top up earnings in work. In practice, though not in the original legislative intent, they now play an important role in alleviating poverty. Entitlement to different benefits varies:

- National Insurance (NI) benefits to cover specific risks, mainly for working people

- A system of non-contributory but means-tested benefits which act as a 'safety net' to provide a minimum income

- A number of 'category benefits' which are neither NI based nor means tested but depend on specific entitlement.

3,066 million people of working age are on some kind of sickness or disability benefit (National Statistics February 2005). Table 4 shows the numbers currently receiving the various benefits[88]. Figure 3 shows the considerable overlap between the key benefits: 62% of recipients receive more than one benefit.

There is widespread misconception about the level of UK benefits. At first sight, Incapacity Benefit (from April 2005, £57.65 - £ 76.45 per week) appears to provide very low wage replacement rates. However, these figures are for the basic, flat-rate benefit and give a false impression of what recipients actually receive (National Statistics 2005). Many receive various

TABLE 4 Number of working age recipients of various disability and incapacity benefits (National Statistics February 2005)

Benefit	Recipients (thousands)
Statutory Sick Pay (estimated)	300
Incapacity Benefit beneficiaries	1454
credits only	924
Severe Disablement Allowance	251
Disability Living Allowance (care and/or mobility)	1556
Income Support with disability premium	1324
Industrial Injuries Disablement Benefit	341
Carer's Allowance *	412

* This is the number of carers of working age, though there is no data on the age of those they are caring for.

Figure 3: Number of recipients (millions) of various combinations of disability and incapacity benefits in February 2005 (National Statistics 2005).

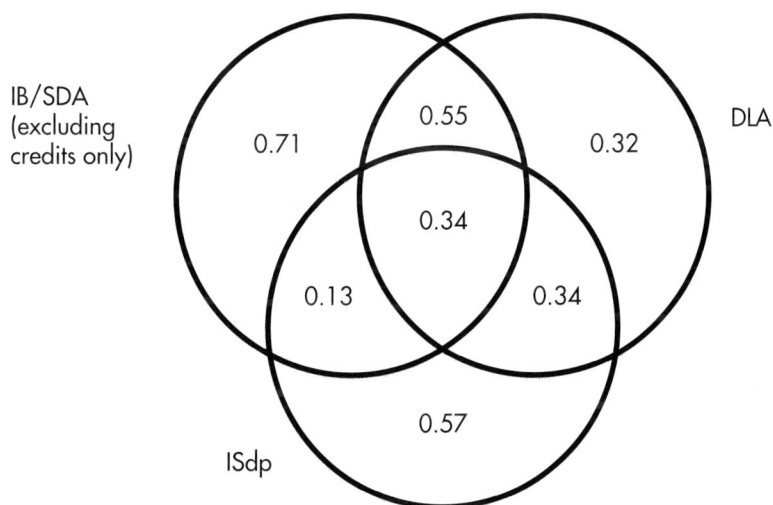

supplements and the average IB payment is currently £84. Many IB recipients (Fig 3) also receive another disability benefit: Disability Living Allowance (DLA) at an average of £58 or Income Support with a disability premium (ISdp) at an average of £87. Total incapacity and disability benefit expenditure of £20 billion per annum (see following paragraph) is paid to just over 3 million people, which implies that the average total disability benefits are about £6,500 per recipient per annum. That still does not allow for possible entitlement to Housing Benefit (average £61 per week), Mortgage Interest Payments or Council Tax Benefit (average £13 per week). Some IB recipients have other sources of income: 70% are married or cohabiting; 18% have a partner who is earning; 6-9% have a partner who is also on IB; some partners receive Carer's Allowance (average £45 per week). Unfortunately, it has not been possible to obtain current DWP data on the total amounts paid to individual recipients. However, Grundy *et al* (1999) found that average gross weekly household income in 1996/97 ranged from £146 for a disabled adult living alone (29% of the disabled) to £395 for a disabled adult living with a partner and children (32% of the disabled). That compared with average UK male earnings at the time of £436 gross per week. It appears that many IB recipients receive much more generous benefits than commonly believed, but there is wide variation and an important minority still live in poverty (Grewal *et al* 2002, OECD 2003, CPAG 2004).

Sickness absence is generally estimated to cost British employers £11-12 billion per annum (CBI 2004, CIPD 2004) though Bevan & Hayday (2001) considered that was seriously under-estimated[89]. Various studies show that about 10% of long-term sickness absence accounts for three-quarters of the costs. DWP disability and incapacity benefits now cost £20 billion a year (of which £6.7 billion is for IB)[90] compared with only £3.5 billion for unemployment benefits. That is a fifth of UK benefit expenditure or 5.6% of total government expenditure. There are no estimates available of the cost of ill health retirement, but it is likely to be of the same order of magnitude. Combining these data, sickness and disability costs UK *at least* £35-65 billion per annum[91], which compares with £60 billion expenditure on the NHS or £49 billion on education. To reduce these figures to a personal level, sickness and disability costs every taxpayer about £650 per annum to pay for DWP disability and incapacity benefits, and probably the same again built into the price of goods and services.

4.2 The Beveridge reforms (1946-48)

Without discounting earlier developments since Elizabethan times and particularly in the late 19th and first half of the 20th century, current UK concepts of 'the welfare state' date from the Beveridge Report and the post-WWII reforms (Beveridge 1942, National Insurance Act 1946). Indeed, the Beveridge Report is still seen in Britain and throughout the world as a kind of 'Magna Carta' of the welfare state. Beveridge's enduring vision was to create an all-encompassing social safety net for the whole population 'from the cradle to the grave', with strong liberal and social democratic overtones. It was underpinned by Keynesian demand management, the prospect of economic growth, and the maintenance of full employment. It expressed the high degree of social solidarity that was probably unique to wartime Britain in 1942, which saw comprehensive social reform both as an essential element in boosting wartime morale and the basis for democratic post-war reconstruction. The concept of citizenship on which it was based was subsequently articulated most clearly by Marshall (1950). However, the Beveridge proposals were very much designed for the social context of their time: founded on a life course of more or less full-time uninterrupted male employment, 'dependent' wife and children, and relatively short retirement. Other groups of people, including women, children, elderly and disabled people were not included in the 'universal' benefits and received highly conditional forms of welfare. Although this seemed like a social revolution in the disciplined and austere wartime 1940s, in the cold light of retrospect the practical reality appears much more selective and austere (Hills *et al* 1994, Harris 1999).

In the Beveridge proposals, sickness benefits were based on social insurance for those who were gainfully employed, which was operationalised as entitlement based on National Insurance contributions. Benefits were 'not for persons who, since they have no earnings, do not lose income if sickness prevents them working'. According to social and employment patterns of the time, the focus was on male bread-winners with some allowances for their dependent families. Funding of the scheme never followed true insurance principles, but was always 'Pay As You Go' and depended on a (growing) share of general taxation. Thus entitlement was granted by society and, contrary to widespread belief (Stafford 1998), was never a 'right' paid for by past contributions. As a general principle, Beveridge proposed that all benefits should be at the same flat rate, with additional support for the extra costs of prolonged disability and additional 'compensation' for industrial injury 'sustained while serving in the national interest'[92]. Concern about potential disincentives, combined with the post-war economic situation and Treasury resistance, resulted in benefit rates that provided little more than subsistence (Tomlinson 1998).

There has always been a tension between individual effort and responsibility vs. state provision of social security, and one of Beveridge's achievements was to strike a balance between collectivism and individualism[93]. It is often forgotten that Beveridge stressed that the welfare state cannot and should not be a complete replacement for individual effort: 'Social security must be achieved by co-operation between the State and the individual. The State should offer security for service and contribution. The State in organising security should not stifle incentive, opportunity, responsibility - -.'

Ahead of his time, but consistent with recent DWP thinking, Beveridge also stressed that social security could not be considered and would not be successful in isolation. His plan assumed:

- 'The establishment of comprehensive health and rehabilitation services for all citizens who need them'. The National Health Service was one of the major successes of the post-war reforms, but UK never developed any national rehabilitation service (BSRM 2000).

- 'The maintenance of employment and avoidance of mass unemployment'. Beveridge accepted there would always be a low level of structural unemployment (he assumed about 3%), but pointed out the costs of benefits and practical limitations of rehabilitation for 'men by the million or the hundred thousand'.

In the light of subsequent trends, there were three major weaknesses to Beveridge's plans for sickness benefits. First, he focused on sickness and took no account of disability. Second, he paid little or no attention to the assessment of sickness or incapacity for work. Perhaps, in the idealistic mood of the times, he assumed that only those who were truly sick and incapacitated would claim benefit. He may have taken for granted the ability of doctors to assess incapacity when issuing sick certificates. Alternatively, he may have been fully conscious of the potential difficulties but also the lack of any clear solution, so simply sidestepped what could have been a major political and practical obstacle to his plan. Third, sickness benefits covered sickness without time limit, but Beveridge seems to have assumed that, with universal health and rehabilitation services and welfare, most recipients would soon be fit to return to work. Unfortunately, even a small percentage failing to return to work adds up to a large number over time, but Beveridge did not seriously confront the problems of longer-term sickness, or distinguish indefinite extension of sickness benefit from early pension. More generally, Beveridge simply appears to have taken for granted that 'the sick' 'need' social security benefits, without really considering what that meant.

4.3 Social security reforms from 1971 to 1985

Since 1948, there have been major social changes (Box 1) that Beveridge's generation could not have envisioned and which impact on sickness and disability benefits. The benefits system has inevitably changed in response to changing needs as well as economic and political pressures, but it has not kept pace with change.

More fundamentally, the very concept of the 'welfare state' is not fixed but is subject to ideological reconstruction (Whiteside 1996). The conventional view today is that the British welfare state was the product of post-war political consensus and wide-ranging desire for social reconstruction and reform, which reinforced the duty of the state to provide security for all. However, that view only emerged retrospectively: the term 'welfare state' was not employed till 1951, and the description concentrates on those elements that survived the demise of the Labour government in that year. The welfare state today comprises those social policies that governments of all political persuasions have been prepared to support (for whatever reason) over the last half century - or, perhaps more accurately, those policies that there has been too much political and public resistance to dismantle. From the very beginning, the seemingly inexorable growth of social security expenditure and economic and political pressures have produced a shift away from the original Beveridge ideal of 'universal' social policies, towards more selective 'targeting' of social expenditure to those most in need (Gilbert 2000).

Gradually increasing awareness and changing social attitudes to disability from the mid-1960s (Swain *et al* 1993, Oliver & Barnes 1998) and OPCS surveys in 1968-69[94] which showed that many long-term sick and disabled people were living in poverty (Harris *et al* 1971)[95] led to considerable expansion of the welfare system during the economic prosperity of the 1960s - mid 70s (Bolderson 1991). Growing numbers of long-term sickness claimants towards the end of the 1960s led to the introduction of Invalidity Benefit (IVB) in 1971. These were initially introduced to Parliament as 'measures for the chronic sick' but there was concern that changing the name from 'sickness benefit' to an 'invalidity pension' after 6 months would carry the wrong messages and create negative expectations about work (Walley 1972). IVB payments were slightly higher than sickness benefits, on the grounds that the long-term sick and disabled had greater needs (Harris *et al* 1971), and IVB also gave entitlement to additional benefits.

Non-contributory Invalidity Pension in 1975, replaced by Severe Disablement Allowance (SDA) in 1984, provided for severely handicapped persons of working age who had never worked or had not paid sufficient NI contributions to establish entitlement to IVB. Claimants had to have onset of permanent disability before age 20 years and to be incapable of all work due to at least 80% disablement. Assessment for SDA was based on 'loss of faculty' (i.e. impairment) which was defined as 'any loss of power or function of an organ or part of the body which is a cause of inability to do things. A loss of faculty may be physical or mental and is taken to include disfigurement' (DHSS 1985a). Disablement was an assessment (expressed in percentage terms) of 'the overall effect of the relevant disabilities, i.e. the overall inability to perform the normal activities of life' (DHSS 1985a). This was the first time 'loss of faculty' was used for anything other than injury, and this attracted criticism as an inappropriate measure of need for SDA, despite its longstanding acceptance for the compensation of war and industrial injuries.

Separate benefits were introduced to cover the extra costs of disability: Attendance Allowance for those who required a lot of care and attention (1971) and Mobility Allowance for those who were unable or virtually unable to walk (1976). Invalid Care Allowance was introduced for carers (1976). Entitlement was based on the assessment of specific disabilities and needs.

Thus state support for the long-term sick and disabled increased substantially from the 1970s onwards. Conversely, however, support for short-term sickness was progressively moved to employers in the form of sick pay from employment contracts and Statutory Sick Pay from 1982 onwards.

4.4 Income Support with disability premiums (ISdp)

The 1985 social security reforms introduced 'disability premiums' as a pragmatic measure to address poverty among disabled people and to overcome benefit traps. It had the worthy aim of directing additional help to some of the poorest and most disadvantaged members of society (DHSS 1985b & c). However, the means of achieving that goal was quite illogical, based on a combination of political expediency, lobbying and concessions at committee stages.

About 45% of new awards of IB and almost 40% of the IB caseload are now 'credits only' and this is the fastest growing category of IB (DWP Administrative data). These claimants fulfil the PCA criteria for incapacity, but they do not have sufficient NI contributions for entitlement to

IB, so they do not receive any IB payments. Instead, they receive NI 'credits' which maintain their contribution record and may also provide entitlement to various other social security benefits.

Some recipients of Income Support, Job Seekers Allowance and some other benefits (which are based on quite separate entitlement criteria) receive additional 'disability premiums' because they are also sick or disabled. Thus there are various forms of entitlement to these disability premiums, but the most important from the present perspective are receipt of IB credits or receipt of DLA.

4.5 Social Security Advisory Committee 1988

The Social Security Advisory Committee considered the strengths and weaknesses of existing benefits for disabled people and options for improvement (SSAC 1988). They recommended that the Government's strategy should be to move towards 'a coherent system of cash benefits to meet the costs of disability so that more disabled people can support themselves and lead normal lives'. Although recognising that disability is not homogeneous, the Committee agreed with representations from various disability groups that disabled people have two main needs in common - income support and extra costs of disability. It laid out four guiding principles:

i   the social security system should provide an adequate basic income for all disabled people who cannot support themselves fully, with parity of income between all groups;

ii there should be help towards the extra costs which people incur because of their disabilities, assessed in relation to their particular disabilities;

iii the benefit structure should provide incentives for disabled people to achieve independence through employment;

iv benefit entitlement rules should be readily understandable, disabled people should have ready access to social security offices and should be able to obtain help with a minimum of delay and inconvenience.

SSAC (1988) argued strongly for the first principle of parity: disability benefits should not vary with how disablement occurred, nor with NI contributions, nor be means-tested. Their argument was that disability benefits are not a matter of individual insurance and actuarial-based payments but are a means of pooling the risks for the whole community, so entitlement and benefits should be based on need. It simply re-affirmed the second principle. Perhaps for the first time, the third principle recognised openly that disability does not always mean total incapacity and that many disabled people, even some with severe impairments, want to and do work and support themselves. It recommended improved service delivery to support this, that the benefit system should avoid disincentives and instead provide positive incentives to work, and that a benefit should be devised to supplement the income of disabled people who were able to do some work but not fully able to support themselves. They suggested that the extent to which a system measures up to these guiding principles gives an indication of the degree to which it meets financial need with equity and in a way that helps and encourages disabled people to be as independent as they can.

SSAC (1988) acknowledged the lack of any clear, precise definition of disability (based at that time on the International Classification of Impairments, Disabilities and Handicaps (WHO 1980)) and 'that there is no generally applicable method of assessing disability or translating its effects into cash terms'. Nevertheless, they were critical of medical assessment at that time, because it gave insufficient weight to the views of GPs and other caring health professionals and because medical assessment of impairment did not correlate with severity of disability. Instead, they supported a needs-based assessment relying as far as possible on self-assessment by claimants. However, they did not consider the practicalities, potential problems or likely impact of such an approach and, once again, they simply seem to have accepted without question that being disabled justifies disability benefits. They also failed to consider how 'disability benefits' might relate to longer-term sickness.

4.6 Incapacity Benefit

The 1995 reforms were undertaken because of continued growth in caseload and expenditure on IVB, which was considered likely to become unsustainable (DSS 1993, Social Security Benefits Agency 1993, 1995):

1   Increasing costs that were perceived to be out of control.

2   Massive growth of numbers on IVB despite improving objective measures of health.

3   Inflow had remained more or less constant but outflow had fallen and more people were staying on benefit longer.

4   GPs were uncomfortable with their gate keeping role. Controls had become lax. Consideration of non-medical factors led to people receiving IVB who were not incapable of work on medical grounds alone.

5   IVB had become a cover for hidden unemployment and a route to early retirement. (With particularly wrong incentives and caseload growth in men aged >50 years; IVB continued after retirement to age 70 for men and 65 for women.)

6   Relatively generous rates of benefit (especially compared with unemployment benefit) created the wrong incentives. (E.g. for the over 50s, average levels of IVB payments were twice those of unemployment benefits.)

Incapacity Benefit (IB) was introduced in April 1995 as the main National Insurance benefit for people who are unable to work because of sickness or disability, replacing previous NI sickness and invalidity benefits. Most short-term sickness was now covered by Statutory Sick Pay and the main focus of IB was on long-term incapacity. The basic purpose of the reforms was to focus the benefit more closely on those people who were 'genuinely and medically incapable of work', and the key to this was a new medical test of incapacity. The three main elements of the reforms were (DSS 1993, Social Security Benefits Agency 1993, 1995):

- A new benefit structure (IB) with clearer and more robust rules of entitlement

- A functionally based test of incapacity (the *All Work Test* – now the *Personal Capability Assessment*). This was completely new and radically different from any previous test either in UK or abroad.

- Bringing this benefit into the tax system. Limiting it to people of working age (i.e. stopping at retirement age). Various older age-related and earnings-related elements of IVB were abolished (affecting mainly men aged >50 years who were also most likely to have occupational pensions).

The Social Security Contributions and Benefits Act 1992 defined incapacity for benefit purposes as 'incapable of work by reason of some specific disease or bodily or mental disablement - - "work" meaning work which the person can reasonably be expected to do'. However, assessment for IVB was not confined to medical factors. As early as 1951, Commissioners had ruled in decision R(S)11/1951 that 'a person is incapable of work…. if, having regard to his age, education, experience, state of health and other personal factors there is no type of work he can reasonably be expected to do'. The effect of that decision and others had been to reduce the focus of IVB on the medical condition and to relax award of benefits. To tighten this up, Incapacity Benefit was based on the principle that 'capacity for work should be determined solely by considering the effects of the medical condition' - - without making any allowance for non-medical factors such as age, skill, or the availability or likelihood of obtaining work. The argument was that the health condition is the primary reason for not working, the basis of entitlement to IB, and what distinguishes incapacity from unemployment (Social Security Benefits Agency 1993). There was considerable opposition to this principle from disability groups and medical bodies who argued that, in reality, employability does also depend on these non-medical factors. However, Government stuck to its grounds on this key principle, without which the gateway would not have been tightened and the reforms would have foundered. During the first 28 weeks, incapacity is for the person's usual occupation, but after 28 weeks it is for work in general ('all work') and not only the claimant's previous occupation.

The Social Security Incapacity for Work Act 1994 defined incapacity as 'incapable by reason of some specific disease or bodily or mental disablement of doing work which he could reasonably be expected to do' (for the *own occupation test*) or 'by reference to the extent of a person's incapacity by reason of some specific disease or bodily or mental disablement to perform such activities as may be prescribed' (for the *All Work Test*). During the development of the *All Work Test*, incapacity was progressively operationalised as:

> 'a level of functional limitation (in each functional area) - - - which would very likely substantially reduce capacity for work of any kind' (Social Security Benefits Agency 1993);

> 'where capacity was so reduced that a person should not be expected to work for the purpose of deciding benefit entitlement (Social Security Benefits Agency 1995);

and

> 'people whose medical condition is such that it would be unreasonable to expect them to seek or be available for work'[96] (DSS 1996).

It is important to emphasise that, in principle, 'passing' the *All Work Test* and receipt of IB was never intended to mean total incapacity for all work. In a Parliamentary written answer (28.10.98), the Secretary of State pointed out that the *All Work Test* 'does not mean that people who satisfy the test are unable to do any work at all: it simply establishes that their incapacity is such that it would be unreasonable to expect them to seek work as a condition for getting benefit. In practice, many people who satisfy the *All Work Test* may be capable of doing some work given the right help and support'.

Historically, IB differs from JSA in three ways: no requirement to actively seek work; it is payable for as long as entitlement conditions are met (whereas JSA is time-limited to 6 months); and increase in the benefit rates over the first year.

The policy requirement of the test for IB was to identify chronically sick or disabled people who, 'by reason of some specific disease or bodily or mental disablement', could not be expected to work (>16 hrs/week), or to compete in the open labour market. This was operationalised 'by reference to the extent of a person's incapacity - - - to perform such activities as may be prescribed' i.e. the functional areas subsequently prescribed in Regulations for the *All Work Test*. Assessment for IB remained based primarily on information provided by the claimant on how their medical condition affected their functional capacity for work, and information provided by the GP about that medical condition, rather than quantifying impairment and/or assigning a medical diagnosis. 'This is intended to allow you to give information about the effect of your medical condition and the resulting physical or sensory disabilities upon your capacity for all types of work' (CPAG 2001). However, in line with European trends (MISSOC 1996), IVB trends and experience of Disability Living Allowance suggested the need for stricter cross-checking of the claimant's self-report and some degree of 're-medicalisation' of the adjudication process. This became 'self assessment with (medical) confirmation where necessary' (Lonsdale & Aylward 1993, 1996). Routine decisions are made by lay adjudicators, but all claims are scrutinised at various stages by a doctor and no claimant can be disallowed IB without a medical assessment.

Several alternative approaches were considered when developing the All Work Test. Simply tightening up existing assessment procedures was not considered to be robust enough to ensure that benefits would be targeted on those who were incapable of work because of the effect(s) of their medical condition. A new test of impairment, although used in some other countries such as the US and Australia, was considered to be too cumbersome, difficult and costly to administer[97], and impairment of different bodily parts was poorly related to capacity for work (Fig 1). Existing DSS assessment of disablement, as used for Industrial Injury Disability Benefit and Disability Working Allowance (DWA), was again considered to be too cumbersome, difficult and costly to administer, and inappropriate to assess incapacity for work. Indeed, many recipients of IIDB and DWA were working. Functional Capacity Evaluation - performing a standardised set of movements and tasks with objective measurement and assessment by a specially trained physiotherapist or occupational therapist (King *et al* 1998, Pransky & Dempsey 2004) - was widely used in the US and fulfilled many of the goals in principle, but was likely to be very time-consuming, cumbersome and costly, and might be regarded as too demanding and intrusive by some claimants. There was insufficient scientific evidence to justify the use of 'iso-machines' (Newton & Waddell 1993), which were also expensive, very time-consuming and impractical for the large numbers requiring assessment. After rejection of these various alternatives, the chosen test focused on medical incapacity and the claimant's inability to perform a range of activities related to work.

The *All Work Test* was developed from well-established measures of disability (OPCS 1985-88), input from a panel of 80 medical and non-medical experts and disabled people, and extensive pilot studies and consultations, which took 3 years from initial work to national implementation (DSS 1993, 1994, Social Security Benefits Agency 1993, 1995). There was an intensive publicity campaign, and an extended programme of staff training, monitoring and evaluation. That very strong evidence base has never been seriously challenged and, despite the criticisms, there is now broad acceptance of the test. A considerable body of Appeal Tribunals' and Commissioners' decisions have consolidated the present adjudication system.

The new test for IB differed from the previous test (for IVB) in that:

- It was a more objective assessment that considered the effects of the medical condition only, and not other factors such as age, education and training, job availability, etc.

(Consultation produced objections that incapacity did not depend solely on the medical condition but also on personal, psychological and social factors. However, the Government held to this principle on the grounds that this was a test of medical incapacity and not of the likelihood of getting work, it was the medical condition that distinguished the long-term sick and disabled from the unemployed, and therefore the test was about the effects of the medical condition alone.)

- It considered capacity for work in the abstract i.e. functional capacity to perform a range of activities associated with work, rather than for specific occupations. (Though consultation showed particular concerns about the ability to assess this in fluctuating, subjective (e.g. stress, pain, fatigue) and mental health conditions.)

- It had a clear lower threshold at which the effects of the medical condition began to affect capacity for work; and a benefit threshold above which it would be unreasonable to expect the claimant to work, but below which he or she could be expected to work: i.e. the point at which ability to perform work-related tasks was substantially reduced, *not* at which work became impossible.

- The GP's role as gatekeeper to the long-term benefit was greatly reduced, though GPs would still be required to provide factual information on the medical condition and diagnosis. (GPs generally welcomed this in principle but there were many practical objections and opposition to cooperating with the changes in practice. Some disability groups objected to losing a perceived GP advocacy role.)

Some parts of the disability lobby and academics disputed the entire logic and rejected the entire notion that (in)capacity for work can be measured objectively. They had fundamental objections to the OPCS methodology (Abberley 1991, Barnes 1991) and asserted that functional ability is a very poor measure of a person's ability to carry out paid work (Barnes & Baldwin 1999). More specifically, the main things that the lobby proposed (and continues to advocate) were that:

- more account should be taken of the claimant's own perspective (i.e. the AWT is too medicalised)

- more recognition of non-health related factors (i.e. even if claimants are not strictly incapable of work, they might have no realistic prospect of working)

- more generous treatment of claimants with fluctuating conditions (which again might mean they are not strictly incapable of work, but they are unlikely to work in practice)

- more sensitive treatment of claimants with mental health conditions (because undergoing the AWT and adjudication on benefits might aggravate stress and anxiety).

However, all of these changes would effectively return to the previous IVB regime, exacerbate the fundamental problem of subjectivity and significantly loosen the gateway to benefits.

In practical terms, claimants initially access IB through sick certification from their GP, and continue to receive benefits till DWP adjudication is complete. Just under 20% of claimants have serious and exempt conditions and are awarded IB without further assessment[98]. All other claimants complete a self-assessment form about how their medical condition affects 14 functional areas that are related to work, e.g. walking, sitting, lifting, etc. Preliminary studies confirmed the lack of direct correlation between incapacity for work and an unadjusted functional severity score. So, in developing a measure of (in)capacity based on these functional restrictions, it was necessary to estimate how incapacitating each functional restriction was in its own right and in combination. The threshold of impact on work for each descriptor was therefore based on what at least 80% of the panellists judged to be 'reasonable'. Combination' scores were developed empirically (in house) as a theoretical construct and then validated in an evaluation study. Modelling showed the scoring was robust: changing the threshold by a point made little difference to the number of claimants found incapacitated (Social Security Benefits Agency 1993, 1995).[99]

The process carefully distinguishes the responsibilities of Medical Advisers[100] who consider and evaluate the medical evidence and lay Claims Decision-Makers[101] who make the final decision on award of benefits. A doctor reviews the claimant's self-report questionnaire, together with all medical certificates, any factual reports and the claims history and makes a balance of probabilities decision on whether or not the claimed level of functional restriction is consistent with and supported by the medical evidence - with quality control of this process (Aylward 2003). Consistency depends on a logical relationship between the manifestations and consequences of the illness, reported limitations and incapacity. If consistent, a lay adjudicator scores the patient's questionnaire and if functional restrictions reach the threshold, the claimant is awarded IB. If the doctor considers the initial evidence inconsistent or the score does not reach the threshold, the claimant is referred for an independent medical assessment. A Medical Adviser interviews and examines the claimant and his or her medical condition, and provides an objective, justified and quality controlled rating of each of the same 14 functional areas using the standardized descriptors and scoring. He does this with reference to the diagnosed medical condition(s), the consistency of the claimant's stated functional limitations, and his own findings. The Medical Adviser's report is then returned to the Claims Decision-Maker who makes the final decision on award of benefit. Overall, about 79% of claims for IB are allowed; 6-7% of disallowed claimants appeal and about 40% of these appeals are successful.

In light of recent trends, it is worth looking more closely at the section of the *All Work Test* dealing with mental health conditions. Consultation showed widespread concerns about the operation of the AWT for such conditions, so account was taken of the advice of the Royal

College of Psychiatrists and a number of safeguards were built in. These included exempting claimants with severe psychiatric illness from the AWT, seeking the views of treating doctors on the likely effect of a decision on capacity for work, and allowing for 'exceptional circumstances' (non-functional criteria). In particular, claimants with severe mental health conditions (e.g. schizophrenia or bipolar depression) are assessed primarily on the medical evidence provided by the treating GP/psychiatrist and are not expected to complete a questionnaire. The real problem is with 'severe' mental health conditions, where severity is based on the severity of symptoms or psychological distress. During consultation, there were various objections that the *All Work Test* failed to take sufficient account of subjective symptoms such as pain, fatigue or stress and could not deal with fluctuating conditions. The Department's counter argument was that the claimant's questionnaire included the effect of such symptoms on the standard 14 functional areas[102]. The Medical Adviser also took account of subjective symptoms and possible fluctuations, and considered four additional areas of psychological functioning that are important in the work situation: completion of tasks, daily living, coping with pressure, and interaction with other people.

The fundamental problem is that assessment of functional areas and limitations in mild/moderate mental health conditions is based more or less entirely on claimants' self-reports that their physical and psychological functioning is limited by their self-reported mental symptoms. There is obvious circularity in this argument. In practice, pilot studies showed little correlation between psychiatric morbidity and the severity of disturbances of mood, behaviour or cognition. Qualitative studies showed that Medical Advisers had more difficulty and lower reliability in assessing psychological functioning. There is also some evidence that Medical Advisers and Claims Decision-Makers are reluctant to disallow claimants whom they perceive to be sick or disabled even if they score below the threshold. In retrospect, the mental health section did not go through the same rigorous process of development and validation as the rest of the *All Work Test* and the fundamental weaknesses remain.

During the development phase, particular difficulty was found with the concept of stress at work and it was accepted that was not fully covered. The recognised problems included all the ambiguities and limitations of diagnosing and assessing 'stress', the question of any causal link to work, and setting a threshold from what is normal (Wainwright & Calnan 2002, IIAC 2004). One solution was to focus on recognised mental health problems.

It should be emphasised that the *All Work Test* is not simply the self-assessment questionnaire or the medical assessment but the entire process of scrutiny, examination and adjudication. The claimant's initial self-assessment questionnaire, the Medical Adviser's report and the Claims Decision-Maker's judgment all focus on the same functional areas and descriptors. The *All Work Test* provides a more substantial bulwark against the weakness of a purely self-reporting system, while retaining full allowance for the claimant's own account of his or her functional limitations and restrictions. At the same time, this is not a purely 'medical' decision: the final decision on benefit is not by a Medical Adviser, but by the lay Claims Decision-Maker who must consider not only the medical evidence but all of the other evidence.

Assessing incapacity for work is a complex problem that no social security or insurance system has managed to resolve satisfactorily. Nevertheless, the *All Work Test* is considered to be amongst the best developed and most stringent in the developed world (OECD 2003) and has been copied in the original or an amended form by several countries, including Iceland, Ireland, Italy, Norway, the Czech Republic and Slovakia.

4.7 Support into work policies

The principle that it is 'a good thing' to encourage and support sick and disabled people to (return to) work if possible is shared by disabled people and their organisations, by the general public, and by all political parties (albeit for different reasons) (Council of Europe 1996, 2003a, OECD 2003, DRC 2004b). There is some danger of this becoming 'motherhood and apple pie', and it is important to focus on specific and practical interventions and then subject them to robust evaluation. The first and second groups generally feel this should be voluntary rather than compulsory; the third group hold conflicting views on that question.

Given the extent of the problem, in the past there was a serious lack of large-scale DWP engagement with this client group. Only about 1.5% of IB expenditure is spent on helping IB recipients into work, compared with 27% for JSA. That approach took no account of the evidence that:

- many IB recipients (up to 75%) do retain some capacity for some work, and many (about a third) say they want to work;

- in many cases (up to 75%), psychosocial issues are more important than the actual health condition in the development of long-term incapacity and in return to work;

- for many people, such issues can be better addressed by a range of largely non-medical interventions

- for virtually all conditions, the longer a person remains off work the greater the obstacles to return to work and the less likely it is that they will ever return.

That was the rationale for a radical shift in DWP policy since the late 1990s[103] from purely passive provision of financial benefits to more active support into work:

i. A greater focus on helping claimants to overcome barriers to (return to) work.

ii. Concentrate on stopping the flow of new short-term cases becoming chronic, but also maintain programmes and checks for the long-term stock.

iii. Develop and rigorously evaluate packages of intervention and support to help move IB recipients into the labour market.

That is one of the main thrusts of Government policy under *A New Contract for Welfare* (HM Government 1998a, 1998b, Welfare Reform and Pensions Act 1999). 'Work for those who can' means providing positive opportunities, interventions and incentives to support return to work; 'security for those who cannot' implies that most resources should go to those with greatest needs (HM Government 1998a). The goal is to enable more people with health conditions or disabilities to access, remain in, or return to work. The 1998-99 reforms proposed a series of structural and process changes that aimed to:

- Facilitate optimal early management

- Encourage work retention rather than incapacity

- Emphasise abilities rather than functional limitations

- Contribute to cultural change among health professionals

- Support re-education, re-skilling and rehabilitation back to work

- Promote radical change in the workplace culture to improve equality and opportunity.

However, these never really got off the ground and did not lead to much change in practice.

The policies set out in the Green Paper *Pathways to work: Helping people into employment* (DWP 2002) were the first significant step to realising this vision. Despite previous hostility, these gained widespread support from all major medical, welfare, disability and employer/TUC lobby groups and most academics in this area (DWP 2003c). The robust defence of the policies that underpin Pathways, the co-operative implementation and the early results have significantly shifted attitudes to IB reform. This is because, despite their relative toughness, they have been presented positively as better, evidence-based support for IB recipients to get back into work:

- A better framework of support (particularly in the early stages of a claim)

- Direct access to a wider range of help

- Improved, visible financial incentives

Consultations showed that the Green Paper was general welcomed, with appreciation of the new tone and language used. There was wide support for addressing the barriers to work faced by IB recipients, the need for early intervention, and the Government's recognition of the need to provide extra help and support (DWP 2003c). The one serious criticism was that the Green

Paper failed to deal adequately with the role of employers (DRC 2003b, Stanley & Regan 2003). In fairness, the Green Paper did recognise this need but did not deal with it in detail because it was a matter for other Government initiatives (HSE 2000, 2004, CBI 2000, DWP 2003a & b, 2004). Nevertheless, this was in marked contrast to similar Australian proposals for welfare reform, which placed equal or even greater emphasis on the obligations on employers (FACS 2002). There is clearly a need to present these policies in a balanced way.

Reintegration policies since 2000 have been supported by:

1. The Department of Social Security and the Department for Education and Employment were amalgamated in summer 2001 into the Department for Work and Pensions to provide a more unified service.

2. The major structural change was the Single Gateway that provides access to all social security and employment services, with the progressive development of Personal Advisers and Jobcentre Plus.

3. The New Deal for Disabled People (NDDP) (February 1999), New Deal for 50 Plus (April 2000) and Personal Advisers provided individualized support and access to a variety of case management programmes (**www.newdeal.gov.uk**). All new IB clients in integrated Jobcentre Plus offices now have a mandatory work-focused interview with a Personal Adviser at the very start of their claim. The New Deal for Disabled People is now funded to help around 30,000 a year find work. The quality of support offered through both these routes has improved notably over the last 18 months although there remain significant challenges around the Personal Adviser's skills in raising return to work issues amongst this client group.

4. The *All Work Test* was changed to the *Personal Capability Assessment* from April 2000, to provide extra information on what the claimant was able to do 'which would be potentially useful to claimants and their personal advisers to decide what might be done to assist a return to work' (HM Government 1998c). [However, the test remained the Gateway to IB with the same structure and threshold, and the first part of the claim and adjudication process remained unchanged. The *primary* purpose for claimants, medical assessors, adjudicators and DWP remained to assess *in*capacity for entitlement to benefits. The concept of assessing remaining functional capacity is entirely laudable, but it was very much secondary and little has been done (at least so far) to make use of this information for rehabilitation or return to work interventions. There remains an underlying ambiguity between incapacity and capability[104]. Not surprisingly, there is no evidence this re-naming has had any significant impact on attitudes, practice or outcomes.]

Action was also taken to reduce benefit disincentives:

1. To strengthen the link of IB to work, entitlement was tightened to earnings above a certain level and NI contributions for one of the last three complete tax years. This was expected to reduce the numbers on IB by 120,000 over 10 years.

2. Changes to various IB permitted work, earnings and linking rules to reduce benefit traps, disincentives and the financial 'risk' of return to work.

3. Claw-back of IB (50p per £1) for any occupational or private pension >£85 per week from April 2001. (Though this only affected 10% of IB recipients.)

4. Severe Disablement Allowance was incorporated into IB from April 2001.

These reforms actually had quite modest impact on limited numbers of recipients but faced fierce political opposition, particularly to reform 3 and to a lesser extent to reform 1.

Measures to ease the transition into work included allowances for therapeutic work, voluntary work, Work Trial, Jobfinder's Grant, Jobmatch projects and the 52-week linking rule (Corden & Sainsbury 2001). More recent, positive policies to 'make work pay' include the national minimum wage, the Disabled Person's Tax Credit (now replaced by the disability element of the Working Tax Credit) and the Disability Income Guarantee. One of the greatest financial barriers for many IB recipients coming off benefits is that they are only likely to obtain low-paid or part-time work. Arguably, this is the most important financial barrier and the most important economic policy intervention. There is some evidence that moving into work needs to provide a net gain of > £40-50 per week to provide any real financial incentive (Dorsett *et al* 1998, Corden & Sainsbury 2001, *Pathways*).

Much is currently being done to develop better support to help sick and disabled people back into work, though many of these initiatives have still to deliver tangible results:

- The Prime Minister's Strategy Unit report on 'Improving the Life Chances of Disabled People' (Strategy Unit 2005), building on what has already been achieved in the Disability Discrimination Act 1995 and the Disability Discrimination Amendment Act 2005 (accepting that much still remains to be done to eliminate discrimination and disadvantage).

- The Social Exclusion Unit (2004) report on what more could be done to reduce social exclusion among adults with mental health conditions, and to enable them to enter and retain work[105].

- The Department of Health white paper on public health places greater emphasis on occupational health issues and outcomes (Dept of Health 2004a, DWP 2005)

- Health and Safety Commission and Executive strategies to improve health and safety at work, including initiatives to improve sickness absence management (HSC 2000, 2004, HSE 2000, 2004, DWP/HSE 2004, NAO 2004).

- Government accepts the need to improve occupational health services in the UK, in order to promote health at work, and to reduce the impact of sickness, injury, and disability (HSE 2000, HSC 2004, DWP 2005). A minority of workers in the UK[106] have access to effective occupational health support, and much remains to be done to provide occupational health services to all UK employees, particularly in SMEs. One area where the NHS has made substantial progress since 2001 is NHS Plus – a network of more than 100 NHS occupational health departments which provides a quality, evidence-based Occupational Health Service to the whole NHS workforce and also sells services to employers (**www.nhsplus.nhs.uk**). HSE is currently developing other innovative partnerships in the public and private sector, to provide occupational health, safety and rehabilitation support (OHSRS). A number of pilot studies are planned or underway, evaluation of which will enable HSE, DWP and employers to judge the cost-effectiveness of OHSRS for improving health at work and reducing sickness absence. For example, HSE has just announced that it will pilot Workplace Health Direct (HSE 2005) from January 2006 for two years. This is a new and potentially groundbreaking scheme, which is the culmination of much discussion and development with the various stakeholders. It is a national advice line targeted at SMEs and will provide free and confidential, work-place focused occupational, health, safety and return to work advice to both employers and workers. The goal is to help reduce the incidence of illness and injury in the workplace, manage sickness absence better and facilitate early return to work.

- There is now broad acceptance of the need to improve rehabilitation in UK and Government is developing a Framework for Vocational Rehabilitation (DWP 2002, DWP 2004).

- *Improving Health in Scotland; Design for Living* and other programmes in Wales[107]; *Working for Health* in Northern Ireland.

- Demonstrating its commitment at the highest level, Government has set up a Ministerial Task Force (the Health, Safety and Productivity Task Force) to develop proposals for reducing sickness absence and improving occupational health and rehabilitation.

4.8 Incapacity Benefit trends

The number of people on Invalidity Benefit increased from about 700,000 in 1979 to 2.6 million in 1995 (Fig 5). This is generally considered to be largely for non-health reasons: industrial restructuring; labour market characteristics (particularly local unemployment rates, marginal employability and disadvantage in the labour market); tightening of the regime for unemployment benefits combined with a weak gateway to Invalidity Benefit; more women working and eligible for benefits; the rising age of recipients and more recipients with multiple disadvantages and health-related characteristics associated with longer duration; higher benefit levels and disincentives to work – particularly for men aged > 50 years; although never official policy, rising IVB was condoned as a means of reducing headline unemployment rates, and became a route to early retirement (NAO 1989, Lonsdale 1993, Lonsdale & Aylward 1996, Dorsett *et al* 1998, Huddleston 2000, Waddell *et al* 2002, Howard 2003). This increase also occurred against a background of increased public awareness and acceptance of disability, changed attitudes to health, sickness and work, and labour market marginalisation of less able workers (Walker & Howard 2000). Inflow increased to over 1 million a year in the early-mid-90s but, critically, outflow also fell and more people stayed on benefits longer. Underlying the duration effect and the fall in outflow was a fundamental change in the characteristics and behaviour of IVB recipients.

Contrary to some sensational headlines, IB is not now escalating out of control as IVB did in the 1980s and early 90s (Hills & Gardiner 1997)(Figure 4). While there are certainly continuing problems and a need for reform, there is no 'crisis': indeed, talk of crisis and panic measures is likely to be counter-productive. Since 1995, the rate of increase has fallen dramatically and the number of recipients has only risen slightly to a peak of about 2.7 million. Over the past 18 months caseload growth has effectively been zero[108]. Internationally, the UK has about the EU and OECD average for the proportion of people of working age on incapacity benefits (OECD 2003) though comparisons should be made with caution because of the wide variation in benefit systems. Unlike the UK, most other countries continue to experience significant increases in caseload (e.g. in New Zealand the caseload has increased by over 10% and in the US by 1 million in the past 2 years).

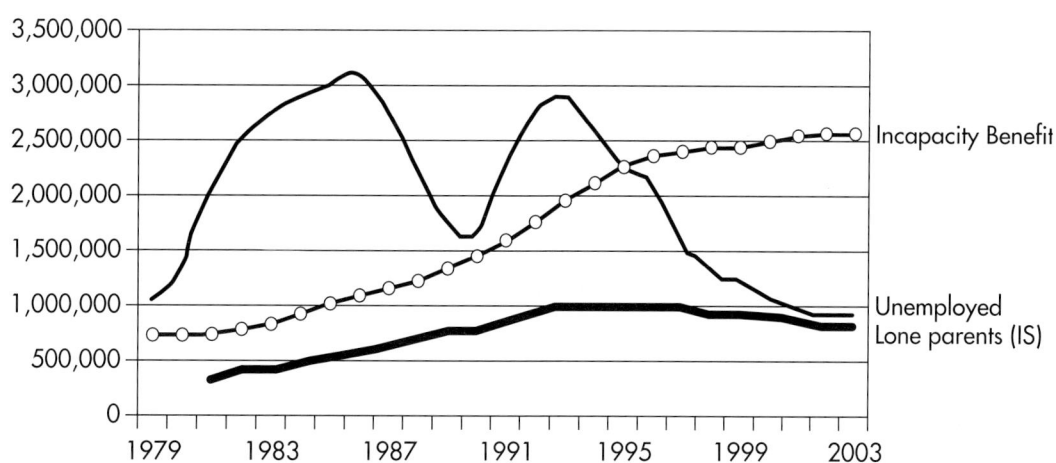

Figure 4: Trends in key working age benefits (DWP administrative data).

It is important to re-emphasise that the rise in the IB caseload is not due to any epidemic of disease. Most objective measures of population health are slowly but steadily improving (Dunnell 1995), e.g. male life expectancy at age 60 increased from 16.8 years in 1985 to 19.6 years in 2000 (**www.statistics.gov.uk**). There was apparently a slight deterioration in subjective health in the 1980s and 90s (Figure 5), though preliminary data from more recent surveys suggests that may have stabilised. In any event, these subjective reports are paradoxical (Barsky 1988) and not nearly enough to account for IB trends. IB trends appear to represent a social and cultural phenomenon, rather than a change in the health of the nation.

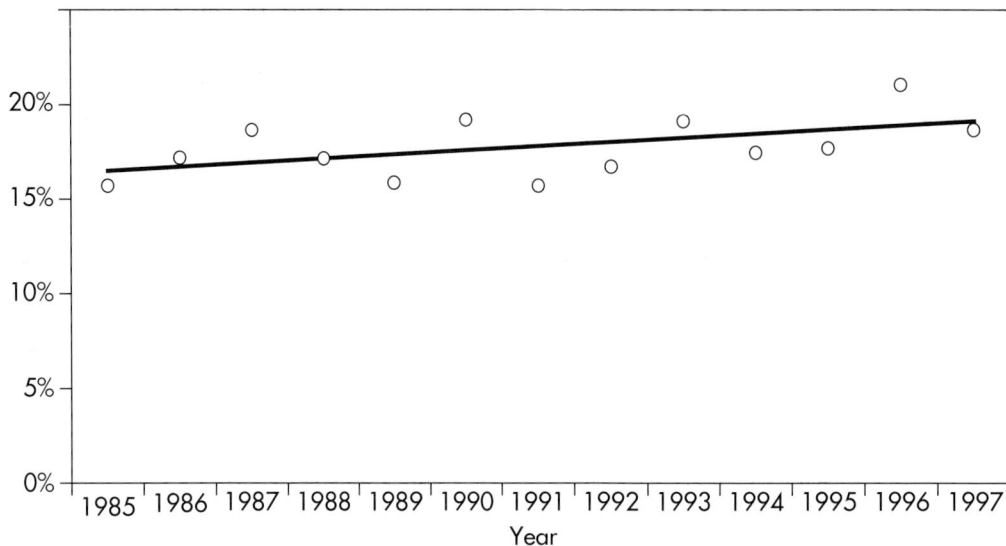

Figure 5: UK surveys of subjective health (1985-98): the proportion of working age people reporting a limiting long-standing illness.

The number of new claims ('inflow') rose to a peak of about 1 million per annum in 1995, since when it has fallen 30% to about 700,000 (Fig 6). This fall appears to be primarily because of (a) the general economic situation and (b) the impact of the reforms introduced in the mid-1990s which tightened the gateway and reduced financial incentives, particularly for men aged > 50 years. The evidence suggests that the overall reduction in inflow is related more to the lower financial incentives for older men to claim IB, as there has been no notable reduction in inflow for other age groups of IB claimants or those claiming the disability premium to Income Support. If there was a general *All Work Test* effect (as opposed to a financial incentive effect) one would expect to see reductions in inflow more widely across gender and age groups.

Despite this drop in inflow, the number of recipients initially continued to rise (albeit much more slowly – Figure 4) because outflow also fell (Figure 6): a) lower inflow means fewer short term recipients who generally make up most of the outflow, and b) the remaining inflow includes more with poorer personal characteristics and poorer labour market prospects, who are harder to get back to work (the 'selection effect'). Thus the average duration on IB increased. These outflow and duration trends are a major cause for concern. To put them in perspective, however, UK has the highest outflow of long-term recipients of any OECD country – about 5% per annum, while most countries only have about 1% (OECD 2003)[109].

The number of IB claimants receiving 'credits only' rose steadily from 45,000 in 1979 to 512,000 in 1995, since when it has continued to rise to 870,000 in the latest available statistics. Since the disability premium for Income Support was introduced in 1985, the number of ISdp recipients has risen to about 1.1 million.

Despite what has been achieved since 1997, IB trends are in marked contrast to the significant improvement in the numbers of unemployed on JSA and of lone parents on Income Support (Figure 4). Moreover, 40% of new IB claimants still become long-term recipients (compared with only 5% for JSA); 74% of current recipients are now on benefit > 2 years; and although the number of men aged 50-64 has declined sharply in recent years, about half the current recipients are aged >50 years. These characteristics plus demographic trends and equalisation of the pension age could place renewed pressure on the caseload again in years ahead.

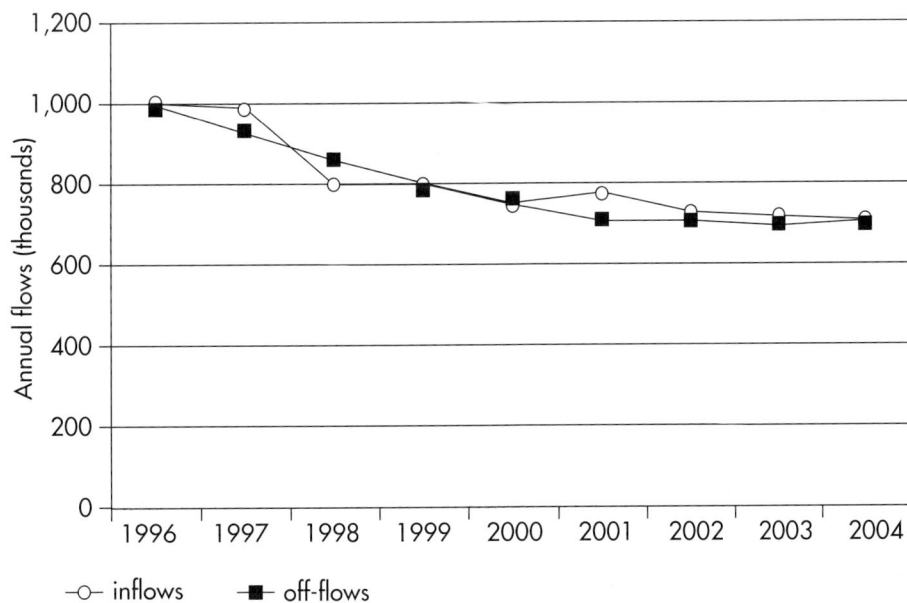

Figure 6: Annual IB inflows and outflows, 1996-2004.

In the 1980s the growth in the IVB caseload was largely due to musculoskeletal conditions, which outnumbered 2-3X the relatively stable numbers with mental health conditions. Since the mid to late 1990s, there has been a dramatic shift in the diagnostic pattern of incapacity from musculoskeletal to mental health diagnoses (Figure 7). The vast majority of this increase is in mild/moderate mental health conditions. Interestingly, there was a geographical dimension to this diagnostic trend, starting in the SE of England and spreading progressively to the rest of the country, which supports the argument that it is a social rather than a biological phenomenon.

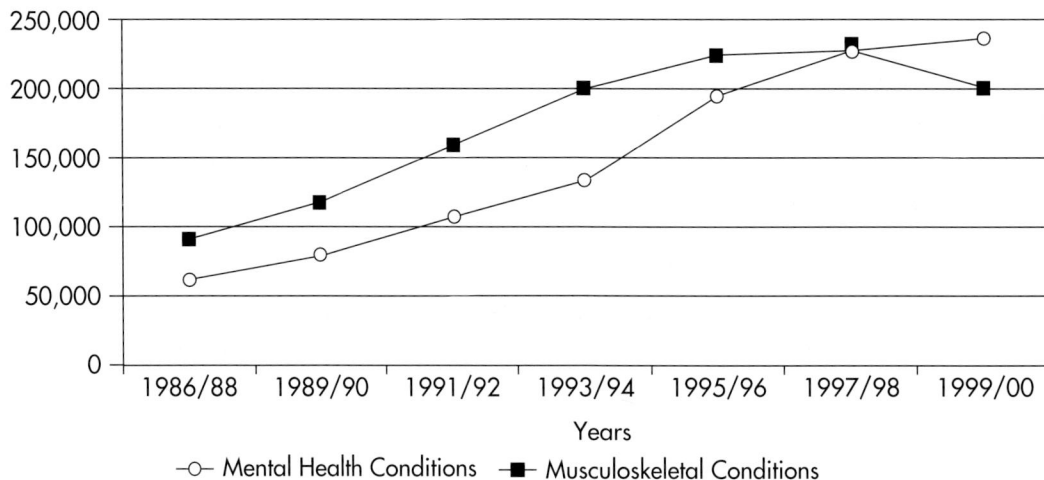

Figure 7: The shift in the relative numbers of IB claimants with musculoskeletal and mental health conditions.

Mental or behavioural disorders now account for 42% of the IB caseload compared to 16% in 1996, and if claimants with a secondary mental health diagnosis are included the proportion rises to more than 50%. They are significantly associated with chronic pain conditions. Absolute inflow of mental health conditions has remained stable since 1996, while the inflow of all other conditions has fallen by about 40% (Figure 6). However, claimants with mental health conditions have much lower outflow (around half in 12 months compared with nearly three-quarters for other conditions) and longer average claim duration. The difference in outflow is not accounted for by any difference in the rate of failing the PCA, which is about the same for mental health and other conditions, but by other (largely non-DWP) barriers to returning to work. These findings are broadly the same across gender and age.

Several conflicting pieces of evidence need to be reconciled to make sense of these mental health trends:

• UK epidemiological surveys show no significant change in the population prevalence of most neurotic symptoms, overall rates of neurotic disorders or rates of psychotic disorders between 1993-2001 (ONS 2000, 2003). Importantly (just as with back pain and musculo-skeletal disorders in the 1970s-90s) there is no evidence of any 'epidemic' of mental illness (Wessely 2004).

- It seems unlikely that clinical and occupational management of mental health conditions are significantly better or worse within this relatively short time. IB inflow has remained stable, though the reduced IB outflow suggests that, if anything, social outcomes may be worse.

- There is some evidence of increased social acceptability and reduced social stigma, discrimination and exclusion of mental illness (Wainwright & Calnan 2002, Social Exclusion Unit 2004). While that is clearly desirable, it is also likely to make sick certification, sickness absence and benefit claims for mental health disorders more socially acceptable. Although IB inflow with a primary mental health diagnosis has remained stable, there has been an increase in the numbers with a secondary mental health diagnosis.

- There are questions about the effectiveness of the mental health section of the PCA. The fundamental problem is that claims, medical assessment and decisions on benefits for mild/moderate mental health conditions are based primarily on self-reports of subjective symptoms and limitations.

- Since the introduction of Incapacity Benefit and the *All Work Test* in 1995, there has been a 40% fall in inflow of all other conditions but not of mental health conditions.

The relatively stable inflow of mental health conditions and the comparable PCA failure rate suggest that growth in the mental health caseload is not a direct effect of weaker control mechanisms in an 'easier' mental health section of the PCA. Rather, the introduction of Incapacity Benefit and the *All Work Test* had a major effect on all other conditions, but no significant effect on mental health conditions. This could be because:

- the reforms (as opposed to the AWT/PCA itself) had less impact on mental health conditions than on other health conditions (which could be a differential effect because of the nature of the conditions, because the controls are less effective, or because of different perceptions or behaviour by claimants and/or health professionals),

and/or

- any reduction in inflow of mental health disorders due to the reforms was counter-balanced by an increase due to extraneous (non-DWP), social influences.

Whichever, or whatever other explanations there may be, the failure to reduce inflow, decreased outflow and increasing caseload reflect a relative failure of control mechanisms.

The clear original intent of sickness and incapacity benefits was wage replacement for workers who had to stop work because of injury or illness (Beveridge 1942, HM Government 1998c), but in practice that is no longer the case. Table 5 shows that only 40% of IB claimants are

Table 5 Employment status at commencement of IB (DWP administrative data).	
Employment status at commencement of IB	**%**
Employed (mostly via Statutory Sick Pay)	28%
Self-employed	12%
Job Seekers Allowance (sometimes after short periods of sickness on JSA)	25%
Economically inactive	30%
Other	5%

employed or self-employed at the time of commencing IB. The majority have no recent contact with the labour market and about a third have not worked for more than 2 years before commencing IB.

Historically, benefit recipients were predominantly male because fewer women worked, many worked part-time with earnings below the NI threshold, and many were married and opted out of full NI contributions. Over the past 25 years the position of women in society, the labour market and the NI scheme has changed and women now account for over one-third of IB recipients.

The proportion of people on IB increases 5-fold between age 20-60 years. Half of all IB recipients are now aged >50 years, and 79% of these older recipients have been on IB for more than two years. It is highly probable that most of these people are completely detached from the labour force and will not return to work before they reach retirement age. It should be re-emphasised that most of this early retirement, particularly in blue-collar workers, is involuntary and that most of these claimants have a genuine health problem, even if that health problem may not have been the main reason for stopping work and would not totally incapacitate them for all work (Loumidis *et al* 2001b, Alcock *et al* 2003).

There is a major problem of regional variation in IB rates, which are particularly high in the ex-industrial areas of Wales, Northern England and central Scotland. There is strong inter-relationship between regional deprivation, local unemployment rates, social inequalities in health, disability and receipt of various social security benefits, which is difficult to disentangle (HMT 2003). The inter-action between health and employment depends on the regional and socio-economic context (Whitehead *et al* 2005). This is partly a matter of health: people in deprived areas not only have lower life expectancy but spend twice the number of years in poor health (Haynes *et al* 1997, Doran *et al* 2004, Bajekal 2005). From another perspective, Alcock *et al* (2003) and Beatty & Fothergill (2004) argue that approximately 1 million of the 2.7 million IB recipients represent 'hidden' unemployment. Although these claimants have a health condition that limits their ability to work to greater or lesser extent, if there were full employment many of them probably would be working. This interpretation is supported by the fact that only 50-60% state that illness or injury was the principal reason for their last job ending (Loumidis *et al*

2001b, Alcock *et al* 2003). This reflects demand-side factors (redundancy, job availability, etc), but claimants in the deprived regions also have multiple disadvantage on the supply-side (age, education, skills, motivation, culture, etc) which appear to be more important (Berthoud 2004). So policy must include increasing the demand for labour, creating a fairer distribution of work, and increasing the rewards for work (Commission on Social Justice 1994), and government is well aware this has a regional dimension (HMT 2003). Nevertheless, the balance of the evidence is that supply-side interventions focus better on the underlying problem.

Financial incentives clearly influence human behaviour, though the strength of the effect is often overstated and it is only one among many influences. The best available evidence, mainly from workers compensation studies in the United States (Loeser *et al* 1995), suggests that a 10% increase in workers' compensation benefits produces a 1–11% increase in the number of claims, and a 2–11% increase in the average duration of claims. There is suggestive evidence from social security trends in the US, the Netherlands and the UK of a similar effect in incapacity and disability benefits (Waddell *et al* 2002). Figure 8 shows the predicted gains for IB recipients returning to work, using the DWP Policy Simulation Model. UK wage replacement rates are not high by international standards and there is a clear financial incentive for most IB recipients to return to work. However, it is worth noting that a significant number would actually be worse off, particularly in low-paid, part-time work, which is all that some of them may be able to get and/or do. The financial disincentives to work are much greater for IB than for benefits claimants generally. For example:

Figure 8: Predicted gains/losses to IB recipients entering work at the minimum wage in 2004-05 (not allowing for tax credits).

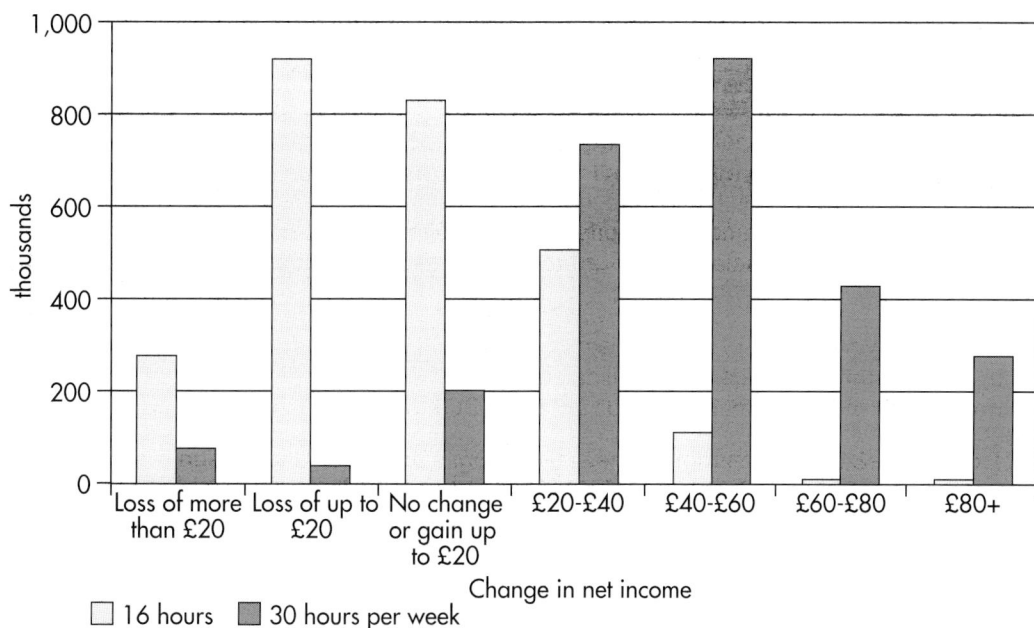

- At 16 hours per week on the minimum national wage, 44% of IB recipients would be worse off compared with only 2% of lone parents;

- At 30 hours per week on the minimum national wage, 39% of IB recipients would be less than £40 a week better off, compared with only 3% of lone parents.

This analysis is support by the limited empirical evidence that is available. Dorsett *et al* (1999) followed up people leaving Incapacity Benefit between June - November 1996 and found their net weekly income at the end of their benefit claim was £171 and at interview 5-10 months later was £177. However, there were two sharply divergent courses of leaving benefits. One third left voluntarily, 68% of whom returned to some form of work and their income at follow-up rose to £234. The other two thirds were disallowed benefits following the *All Work Test*, only 19% of whom returned to work and their income at follow-up ranged from £130-152.

4.9 Conclusions

1 Over the past 25 years there has been an enormous increase in the number of people claiming and receiving disability and incapacity benefits, though the rate of increase has been much slower since the 1995 IB reforms and has currently plateaued.

2 For many, *but not all* recipients, incapacity benefits have become much more generous compared with the original subsistence levels of 1948, even if they are possibly lower in real terms than in 1979. However, there is no public awareness of this because the flat-rate basic benefits are deceptively low. For certain groups (e.g. those with very poor labour market prospects, or economically secure professional people who also have occupational sick pay or pensions and other sources of family income) there may be little financial incentive to work and insufficient to outweigh the other advantages of the sick role or early retirement.

3 There has been a major shift in the culture, attitudes and expectations that surround illness, sickness and disability. This has increased the range of types and severity of sickness and disability considered to justify benefits (Aylward & LoCascio 1995). Long-term incapacity, claiming and taking social security benefits, and early retirement on health grounds are now much more socially acceptable and taken as a 'right', provided they are 'within the rules' and whatever the actual degree of (in)-capacity for work (Waddell *et al* 2002).

4 The original social and legislative intent to direct benefits to those in greatest need is in accord with public perceptions, but in practice changing perceptions of disability, greater social acceptability and rights, medical certification practice and appeals decisions have led to a much wider range of types and severity of sickness and disability receiving benefits.

5 There is failure to direct sickness and disability benefits to those with greatest needs. Disability policy in general and sickness and disability benefits in particular are still failing many of the most severely disabled people, as shown by social exclusion, (un)employment

and poverty rates. At the same time, many disability and incapacity benefits are going to people with lesser needs for whom they were not originally intended. The more thinly finite resources are spread, the less help is available for those who need it most.

6   Recipients are staying on benefits longer, many to state retirement age, and these benefits often effectively become a route to and (supplement to) income in early retirement.

7   For some people, disability and incapacity benefits have become an alternative and more generous means of support in poverty or unemployment. This has created sick role and benefit traps that obstruct people coming off these benefits, particularly if they do not successfully enter work.

8   For too long, people who could work were consigned to a life on benefits; e.g. those who 'proved' their incapacity to receive IB were often effectively written off and not given any help to make the most of the potential they did have[110].

9   Once people are on IB, physical and mental health tends to deteriorate rather than improve. The benefit system itself creates 'welfare dependency', lowers self-esteem and denies opportunity and responsibility in almost equal measure. The barriers to coming off benefit and returning to work become greater and the chances of doing so become less over time.

Because of the way they have evolved over time to meet such diverse needs, goals, interests, politics and legal challenges, current benefit structures and regulations for sickness and disability are complex, contradictory and at times counter-productive. The present situation is the *ad hoc* outcome of constant pressures to increase the scope of disability and incapacity benefits vs. pragmatic attempts to control claims and costs. IB has become an umbrella benefit for people who are 'incapacitated' for work because of 'sickness and disability'. There is a lack of clear concepts of sickness, disability and incapacity, failure to distinguish between them, and too often simply an assumption (by all parties) that sickness and/or disability automatically mean incapacity for work.

4.9.2 Paradoxes

It should be evident by now that there are many glaring paradoxes in the current situation:

The typical recipient paradox: The typical examples used in the welfare debate are people with severe impairments (e.g. people in wheelchairs or with severe neurological disease) but the majority of people receiving incapacity and disability benefits now have less severe health problems (e.g. stress, back pain, etc).

The health paradox: objective measures of health are improving; subjective reports of health and fitness are remaining much the same; while the number of people on long-term incapacity benefits has increased dramatically over the past 25 years. More people are being certified unfit of work and going on to long-term incapacity, often with less severe health problems where incapacity cannot be understood in purely medical terms.

The failure to recover paradox: With medical discoveries and innovations and increased NHS expenditure, health care and clinical outcomes should be improving but work-related outcomes are actually deteriorating. The transition between clinical 'recovery' and return to work is often neglected and fails. At the other end of the process, IB outflow has not improved but has fallen and more people are staying on benefit longer. This is not explained by the medical condition or health care but more by personal, contextual and labour market factors.

The early retirement paradox: Overall, people are living and staying healthy longer, particularly over age 50 years, but early retirement is increasing, often with less severe health problems (but with little change in early retirement rates due to severe medical conditions).

The disability rights and benefits paradox: There is some unavoidable tension between the right of disabled people to participate as fully as possible in society (including the right to work) and the right to income replacement benefits (the right not to work).

The sickness / disability paradox: There is failure to distinguish sickness and disability. Sickness is traditionally about the right *not* to work; modern disability rights are about the right *to work*. Some benefits and assessments were designed primarily for disability, but most recipients now have longer-term sickness.

The capacity/incapacity paradox: Claimants must demonstrate their *in*-capacity for work to establish and maintain their entitlement to benefits, but obtaining/returning to work depends on demonstrating their *capacity* for work. It is contradictory to expect claimants to attend Work Focussed Interviews at which they must simultaneously demonstrate their incapacity, discuss their capacity for work, and cooperate with return to work initiatives.

Assessment paradox 1: Sickness and incapacity benefits are provided by the state but entry to benefits is outwith the control or even knowledge of DWP. In practice, claimants receive IB and are labelled as 'incapacitated' based on sick certification by their treating GP. DWP then faces an uphill battle to withdraw benefits with reversal of the normal burden of proof, (i.e. there is a presumption of incapacity till proven otherwise rather than a presumption of health till proven to be incapacitated).

Assessment paradox 2: The argument that doctors can't and only disabled persons themselves can assess disability effects and needs has obscured the primary question of whether the claimant has a physical or mental condition that may reasonably be expected to cause long-term disability / incapacity.

The timing paradox: The clinical course is largely determined within the first 1-6+ months of sickness absence. By the time DWP has any direct involvement, the battle is often nearly over and intervention is more difficult and less (cost)-effective.

The labour market paradox: Unemployment has fallen and job availability has increased, but the number of people on long-term sickness and disability benefits remains stubbornly high.

The IB rates paradox: The welfare debate and public awareness focus on the basic rates of IB (currently £57 - £76 per week) but recipients actually receive average disability and incapacity benefit payments of about £6,500 per annum.

The inequality paradox: There is greater economic prosperity and social security expenditure has risen but economic and health inequalities have increased and a large minority of the population still face social disadvantage, exclusion and (relative) poverty.

The expenditure paradox: Despite increasing expenditure on disability and incapacity benefits, a significant minority of long-term sick or disabled people still live in (relative) poverty.

5 PRINCIPLES OF IB REFORM

5.1 Policy goals

1   The most important and compelling goal of IB reform is social justice:

   a   to improve employment rates of sick and disabled people, and

   b   to prevent poverty among sick and disabled people and their dependents (Stanley & Maxwell 2004).

Concurrent administrative goals are:

2   To control caseload and expenditure

3   To improve routes on to and off benefits

Recognising pragmatically that (Lilley 1993, 1995):

   a   there is no simple, cheap or short-term answer (or someone in the world would have found it!)

   b   there is a need for further work to establish the feasibility, costs and effectiveness of any proposed reforms

   c   any proposed reforms are likely to be politically contentious.

The primary reason to reform IB is that it is failing to serve its purpose as well as it should. The original policy intent is to support recipients while they are unable to work due to a long-term health problem or disability. IB is not only failing to provide the most appropriate support to those with greatest needs (as shown by rates of economic inactivity, social exclusion and poverty among sick and disabled people) but has become a barrier to work. This is a social injustice that should be corrected (Stanley & Regan 2003, Stanley & Maxwell 2004). Essentially, the most appropriate balance of financial and other support must be targeted more efficiently (Gilbert 2000).

There is broad agreement that the benefit system is too complex, difficult to understand and needs to be simplified and more transparent (Williams *et al* 1999). No country has ever managed to achieve the universal goal of simple, fair and easy-to-use sickness and disability benefits but, nevertheless, the social security system should strive as far as possible to meet the following ideals (Ploug & Kvist 1996, Kingson & Schulz 1997, Field 1998, White 2004b):

- Principles that are clear, fair and just, and generally agreed by all stakeholders *

- Deliver adequate benefits to those for whom they are intended, and at the same time do not give to those for whom they are not intended; prevent abuse

- Principles and process should be explicit, transparent and understandable *

- Gateways to benefit should be clear, easy to understand and use *, and enforceable

- The system should be simple and administratively efficient, yet sufficiently flexible and 'human' to take account of individual circumstances[111].

- Workable and deliverable in practice (using existing or realistically foreseeable resources)

- Provide incentives that encourage rather than discourage desired social behaviour (e.g. 'make work pay' and 'work for those who can'). Avoid perverse incentives

- Avoid benefit traps, discrimination and stigma, and undesirable or unforeseen side effects

- Do not further disadvantage those recipients who are already the most disadvantaged

- Fulfil all the goals and at the same time avoid all the pitfalls!

* To the claimant, the man in the street and the person doing the assessment.

That is broadly consistent with the goals of disabled people. The primary goal of the Disability Rights Commission is: 'a society where all disabled people can participate fully as equal citizens' (**www.drc-gb.org**). Disability groups have campaigned continuously since the mid-1960s for the replacement of the current patchwork of benefits by a more coherent benefit system that covers income replacement, extra costs and compensation, with benefit levels based on the severity of disability rather than its cause (UPIAS 1976, Barnes & Baldwin 1999).

The extent to which these goals are realistic will depend on a balance of costs, political judgment and public acceptance.

Policy reforms depend on corresponding changes in the organisational structure and culture to implement and deliver them (Berthoud 1998, Watson & Patel 2004). That raises issues of staff resources, competencies, training, practices and commitment.

5.2 Initial premises

Sickness and disability policy is a complex area that should not be over-simplified. Welfare reform must allow for the heterogeneity of claimants, the complexity of sickness, disability and incapacity, and the interaction of health-related, personal and social issues. However, academic analysis must not lead to the nihilistic conclusion that it is all too complicated to do anything about it. In the real world, action depends on pragmatic assumptions. The following premises are based on the above analysis and may serve as the starting point to considering IB reform:

1 Society provides specific 'incapacity' benefits (i.e. distinct from unemployment benefits) as income replacement for people of working age who are unable to work because of sickness or disability[112].

2 Individual entitlement to incapacity benefits is based on a physical and/or mental condition or impairment[113].

3 Only the individual can describe the personal experience of illness and disability, and this generally provides the basis for health care. When the individual claims financial support for disability and incapacity, however, society has the right to decide on legitimacy and entitlement, based on principles of social justice, fairness and reasonableness, and taking account of the needs and aspirations of sick and disabled people themselves.

4 There are powerful social and financial incentives to sickness and social security benefits, which must be balanced by equally strong social and financial incentives to work, and subject to adequate social control mechanisms.

5 Self-report of incapacity is insufficient on its own and requires some kind of check - because of the moral hazard of the benefit system, human nature and behaviour, and the natural pursuit of self-interest. Human beings are driven by both self-interest and altruism (love for others) but self-interest is generally dominant. Self-interest (as opposed to selfishness) is human nature, there is nothing morally wrong with that, and it must be allowed for. It must be recognised and acknowledged that the structures and (dis)-incentives of the social security system influence claimant behaviour, and the present structure sometimes has deleterious effects - 'welfare dependency'. Social security structures should work with rather than against human nature, work with self-interest, and encourage rather than discourage desired social behaviour. Social security should help people to help themselves, to move from dependency to fulfilling their potential (Field 1996, 1997).

6. Social security rules and control mechanisms are based on a presumption of personal responsibility for one's actions (Chap 3.6). Claimants are answerable to whether it would be 'unreasonable to expect (me) to seek or be available for work'. The principle of 'reasonableness' is sufficiently broad to allow for the nature and severity of the health condition, and social circumstances.

If these premises are not accepted, it is submitted that rational reform of sickness and disability benefits is not possible.

5.3 The crux of the problem

Historically, the UK social security system for sickness and disability was about the passive provision of financial benefits and did not provide any active support for rehabilitation or reintegration (BSRM 2000, Waddell *et al* 2002). It 'chained people to passive dependency instead of helping them to realise their potential' (HM Government 1998a)

IB not only fails to provide positive support: it has actually had a negative impact. The whole focus is on 'incapacity': too often, the IB regime has effectively written people off and locked them into a lifetime of dependency on benefits. It has become a dumping ground for DWP's and other agencies' failures. The very name 'Incapacity' Benefit and some of the terms in the legislation and regulations are unfortunate and unhelpful because of their connotations of total incapacity for any work. Despite emphasising that 'passing' the PCA is simply an administrative cut-off at which it would be unreasonable to expect the claimant to work, the legislation and regulations effectively demand that recipients are incapable of work every day that they are on the benefit. Claimants need to demonstrate – sometimes repeatedly – their incapacity for work in order to gain the benefit. Many recipients are then afraid that showing any sign of trying to return to work is inconsistent with their 'incapacity' status and could risk losing benefits, while returning to work could jeopardise future claims. As Hadler (1996a) pointed out: 'If you have to prove you are ill, you can't get well'. These perverse incentives lead to negative perceptions, attitudes and expectations among many IB recipients - and their families, friends, and fellow workers - that they are permanently incapable of any work at all. Health care professionals, employers and personal advisers often share and reinforce these beliefs. In the past, DWP acted as if incapacity were a purely medical problem and left recipients passively on benefit awaiting 'cure' from the NHS as the only route off benefits. So receipt of IB often reinforced incapacity and became a barrier to work (Stanley & Regan 2003, Stanley & Maxwell 2004, Sirvasta & Chamberlain 2005).

That negative impact of the IB regime was compounded by three key 'medical' issues that underlie current IB trends:

- The increasing proportion of long-term 'incapacity' associated with less severe, 'common health problems'

- Failure to distinguish longer-term sickness from permanent disability

- Failure to acknowledge that many people on 'incapacity' benefits are capable of some work.

Tragically, the IB regime created needless incapacity in some people whose incapacity should have been avoidable, if they had been given the right opportunities and support.

It is clear that sickness or disability does not and should not *necessarily* mean incapacity for work. The Government's philosophy of 'work for those who can, security for those who cannot' (HM Government 1998a) might then be expanded:

- Work is the best form of welfare for people of working age who can be helped to (return to) work;

but this needs to be balanced by

- a strong framework of support for those who are unable to work.

The critical questions then are how to distinguish between those who can and those who cannot work, and how to deal with the most marginalized who do not fall neatly into either category - partly because of their personal characteristics and circumstances and also because of the local labour market (SSAC 2002).

To address these fundamental problems, three key elements should underpin reform:

- Better clinical and occupational management of common health problems and longer-term sickness (Waddell & Burton 2004b).

- Re-structuring and re-naming the benefit to 'unbundle' sickness, disability and incapacity for work (OECD 2003).

- A much stronger focus on a new system of support (*Pathways*) and encouragement of 'work for those who can' (HM Government 1998a & c).

Re-naming the benefit requires careful consideration. Names are important because they help to crystallise thinking and encapsulate a set of ideas and beliefs. They are a kind of social and linguistic shorthand. There is clinical evidence that diagnostic 'labelling' of patients can have a powerful influence on the perceptions, attitudes and behaviour of patients, health professionals, employers and society at large (Waddell 2004b) and the same is true of social security benefits (as discussed earlier). Most important, they can be developed into brand names, symbols and images with a particular set of connotations, and it is vital that these are positive and promote the kinds of perceptions, expectations and behaviour that are desired.

5.3.2 Longer-term sickness

These perverse effects of 'incapacity' are most relevant in claimants with 'longer-term sickness', which forms the major part of current IB (and DLA) problems. For the same reasons, that is hardest to fit into any restructured benefit. It is worth summarising some key facts.

Sickness is essentially a temporary status that is normally expected to recover, sooner or later, and to greater or lesser degree. Illness *can* cause permanent disability but that is then a different condition; longer-term sickness *per se* is not equivalent to permanent disability (Figure 9).

Figure 9: the relationship between longer-term sickness, permanent disability and incapacity.

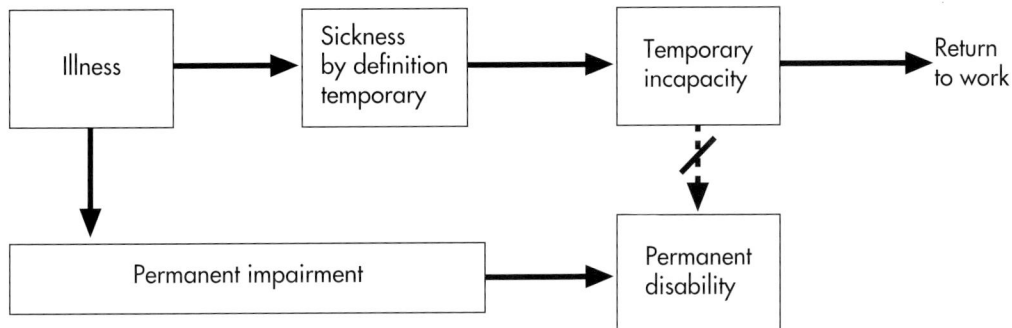

The reality, of course, is that even a small minority who do not return to work as expected can add up to very large numbers. Continued incapacity may be due to:

- Injury or illness producing permanent damage and impairment, leading to permanent disability: e.g. head injury with brain damage.

- The nature of the health condition, which is likely to continue indefinitely: e.g. ischaemic heart disease with chronic cardiac insufficiency.

- Continued symptoms with associated limitation of activities and restriction of participation.

The first two groups are likely to meet any criteria for longer-term incapacity benefits and present little difficulty in defining entitlement, assessment or adjudication. The real problem is the third group whose continued incapacity is based essentially on self-reports of 'feeling unwell' and 'limited'. A person who is unwell may 'feel too ill' *at present* to consider returning to work, but that is not a valid basis for future, permanent incapacity. The argument that, even if they recovered, they could not 'risk' work because it might be 'harmful' to their health is invalid because of the generally beneficial effects of work and the ill effects of long-term worklessness (except in rare conditions where there is clear and specific evidence that work would be 'prejudicial to health' - e.g. an allergy where specific exposure should be avoided). Thus, the *expectation* of continued 'longer-term sickness' is not a sufficient basis for permanent incapacity for all work.

The benefit status of people with longer-term sickness should therefore be distinguished from those on short-term sickness benefits and those with permanent impairments. The most positive approach to longer-term sickness is to address it as essentially a matter of rehabilitation and reintegration. The benefit system must make it clear that there are still expectations of rehabilitation and return to work, recognising that additional support and help will now be required. This shifts the emphasis from passive income replacement to active support into work measures, which the evidence suggests are more effective (OECD 2003). Consultations show that will gain broad support and is most likely to secure the cooperation upon which real change depends (DWP 2003c, DRC 2003b). Given the expectation of recovery and the rights and responsibilities of the sick role, it may also be reasonable to make continued receipt of benefits conditional upon efforts to achieve this end. Providing extra support and help gives the moral justification for expecting individual motivation and effort.

The problem of longer-term sickness will be a major focus throughout this review.

6 OPTIONS FOR REFORM

Some of the options for IB reform that have been mooted in various places will be considered, before trying to develop a more fundamental approach. It will become clear that we do not agree with some of these ideas. These options are not mutually exclusive.

6.1 The first option: 'anti-fraud' policies[114]

The IB caseload has more than trebled since 1979 while there has been little if any change in the nation's health, so it may be argued that about two-thirds of current recipients would have been working under the 1979 regime[115]. We have already reviewed other evidence that around two-thirds of IB recipients have no clear biological or medical reason for permanent incapacity, and that 'incapacity' also depends on (conscious and unconscious) personal, psychosocial and cultural factors. One interpretation is that many current recipients are claiming benefits fraudulently.

That is an over-simplification, but it goes to the heart of the medical, social, political and moral debate about IB reform. It may not be 'politically correct' and it is likely to provoke a storm of righteous indignation from certain vested interests, but the issue cannot be evaded.

No social security system control mechanisms can ever be 100% efficient, and it is to some extent a matter of perspective whether inclusion errors are regarded as abuse or simply the inefficiency of the system. Indeed, such observations often say as much about the philosophical and political perspective of the commentator as about the behaviour of recipients. It should also be clear by now that questions about what constitutes 'genuine' or 'reasonable' incapacity are extremely complex. Despite these caveats, the issue remains, and needs to be addressed.

There is strong medical evidence, supported by benefit trends and wide consensus (DWP 2002, 2003c, ABI/TUC 2002, OECD 2003, DRC 2003b, TUC 2004, CBI 2004), that many IB recipients are physically and mentally capable of some work. They may well have health problems and some limitations and restrictions, but these are not severe enough to stop them working, *if* they chose to do so and *if* they were given the right opportunity, support and incentives. Of course many IB recipients have such severe disabilities that they cannot reasonably be expected to work, but a best guess is that about one third could be helped to (return to) work quite easily, while another third might possibly be helped into work with much greater support and accommodations. It is impossible to set any firm figures, but these kinds of proportions seem consistent with the medical evidence, trends since the 1970s and common experience.

If, instead, many of these claimants with less severe health problems remain on IB, to what extent is that 'fraud'? The strictest definition of fraud is criminal deception (Oxford English

Dictionary), i.e. conscious and deliberate dishonesty with intent to deceive. All the evidence is that true 'malingering' (feigning injury or illness that does not exist, with intent to deceive) is rare[116] (Halligan *et al* 2003). Benefit fraud provable to a criminal standard (e.g. claiming IB and working in the black market) is officially estimated to be <1%[117] of disability and incapacity benefits (ONS 2001, Kitchen 2003), though in view of public and official reluctance to pursue this issue, that figure is almost certainly an under-estimate (Mackay & Rowlingson 1999). Fraud is clearly very serious when it occurs, but fraud in a legal sense does not seem to be the real issue here.

Taking a broader view of 'abuse' (misuse, perversion of – Oxford English Dictionary), there is no doubt that many claimants pursue their own self-interest, and may 'make the most of their symptoms' and 'take advantage of the system'. There is empirical evidence that such attitudes are widespread in contemporary society (Robinson 2003). Various international studies suggest that 20-30% of compensation claimants demonstrate some degree of 'lack of effort' or 'exaggeration' of their symptoms and disability on testing[118] (Halligan *et al* 2003, Green 2003). Similarly, UK employers believe that 15-20% of sickness absence is 'non-genuine' (CBI 2004, CIPD 2004). So it is entirely legitimate to question whether all claimants are as 'incapacitated' as they claim.

That returns to the question of 'motivation' and 'effort' (Chap 3.6), even if judgment must be tempered by allowance for all the other personal and social factors that influence (in)capacity (Chap 3.5). However, there is another side to this argument. Many claimants do *not* receive the most appropriate advice and the optimum clinical / occupational management. Despite recent efforts and some encouraging progress, occupational health and rehabilitation services in UK are still very patchy. Too few people receive the support into work that they need from the NHS or employers. Employer discrimination remains a significant problem, especially for those with mental health conditions. The counter question is then whether the current social, employment and benefit system provides the necessary conditions to enable these people to work?

Given the complexity of the problem, a crude anti-fraud policy is very unlikely to have any significant effect on IB trends. It is entirely right to deal with fraud when it occurs and DWP initiatives have had modest success: the costs generally exceed any recoverable arrears in the individual case but there is overall benefit in the 'halo' effect (Kitchen 2003). However, there is no evidence in UK or internationally that anti-fraud policies have had any significant impact on overall trends (ISSA 1996, Waddell *et al* 2002). On the contrary, that kind of antagonistic approach is more likely to be counter-productive because of its negative impact on claimants', GPs' and employers' attitudes and behaviour. It risks undermining the fundamental cultural shift and cooperation on which any lasting improvement depends.

Rather than unhelpful arguments about the *extent* to which fault lies with the claimant or the system, it is more realistic and more positive to regard many of these claimants as having real health problems that, in themselves, should not be totally incapacitating: but when they are compounded with these other disadvantages and barriers, they easily become so. Overcoming that depends on individual motivation and effort, but that alone is often not enough. It also depends on better advice and support from the NHS / GPs, combined with more positive attitudes and support from employers and the DWP. The onus is on society to provide the proper opportunities, support and incentives as the corollary to expecting greater individual motivation and effort. Ultimately, it is a question of redefining the 'reasonable' balance between accepting that a claimant is entitled to incapacity benefits vs. expecting them to (return to) work despite their health condition or disability, *provided* they are given proper support and opportunity.

6.2 The second option: tighten the gateway to benefits

A more plausible, apparently simple option is to tighten the gateway to benefits. A tougher medical test, stringently applied, would seem to be the most direct way to reduce inflow and hence control caseload and expenditure. However, this fails on many pragmatic issues and on the policy goal of fairness and justness:

- It is naïve and simplistic.

- There are major practical problems and limitations to developing and implementing such an approach.

- The UK evidence is that it would have limited direct impact on inflow or caseload.

- The international evidence is that any effect on inflow and caseload would only be temporary.

- Any impact it had would probably be on the most disadvantaged recipients.

- Many people would not return to work, but move to other benefits (e.g. JSA or IS) or soon return to IB .

- It would be likely to face major political opposition.

It might appear that the simplest way to tighten the gateway to IB would be to raise the numerical threshold of the Personal Capability Assessment. However, that test is already considered by OECD (2003) to be one of the toughest in the developed world apart from the United States. Moreover, this would be difficult to defend on grounds of principle. The original *All Work Test* and the threshold were based on extensive development work, a strong evidence base and broad consensus. Considerable time and resources were put into its implementation and delivery, and it has stood the test of time reasonably well. It would now be very difficult to amend the test significantly (even 'just' by changing the threshold) without an equally strong logic, evidence base and new consensus. Development of any credible alternative would be a major undertaking, requiring a comparable amount of time, resources and costs. Even once a new test was successfully developed, implementing it would involve major reorganisation of the medical service, just as it is finally settling down and working efficiently. In view of the considerable body of Appeal Tribunals' and Commissioners' decisions that already exists, it might be much simpler to address any particular anomalies that have developed rather than start the entire process afresh.

Perhaps surprisingly, there is no clear evidence that introducing measures to tighten the gateway would be an effective method of reducing IB inflow and caseload. This may be because inflow to longer-term sickness is largely outwith the direct control of DWP, and appears to depend more on the prevailing social, occupational and medical culture and practice. The introduction of what was perceived to be a more stringent UK medical test in 1995 probably had little immediate impact on inflow. The steady reduction in inflow since that time, during which the test has remained unchanged, appears to reflect much broader trends.

Although annual inflow to IB has fallen significantly since 1995, outflow has also fallen and caseload initially continued to grow. A tighter gateway means that the 'average' health and employment characteristics of those who are allowed benefits are worse, which leads to longer duration and lower outflow. Moreover, US experience suggests that an extremely tough gateway makes those who do successfully gain benefits even more risk aversive and reluctant to do anything to seek work that might jeopardise their benefits. This helps to explain why the main US support into work programmes for this group have been such a dismal failure (Bruyere *et al* 2003).

Internationally, there is little or no correlation between the tightness of the gateway and numbers on long-term incapacity benefits. For example, UK has one of the toughest tests, but about the EU and OECD average for the proportion of people of working age on incapacity benefits (OECD 2003). The United States has what is universally agreed to be the toughest gateway, but their caseload has increased by 1 million in the past two years and they now have relatively more people on their incapacity benefit than UK. On the other hand, Austria has a permissive gateway, but one of the lowest caseloads.

Thus, tightening the gateway in isolation would not only be ineffective: it would probably have positively harmful effects on certain groups of recipients. It could exclude large numbers of people with genuine health problems that cause genuine difficulty working. Those claimants most likely to be excluded from benefits would be those with mental health and pain-related conditions and those with multiple social, educational and skills disadvantages. For the same reasons, these are the very claimants who face the greatest barriers to (re)-entering the labour force. Without more positive support, simply forcing these people off IB would not necessarily mean they would (re)-enter work: many would simply move to other benefits such as JSA or IS (with or without the disability premium) or soon return to IB with new sick certification. This might improve headline figures, but at a considerable cost of human distress and suffering, and administrative and political hassle, with little or no lasting gain or financial savings.

Where claimants with less severe health problems are disallowed IB they usually move across to JSA. JSA is less generous, time-limited and involves full worksearch conditionality. Despite these tough rules and the clear work focus, claimants who fail the PCA and move to JSA have very poor work outcomes (DWP Administrative data):

- They are less successful in moving from JSA to work than any other category of JSA;

- Only 23% are in work after 12-18 months compared to 95% of the overall inflow into JSA;

- 35% are back on IB

- A quarter continue to rely on other social security benefits.

Moving people with health conditions or disabilities from IB to JSA would simply transfer the problem from one benefit to the other. This would increase the 'unemployment' count (perhaps very substantially) and at the same time fail to address the historical lack of an effective framework for helping these people. The problem would still need to be addressed within JSA and that might be even more difficult, requiring a completely new framework and initiatives. Similarly, despite the overall success of the New Deal for Lone Parents, it has had little success engaging with and helping back to work lone parents on Income Support with health problems.

Some claimants forced off IB or forced on to JSA, which finished after 26 weeks, might then be left without any financial support if they did not meet the different criteria for means-tested Income Support. For example, the US has one of the highest proportions of the disabled population receiving no work or benefit income (nearly 20%) while UK currently has one of the lowest[119] (<10%) (OECD 2003). A significant minority could be pushed below the poverty line, with undesirable consequences for social exclusion, anti-poverty, child poverty and public health policies. That would defeat the goal of social justice and fairness.

Any proposed changes to the test perceived as simply tightening the gateway to reduce expenditure would be likely to meet strong opposition from the disability lobby and political opponents e.g. the American test is harshly criticised for its draconian nature. Gateways were tightened in the United States, the Netherlands, Sweden and Norway at various times during the 1980s and 90s (Waddell *et al* 2002, OECD 2003), leading to professional, public and political antagonism and hostility, and years of appeals and litigation, which made them unsustainable.

In each case, subsequent political and administrative relaxation of the gateway led to a rebound phenomenon that outweighed any gain.

6.3 The third option: time limit incapacity benefits

Another apparently simple option is to time-limit sickness-related benefits. In recent times, this was first seriously proposed by Fordyce (1995) in the United States, who suggested a 6 week limit on workers compensation benefits for acute low back pain without demonstrable pathology. However, the argument is essentially the same for any time limit e.g. 1-2 years. The basic argument is that sickness and the sick role are temporary (at least for many common health problems); many IB recipients have health conditions that 'should' get better, at least sufficient to return to work; so there is no health basis for indefinite or effectively permanent benefits. An appropriate time limit should therefore be set for these 'sickness benefits' after which benefits should stop. That will 'encourage' people to return to work, which is in their own best long-term interests. There is some validity to the starting premise but the proposed solution has fatal flaws in principle and fails in practice.

'Expected recovery times' are certainly a useful guide and form one cross-check on individual progress (**www.dwp.gov.uk/medical**). However, they are essentially a form of average: they generally have little biomedical basis and are simply statistical measures of clinical or occupational groups, especially for functional recovery and return to work. Whatever threshold is set, there will always be a larger or smaller minority who 'fail to recover' but remain genuinely sick and incapacitated for work. DWP data shows that those who do remain on benefits (both by selection and duration effects) are the most disadvantaged group who are furthest from the labour market. They need most positive help to return to work and purely negative incentives like withdrawing benefits are least likely to 'make them' successfully re-enter the labour market. Any arbitrary time limit on incapacity benefits is more likely to move them to other benefits or lead to re-cycling. Thus, arbitrary time limits fail on grounds of social justice, fairness and further penalising the most disadvantaged.

There is also a paternalistic argument about whether the state 'knows better' than individual recipients and their medical advisers what they should do and what is good for them.

These principles of fairness and social justice probably underpin the opposition that has been voiced from many quarters in recent months to even hints of time-limiting incapacity benefits. IB recipients and the medical profession, in particular, will be violently opposed. Surveys confirm strong public opposition to time-limiting sickness and disability benefits, on the grounds that benefits should continue for as long as the person is incapable of work (Stafford 1998). It is likely that political opposition to time limits on benefits would be insurmountable. Even if legislation was successfully pushed through, it would probably lead to complete withdrawal of cooperation that would render other reforms ineffective.

The Workers Compensation Boards of Canada are the only statutory bodies in the world who have attempted to legislate time-limited benefits for chronic pain (Waddell 2004a). The proposals were evidence-based, the logic was clear and widely debated, and the benefit changes were accompanied by a comprehensive, well-funded rehabilitation package. Despite that, Nova Scotia was the only province to pass the legislation; political and professional opposition in Ontario led to proposed legislation being shelved; the other provinces deferred their decisions. When the Workers Compensation Board of Nova Scotia implemented the proposals, it faced fierce legal challenge and appeals which were taken all the way to the Supreme Court of Canada. The Supreme Court finally ruled that arbitrary time limits breached human and constitutional rights of access to services and benefits because they discriminated against certain claimants as a class by failing to consider and assess them individually. Underlying the technical legal argument, the Supreme Court effectively ruled that claimants' pain and suffering must be acknowledged, and that their individual rights were paramount and must not be discriminated against.

These arguments seem to rule out arbitrary or general time-limits on incapacity benefits. Nevertheless, more specific use of time limits might be justifiable in certain circumstances or for certain purposes. Benefits (or elements of benefits) directed to a specific contingency or for a specific purpose might be limited to the duration of that contingency or purpose. For example, short-term sickness benefits might be distinguished from longer-term incapacity benefits. After a set time, recipients might be re-assessed and different levels of entitlement and conditionality imposed. Any benefit (or element) which was specifically directed to supporting and encouraging rehabilitation and return to work might last for the duration of such interventions. However, in view of the likely political opposition, legal challenge and appeals, any such proposals would require a clear and strong rationale, general public and political acceptance as just, and precise defensible legislation.

6.4 The fourth option: cut the benefit rates

The crudest option would be simply to cut the benefit rate for IB to equal, for example, JSA. That would return to Beveridge's basic principle of parity and remove any direct financial incentive for 'sickness'[120].

This would be the most direct approach to reducing IB expenditure. In theory, it could produce massive savings - if implemented immediately for all current recipients; in practice, transitional arrangements would erode most of these savings. There would then be a huge disincentive for existing recipients coming off the benefit and losing their preserved rights, which would be likely to have a very negative effect on outflow.

However, this option would probably have little impact on initial inflow to benefits, which has more to do with 'sickness' and the sick role than benefit rates. It would not address the most serious area of caseload growth – IB 'credits only' or issues of entitlement, conditionality and duration. In practice, all of the current problems of IB would still be there. Draconian cuts would be more likely lead to antagonism and confrontation, undermine the scope to apply any further conditionality, and destroy the real progress that has been made on support into work.

If such a massive cut was imposed on existing recipients, it would have an immediate and serious impact on individual recipients, especially those with long-term sickness or disability. The most serious losers would be the many hundreds of thousands of people who are (just) above means-tested benefit levels but far from well-off. A significant minority would be pushed below the poverty line.

This option runs contrary to the political and public consensus on the need for special provisions for sickness and disability. Large numbers of IB recipients have severe medical conditions or impairments that make it unreasonable to expect them to work. It would be extremely difficult to cut support for such people who have contributed to the system in the past, and who are very unlikely to work again or are still in the process of recovery. Such a benefit cut would also undermine the progress that has been made on disability rights. It is easy to imagine the likely opposition from the disability lobby, public opinion, MPs of all parties and the House of Lords. And it would be likely to destroy any cooperation from the key stakeholders whose cooperation is essential for any real progress.

Crude cuts to basic IB rates across the board therefore seem unrealistic. However, there needs to be much more open information and public debate about the actual total benefits paid to some recipients (Chap 4.1). It might then be possible to reconsider and rationalise some of the more generous benefit packages, particularly when they go to recipients with less severe health conditions. The major proviso is that any changes must not bear unfairly on those who are already the most disadvantaged (Chap 10). Moreover, experience with the 1998-99 reforms shows that even the most justifiable cuts are likely to meet fierce political opposition (Chap 4.7).

6.5 The fifth option: stop automatic increases in IB rates with duration

At present, IB payments effectively increase automatically over time between short-term lower rate, short-term higher rate and long-term IB. This is a hang-over from the time of Beveridge, on the grounds that income replacement needs are greater over long periods. That argument was later reinforced by evidence that poverty is most common among the long-term disabled (Harris *et al* 1971, HM Government 1985a & b, Smith *et al* 2004). However, that is really a question of the adequacy of IB and DLA benefit payments, which should be addressed on its own merits and is quite separate from the question of a progressive scale over the first year on benefits.

The major disadvantage of such automatic increments is that they provide a perverse incentive: the longer a claimant remains on benefits the greater the financial reward. Protected rights through the linking rules reinforce this. This negative incentive is particularly relevant during the first year on benefits, which is exactly the time when chronicity and long-term incapacity become established (Waddell *et al* 2003). Such increases run contrary to all occupational sick pay and insurance schemes, which commonly only provide maximum benefits for 6 months, 50% benefits for a further 6 months, and then fall further to ill-health retirement pension rates.

There is no public understanding and little support for such automatic increments over time (Stafford 1998). It is difficult to see any valid argument for them and there is a strong argument for abolishing them. Instead, any additions or supplements should be designed to meet specific needs or to provide positive incentives for desired behaviour.

6.6 A more fundamental approach

Some of the options considered above are undisguised attempts to cut benefit expenditure, which fail to address the real, underlying problems of IB and are therefore unlikely to produce lasting improvement in trends. Some would decrease rather than advance social justice, and are unlikely to be politically feasible or publicly acceptable.

That is not to deny the need to reform the structure, incentives and control mechanisms of incapacity benefits. There are strong arguments for IB reform, but it must address the underlying problems. IB trends over the past 20-30 years reflect a fundamental shift in the culture that surrounds sickness, disability and incapacity for work: real and lasting change demands an equally fundamental shift in thinking. It must also be done in such a way that it is generally acceptable, gains the cooperation of the main stakeholders and actually delivers the desired results.

Three basic strategies underpin all options for reform of sickness and disability benefits.

- Gateway changes; controlling inflow, directing benefits to those in need

- Benefit re-structuring

- Active support into work policies: e.g. employment/rehabilitation programmes, 'making work pay', conditionality.

Attempts at welfare reform in the UK have generally focused on benefit re-structuring and gateway tightening much more than on active reintegration measures. Yet the historical evidence shows that policies focusing solely on financial benefits have produced disappointing results (OECD 2003). In the past few years, there has been:

- an increasing focus on employment outcomes – as opposed to simply controlling benefit expenditure – across all benefit groups (primarily on anti-poverty and wider economic grounds);

- evidence that the UK gateway to benefit is now tight by international standards and that further tightening alone is unlikely to have much direct impact on caseload;

- emerging evidence that positive support into work interventions and re-integration policies are more effective.

As a result, welfare reform in all OECD countries since the 1990s has placed greater emphasis on (re)-integration (Prins & Bloch 2001, OECD 2003, Prinz 2003, Gilbert & van Voorhis 2003), with four key elements:

- the introduction of anti-discrimination legislation;

- a significant increase in employers' responsibilities towards people with disabilities;

- the promotion of streamlined administration and one-stop service centres;

- the introduction of various forms of work incentives with continued recognition of disability status.

This has led to a more balanced approach – a balance between providing a decent, level of income replacement for sick and disabled people who cannot work, and a realistic set of opportunities, support and encouragement for whose who do have (some) capacity for work (Mashaw & Reno 1996, Reno *et al* 1997). This is a much more positive, active approach (Blair 1997):

- The welfare state should be active, not passive; providing support and services and not just financial benefits.

- The welfare state should combine opportunity and responsibility, as the foundation of society and citizenship.

Box 13: Main developments in UK disability policy (After Burchardt 1999, 2003b)

1995 Disability Discrimination Act

1997 New Deal for Disabled People pilots of Personal Adviser service and innovative schemes launched.

1998 Green Paper: a new contract for welfare

1999 ONE service introduced

2000 Disability Rights Commission became operational

2001 New Deal for Disabled People job brokers service extended nationally

2002 Green Paper: Pathways to work

2002 Jobcentre Plus launched

2003 Job Retention and Rehabilitation pilots (JRRPs) launched

2004 *Pathways to Work* pilots launched

2005 DWP Five-Year Strategy

2005 Disability Discrimination Amendment Act

A balanced approach requires simultaneous advance on many fronts (Box 13). IB has many of the characteristics of a *complex system*: it cannot be reduced to the sum of its parts, but interactions between the elements produce new properties, characteristics and effects (Glouberman *et al* 2000, Glouberman 2001). Gateways, benefit structures and reintegration measures are inter-dependent. An apparently simple change in one element does not necessarily have a direct and predictable effect: it inevitably has repercussions on the other element(s) that may negate or magnify its effects or lead to unexpected or undesirable effects. Change in one element usually necessitates adjustment(s) or compensatory change(s) in other element(s). Thus, to achieve the kind of cultural shift required, there must be a balanced approach with action on all three fronts. And given that real and lasting change depends on modifying the attitudes and behaviour of various stakeholders, and on their cooperation, a positive strategy is also essential.

Setting the positive support elements of policy in place provides the moral and political justification for benefit reform. The order, balance and presentation of these initiatives are then important. A primary focus on controlling benefits is likely to be seen as financially-driven, mean, unjust and unfair. It would face massive political and public opposition, and risk antagonising the key stakeholders needed to provide support into work. That could risk losing both benefit and support into work reforms. In contrast, a *primary* focus on providing positive support and incentives to work, which is then backed up by benefit re-structuring, is more likely to be seen as just and fair, about improving outcomes rather than just reducing expenditure, morally and politically justifiable, and sellable. In view of the sensitivity of the issue and the vested interests, the balance still needs careful packaging and selling. The package should cover all three strategies, but lead primarily on the support into work side.

Social security benefits must also be placed in perspective and context. Benefits are only one, albeit very important, element of the social support that society provides for sick and disabled people (Figure 10).

Figure 10: Social support for sick and disabled people. The elements have been divided somewhat artificially into interventions on the individual and social levels, but there is much overlap and interaction. E.g. support into work interventions usually address both individual and environmental obstacles to (return to) work; social inclusion policies must be implemented at a societal level but also delivered at an individual level.

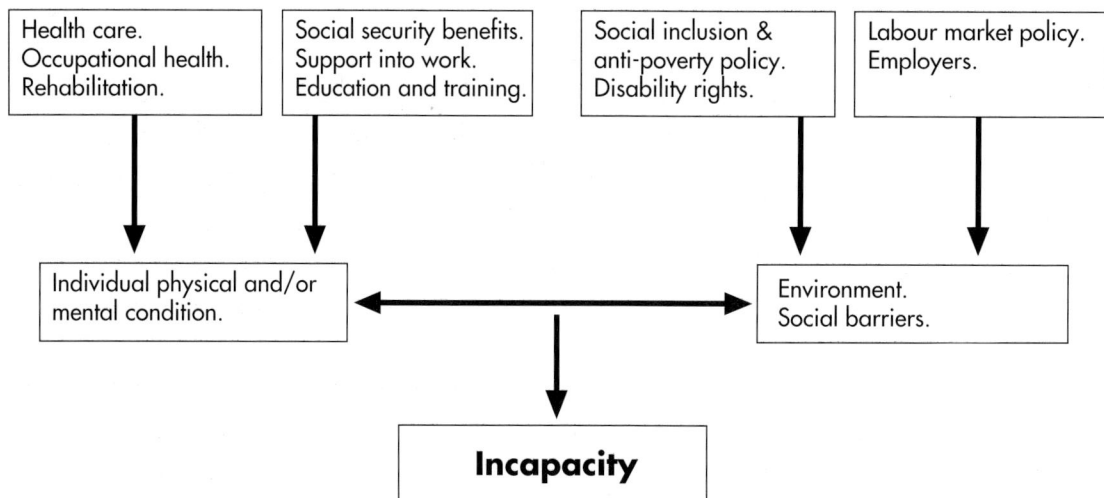

7 THE PRIMARY GATEWAY TO SICKNESS

The Personal Capability Assessment (PCA) is often described as the 'Gateway' to IB, but that is inaccurate. There are two main gateways[121] to sickness and disability benefits with completely different characteristics:

- The primary social gateway to sickness

- The formal DWP gateway to longer-term benefits.

7.1 The primary gateway

The primary gateway to sickness is effectively a 'social' gateway. The initial decision to stop work is commonly made by the individual, with or without the advice or agreement of health professional(s). This decision is influenced by many factors including but not limited to the health condition: the key factors appear to be the individual's perception of his or her symptoms, the nature of work demands and the psychosocial and cultural context. At some point within the first 7 days, sickness absence is legitimised by medical certification from a GP. Individual workers' decisions about sickness absence may also be influenced by company policies, sick pay conditions and sickness absence management, which may give the employer some influence even if no direct part in the decision. At that stage, all stakeholders usually make short-term decisions about acute illness and do not consider possible long-term consequences. However, those people who do not recover but go on to longer-term sickness may drift on to social security benefits without any further clear decision points. So, effectively, early decisions about starting and continuing sickness form the initial gateway to subsequent benefits.

DWP has no direct involvement in administering this primary gateway for the individual claimant and, indeed, has no knowledge of the sick person until the point of claim. For many practical reasons this is unavoidable. DWP can never administer the primary gateway directly, but that does not mean DWP cannot do anything about its operation. Government policy can have a major influence on the attitudes and behaviour of the key decision makers – individuals, GPs and employers – and should attempt to direct them towards the desired goals.

The process of moving from the primary gateway to longer-term benefits can also be improved. More should be done to differentiate clearly between the early stages of a benefit claim and subsequent progress to longer-term benefits. In particular, it should be made clear that sickness benefits obtained through the primary gateway are provisional until formal DWP assessment. This would further reinforce the idea that sickness benefits are temporary, in the expectation of recovery and return to work, and do not carry any automatic expectation or right to permanent incapacity.

The primary gateway operates by a set of inter-dependent elements:

- GP advice on Fitness for Work and sick certification

- NHS care and rehabilitation

- Occupational management

- The 'culture' that surrounds sickness and disability

All of these elements can and should be improved. The changes must be integrated: all ultimately depend on and should contribute to a fundamental change in the culture that surrounds 'incapacity'.

7.2 GP advice on Fitness for Work and sick certification

GPs have a pivotal role as the main source of professional advice about sickness and Fitness for Work, but the profile and quality of practice in this area needs to be improved (Sawney 2002, Pransky *et al* 2002). Up till now, many GPs have lacked the tools and the training to support their patients in returning to work, despite its importance for promoting well-being. To underpin the required change in practice, all health professionals who deal with patients of working age need to:

- Understand the importance of work for health (Box 2),

- Be aware of the implications of (longer-term) sickness absence, the alternative options and the support available to minimise it (Sawney 2002).

- Be interested in and accept some responsibility for rehabilitation and occupational outcomes (BSRM 2000, Waddell & Burton 2004b)

- Consider carefully whether sick certification is really necessary and in the patient's best long-term interests (Sawney 2002, CMG 2004a & b).

Sick certification is one of the most powerful health care interventions (especially for common health problems) and, like any drug or invasive procedure, it is important to consider the indications and contra-indications, the likely impact, and the potential risks and side effects. Many health problems do not need automatic sick certification, and doctors should always consider carefully whether advice to refrain from work is the most appropriate clinical management and whether it is in the patient's best long-term interests. The scientific evidence and current best practice show that it is often better to encourage and support patients to stay at work or to return to work as soon as possible (CMG 2004a & b).

The problems of GP certification are well recognised (Chap 3.8) but nothing has been found to provide the same patient accessibility, quality of advice and cost/affordability to employers and the taxpayer. Current DWP pilot studies are exploring the possibility of extending the role of certification to other non-medical health professionals (Niven 2005). Certain groups of non-medical health professionals are enthusiastic and confident about their ability to undertake this role[122], but there are major questions around education, training, ethics, guidelines and standards of practice[123]. It is unclear if or how this would address the fundamental weaknesses of certification by any health professionals whose primary interests and responsibilities lie in patient care. Moreover, any alternative system could involve more time, resources and costs[124], without any evidence at present that it would be more cost-effective.

The BMA has argued that occupational health practitioners might be in a better position to undertake sick certification. In practice, however, that would mean a major shift in the traditional role of most working OH professionals and many (just like GPs) would require further training in disability evaluation and rehabilitation. Occupational health nurses are among those least in favour of extending certification (Niven 2005). In any event, the severe shortage of all OH professionals in the UK makes this impractical for the foreseeable future. It has also been opposed by employers, who would bear the costs.

Accepting that GPs will always have a key role in sick certification, there is a lot that can be done to improve certification practice. That depends on developing professional knowledge and skills, but also depends on and must be underpinned by a much more fundamental shift in GP thinking and advice about Fitness for Work (Boxes 2 & 19). This is primarily a matter of training and continuing professional education (Sawney 2002, Wynn *et al* 2003). To be credible and acceptable, training and education must be led by the appropriate professional bodies but DWP has the vested interest, expertise and resources to make a substantial contribution (Box 14), which would involve modest expenditure and is likely to be highly cost-effective in the long run. It will be important to sell this as being in doctors' and patients' best interests rather than simply an attempt to control sickness absence and costs.

Improving the quality of advice on fitness for work and standards of certification practice would be greatly helped by the development of effective recording and monitoring systems (DWP 2005), which have been non-existent since 1988. This contrasts with the close audit of NHS drug prescriptions, even though the expenditure consequences of sick notes are much greater. Monitoring would make it possible to:

- Promote the merits of sound certification practice as an integral part of good clinical practice;

- Monitor individual GP certification practice (which is probably the most accessible and 'hardest' measure of advice on work);

Box 14: DWP Information and training for General Practitioners [125]

1. A series of laminated desk aids with advice and guidance on:

- Completion of medical statements [sick notes]
- Helping patients stay in work
- Evidence based recovery times
- Time lines for patient management

2. Videos and DVDs on:

- Information on common health conditions with comments from medical experts
- The benefits of work
- Incapacity Benefit
- The medical assessment

*3. Internet resources (**www.dwp.gov.uk/medical**) and hard copies:*

- Overviews &Guidance on providing medical certificates for Statutory Sick Pay, Statutory Maternity Pay and Incapacity Benefit (www.dwp.gov.uk/medical/medicalib204)

- Approved doctor's and decision makers' handbooks
- Accredited online learning modules:
  - Certification
  - Health and work [with HSE]
  - Common health conditions

4. Commissioned and published research reports and papers

5. Presentations at postgraduate meetings & seminars by Corporate Medical Group doctors.

- Provide feedback to individual GPs, highlighting good and bad practice against evidence-based guidelines;

- Link performance to re-training and re-validation;

- Collect quantitative data for research and policy-making, e.g. on sickness absence, tracking GP workloads and identifying areas for further research, guidance and training.

This would be more feasible if certification were integrated into practice computer systems[126]. DWP plans to pilot computerisation over the next year, with the aim of producing specifications and basic programs for inclusion in the NHS network. National roll-out would require close cooperation with the Health Departments and the NHS. However, it must be recognised that GP representatives may resist recording and monitoring, given their stated desire to end all responsibility for sick certification. Delicate negotiations would be required to reassure them this would not amount to 'policing' of clinical management.

Good clinical practice in this area also needs to be further defined. A recent Swedish systematic review of the literature on sick certification (Alexanderson & Norlund 2004) left many questions unanswered. A more fundamental conceptual review is required to provide a theoretical framework for policy making, research and development, and practice. Original scientific research and pilot studies are required to develop stronger evidence of the impact of good and bad sick certification practice on patients' future health in the UK context[127]. This evidence would need to be developed by academic researchers who are perceived to be independent of DWP. These concepts and evidence then need to be formulated into evidence-based guidance for GPs, by credible professional bodies that are acceptable to primary care physicians. This guidance should be incorporated into undergraduate and post-graduate medical training, continuing medical education, and official DWP/DH guidance (Sawney 2002).

DWP and the three Health Departments of England, Scotland and Wales (Dept of Health 2004a, DWP 2004, Strategy Unit 2005, DWP 2005[128]) are committed to working together with the various Royal Colleges and professional bodies to improve professional education and training about Fitness for Work and clinical management of sickness absence. The DWP Corporate Medical Group is leading this work for the Government (Box 15), but close cooperation and concerted effort will be necessary to ensure training is available and delivered nationally. Progress to date suggests that, with careful handling, this could be deliverable.

Pilot studies are currently testing a possible role for DWP Personal Advisers in GP surgeries. In purely practical terms, this has the potential to provide easier and faster access to employment related services. Perhaps even more important, it could increase awareness of occupational issues and these services among GPs and their patients. It could facilitate links and improve communication between GPs, employers and other key players and help to develop a team approach to return to work. Preliminary reactions have already shown there would be strong professional opposition to any attempt to impose such 'spies in the surgery'. So it would probably need to be agreed on an individual and voluntary basis by GPs, who would have to be convinced of the advantages to them and their patients.

Professional education provides the essential knowledge and skills but is insufficient in itself. Actually changing clinical practice requires a concerted implementation plan and a broad, multi-dimensional campaign to get the messages across and change professional behaviour (Oxman *et al* 1995, COST B13 2003)(Box 16). Professional change is more likely to occur if it is in tune with broader change in society. Experience from Working Backs Scotland (**www.workingbacksscotland.com**) suggests that changing public and patient attitudes may

Box 15: DWP research and development to improve Fitness for Work Advice and certification practice

- Commissioning evidence reviews and developing the evidence base, e.g. on the benefits of work for health, effective methods of sickness absence management and rehabilitation.

- Further development of DWP training materials (As listed in Box 14)

- Reviewing and enhancing undergraduate medical training and post-graduate medical education and training programmes.

- Developing new techniques, desktop aids and tools.

- Defining good practice, standards and protocols

- Developing and pilot studies of computerized certification records and effective methods of monitoring and auditing certification practice.

- Pilot studies of GPs with a special interest, e.g. musculoskeletal, mental health, occupational health.

- Pilot studies of various alternative methods of delivering fitness for work advice and sick certification.

- Pilot studies of various methods of increasing contact and awareness between GPs and DWP services.

- Further development of condition management programmes and materials (as in *Pathways*).

be an indirect but more powerful method of changing professional behaviour. Critically, however, it is worth re-emphasising that change depends on gaining the cooperation of the key health professionals - both their representative bodies and individual GPs. That is why DWP must approach this whole issue sensitively and positively.

In general, a positive approach that recognizes and rewards good practice is more likely to gain professional cooperation. Nevertheless, it must be recognized that there are some GPs whose certification practice falls well below acceptable standards. In extreme cases, the DWP Chief Medical Adviser has the power to take GPs through the NHS disciplinary machinery and to the General Medical Council. There are many practical problems to disciplinary proceedings, which must incorporate appropriate safeguards, and no GP has ever been disciplined in any way for poor work in this area. DWP should work closely with the Health Departments and the NHS to develop greater powers to identify, engage with and remedy the practices of poorly performing doctors. As with most areas of clinical practice (GMC 1998), however, a positive

Box 16: Interventions to change professional practice (Adapted from COST B13 2003)

Most consistently effective:

Interactive educational meetings: e.g. workshops including discussions of practice

Educational outreach visits

Reminders (manual or computerised)

Multifaceted interventions

Professional, financial and other (dis)-incentives.

Variable effect:

Audit and feedback

Local opinion leaders

Local consensus process on practice

Patient mediated interventions

Limited or no effect:

Printed or electronic educational materials, guidelines, etc

Didactic educational meetings and lectures

supportive approach is more likely to elicit cooperation and the required change in professional practice, with disciplinary action held in the background as a last resort.

7.3 NHS care and rehabilitation

The first and most important priority for most ill or injured people is to get appropriate and effective health care[129]. Health care provides essential support and relief for human suffering. However, the effectiveness (or otherwise) of health care also has direct consequences for inflow to, stock, and outflow from sickness and disability benefits, so DWP has a vested and legitimate interest in health care outcomes.

From the perspective of the present analysis, trends of long-term incapacity associated with common health problems represent a massive failure of health care. There is clearly need for a fundamental re-think about NHS services for these people, and it is right and proper that DWP contributes to this debate (Dept of Health 2004a).

The design of NHS services should start with the needs of patients (Box 17). NHS provisions for the investigation and treatment of severe medical conditions are a separate issue that is outwith the remit of this review. The question here is how to improve services for patients with sickness, disability or incapacity, particularly associated with less severe, common health problems. The policy goal is to provide better health care for these people, but these proposals should also lead to more efficient and cost-effective use of NHS resources. This is largely about making better

> **Box 17: Health care needs of patients with 'common health problems', sickness and disability**
>
> Exclude serious medical conditions, reassurance & prognosis
>
> Symptomatic measures
>
> Provide information and advice, including advice about work
>
> Support for self-management of persistent and recurrent symptoms
>
> Restore function
>
> Address psychosocial issues
>
> Overcome obstacles to (return to) work
>
> Fitness for work and occupational health advice and support

and more effective use of existing resources, though there is also a need to develop new condition management programmes that integrate health care, self-care and rehabilitation.

To meet these needs requires a different kind of clinical management. The primary goal of health care is to treat disease and provide symptomatic relief, and it is often implicitly assumed that if this 'makes the patient better' that will automatically restore function and lead to return to work. Since most patients do recover rapidly and return to their normal activities and work, it may be argued that routine health care effectively does rehabilitate. Indeed, modern clinical management of common health problems emphasises the possibility and importance of restoring function as the best means of achieving lasting relief of symptoms (Waddell & Burton 2004b). Unfortunately, because of the poor correlation between symptoms, disability and incapacity (Figure 2) and the influence of other biopsychosocial factors, clinical 'recovery' does not always translate into return to work. For those patients who do not recover, continued 'treatment' alone does not restore function and in particular is not effective for occupational outcomes (Staal *et al* 2002, James *et al* 2002, 2003, OECD 2003). By that stage, restoration of function requires attention in its own right. Clinical management must shift from symptom relief, to symptom management, maintenance and restoration of function, and support into work. These goals are closely intertwined, they run concurrently, and they are inter-dependent. Relief or at least control of symptoms may require continued health care; restoring function must address the broader biopsychosocial dimensions and obstacles discussed earlier (Waddell & Burton 2004b). Quite simply, good clinical management should *both* relieve symptoms and restore function, and these go hand in hand. The ultimate social measure of successful health care is the level of activity and participation achieved (Figure 11).

Figure 11: Interventions and outcomes.

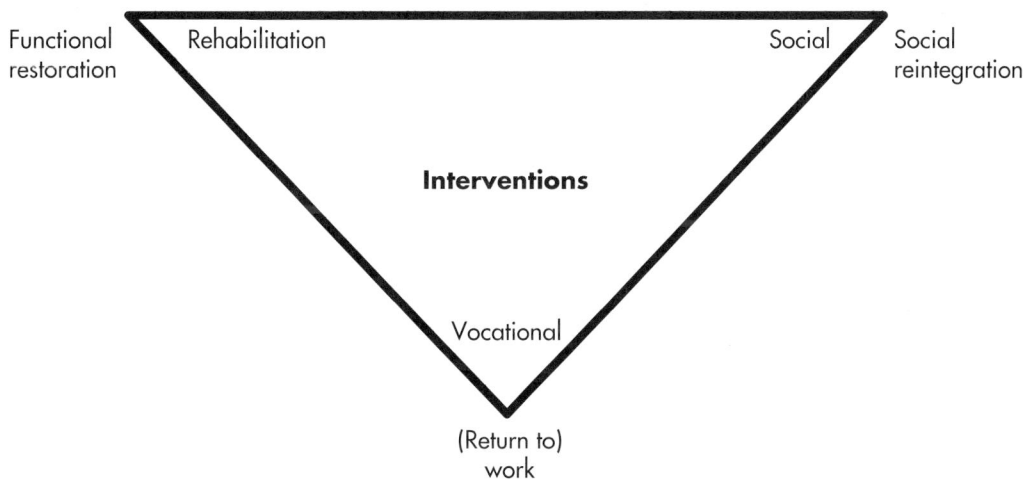

Thus, rehabilitation is *not* a separate, second stage intervention to be delegated to a specialist: restoring function should be an integral part of good clinical management (Waddell & Burton 2004b). That may require a fundamental shift in the culture of health care, in the nature of clinical interventions and in the mind-set of clinicians. All health professionals caring for patients of working age (doctors, nurse practitioners, allied health professionals, occupational health personnel) should have an interest in, and accept some responsibility for, restoring function and occupational outcomes. This does not mean that every health professional must become a 'rehabilitation specialist': rather, it goes to the roots of what good clinical management of people of working-age is all about.

This has a number of very practical implications for routine NHS services for patients with common health problems:

- The needs listed in Box 17 are largely issues of clinical 'management' rather than 'treatment'. Once serious medical conditions have been excluded, services should be designed to provide a more holistic and more socially oriented approach to assessment, clinical management and rehabilitation rather than continued medical focus on investigation, diagnosis and treatment.

- Many common health problems are persistent, recurrent or fluctuating, and largely a matter of self-management: appropriate information and advice is absolutely central.

- The key figure in providing appropriate management and advice is the GP, who must be provided with the appropriate training, skills and resources.

- These services are and should be provided most appropriately in primary care - general practice, physical therapies and occupational health care – which must be provided with the necessary funding and resources (CSAG 1994).

- Timing is vital: the longer the period of sickness absence the greater the risk of long-term incapacity (Waddell *et al* 2003). The service must be designed to take maximum advantage of the window of opportunity between about 1-6+ months for effective intervention to *prevent* long-term incapacity (Waddell & Burton 2004b).

- Health professionals should have the skills and time (when required) to address psychosocial issues (particularly around work).

- Services should be designed to provide simple, safe symptomatic measures *and* to restore function. There should be a much stronger emphasis on rehabilitation. Principles of rehabilitation should be incorporated into routine clinical management (Waddell & Burton 2004b).

- Closer links should be developed between NHS primary care and occupational health services (Beaumont 2003a & b, Sawney & Challenor 2003).

- Key outcome measures and targets of health care should include occupational outcomes.

During the acute stage most people recover and return to work uneventfully: the priorities are to provide symptomatic relief and avoid iatrogenic disability. During the sub-acute stage people are at increasing risk of long-term incapacity: this is the optimum window of opportunity for effective intervention. By the chronic stage most people face increasing obstacles to return to work: they then require more intensive support and rehabilitation.

Individual health professionals must change their clinical practice to achieve the desired goals, but that depends on and is constrained by the services that are available, e.g. referring a patient with back pain for rehabilitation rather than to see an orthopaedic surgeon[130] depends on funding and provision of appropriate services. Patients with 'common health problems' have very different needs from those with 'major killer diseases'. NHS services and funding are designed primarily for the investigation and treatment of 'medical' conditions; the problem is that they are largely inappropriate and even harmful for patients with many common health problems. At the same time, primary care and specialist services are swamped by patients with less severe problems for whom they were not designed. Provision of more appropriate alternatives should free up these specialist services and help to reduce waiting lists.

The emphasis in this discussion has been on improving routine primary care because that is where most patients are and, because of numbers, always will be managed. But it must be acknowledged that a minority of patients will always fail to respond and need additional help and support. Rehabilitation in the UK has always had limited priority and resources and there is wide recognition and acceptance of the need to improve rehabilitation services, in order to reduce the impact of sickness, injury, and disability (BSRM 2000, DWP 2002, 2003c, 2004a). The limited specialist rehabilitation services in UK currently focus on severe medical conditions (such as head injury with brain damage, severe neurological conditions, etc), on young people with severe physical or mental impairment, and on the increasing number of elderly and infirm people (Nocon & Baldwin 1998). These services are clearly important, they need to be developed and better resourced, and they should have a much higher clinical and academic profile. But patients with long-term incapacity associated with common health problems need a very different kind of service that must be designed to meet their specific needs, which will require further research and development. In view of the biopsychosocial nature of incapacity (Waddell 2002) and obstacles to (return to) work (Waddell & Burton 2004b), this is not purely a matter of health care and the NHS cannot do it alone. It must be done in collaboration with employers and other Government services (DWP 2004).

Underlying change in NHS services and practice there must be a change in policy, and DWP should contribute to developing more comprehensive Department of Health (DH[131]) priorities around this area. DH has always had a very 'medical agenda' rather than a social agenda on health. Priority areas and targets in the NHS Planning Framework and the Public Service Agreement Objectives (Dept of Health 2002a) centre on 'major killer diseases' such as cancer and coronary heart disease, mental health, waiting times for appointments and treatment, health care for older people and improving life chances for children. Although mental health is included, DH priorities and targets are about severe mental illness, psychiatric services and suicide. There is little or no place for the less severe 'common health problems' that cause most long-term incapacity. Potentially the most relevant priority is about 'reducing health inequalities'. There is widespread Government recognition that this is primarily an issue of poverty and social disadvantage (Graham 2004), but again DH focuses on 'medical' issues such as pregnancy, infant mortality, cancer and coronary heart disease. Inequalities in life expectancy are included but only addressed as mortality from 'killer diseases' and 'risk' factors like smoking. DH targets focus on process measures of service delivery and medical outcomes of diagnostic and mortality rates. The recent Public Health White Paper (Dept of Health 2004a) again focused mainly on 'medical' risk factors such as smoking, alcohol, obesity, exercise and safe sex.

DH thinking on disability reflects the same emphasis on severe 'medical' conditions. DH (**www.dh.gov.uk**) has had an interest in learning disabilities and 'physical and complex disabilities' for many years, but these are generally severe impairments. More recently, DH has made Chronic Disease Management a high priority (Dept of Health 2004b), but again the emphasis is very much on *diseases* such as arthritis, asthma, diabetes, severe respiratory disease and stroke. The National Service Framework for longer-term conditions could potentially provide a broader arena to address issues of disability and incapacity. That NSF currently focuses on the needs of people with neurological disease and brain or spinal injuries, but hopefully that could be expanded in future. The Expert Patient Programme (Dept of Health 2002b & c) could provide another avenue. That currently focuses mainly on the management of 'chronic diseases' such as arthritis, manic depression and multiple sclerosis, but the principles are relevant to less severe, common health problems and this again could be expanded in future. The DH and the Disability Rights Commission have recently drawn up a Framework for Partnership Action on Disability (Dept of Health/DRC 2004). Currently, this is concerned with access and equality of health services for disabled people, but potentially it could provide the basis for a more comprehensive debate on NHS priorities.

There are powerful health, social and economic arguments that DH must take a broader view of 'health care'. It is not enough to define health care in purely medical terms of treatment for disease: *health care* must incorporate a broader social perspective (WHO 1948, 2003, 2004). Of course killer diseases are important and need high quality and effective health care, but they are the mechanism rather than the root cause of social inequalities in health. 'Common health problems' now account for a larger proportion of 'ill health' – in terms of primary and secondary health care consumption, sickness and disability, long-term incapacity and ill health retirement. They form one of the main links between poverty and social disadvantage, social inequalities in health and premature mortality.

DWP and DH have a shared interest in improving public health (Dept of Health 2004a), with the goals of improving the health of the nation, lowering health care consumption, reducing sickness absence, long-term incapacity, ill health retirement and the disability and incapacity benefit caseload, and improving healthy life expectancy. This requires closer collaboration between DWP and DH to develop a more balanced set of priorities and targets that include disability, rehabilitation and support into work.

The recent Public Health White Paper (Dept of Health 2004a) included a chapter on 'work and health', which provides one of the first and best examples of 'joined up thinking' by DH and DWP in this area. Much more needs to be done to develop this line of thinking and to move it to the forefront of DH thinking and NHS practice. Encouragingly, the Scottish Dept of Health (Scottish Executive 2004) is taking a more holistic approach to 'healthy working lives', *Design for Living* and other programmes in Wales (Welsh Assembly 2005) sets out an ambitious 10-year health care delivery and public health strategy, while Northern Ireland's Dept of Health focuses on 'poor health and social well being experienced by disadvantaged people, groups and areas' (Secretary of State for Northern Ireland 1999).

7.4 Occupational management

Many employers[132] have low awareness and understanding of disability (NEP 2005). Many are unaware of the true cost of sickness absence (Bevan & Hayday 2001). Many also seem to assume that sickness and incapacity are matters for health care and that they cannot do anything about or take any responsibility for sickness (apart from 'risk prevention'). That is all untrue. Occupational health, especially for common health problems, is not a matter for health care alone: it is a much broader public health issue of 'health at work'[133]. There is a strong business case and increasing senior management awareness of the need for more effective occupational management of health at work (CBI 2000; Zadek & Scott-Parker 2001; ABI/TUC 2002, EEF 2004a & b, NEP 2005[134]). However, many businessmen and small employers lack awareness and understanding of these issues, may feel the business case does not apply to them, and are suspicious of Government advice. More needs to be done by business leaders to change this culture (TUC 2000, 2002, NEP 2005).

The Health and Safety Commission's ten-year strategy (HSC 2004) to improve health at work has three core aims:

- to stop people being made ill by work

- to help people who are or have been ill or injured to return to work, and

- to improve work opportunities for people currently not in work due to ill health.

Over the past few years, a more holistic view of 'health at work' has begun to emerge, leading to a more positive approach to promoting health at work rather than the traditional, more negative approach of preventing harm from work. 'A healthy working life is one that continuously provides the opportunity, ability, support and encouragement to work in ways and in an environment that allows workers to maintain and improve their health and well-being. This is not only a matter of disease or disability: it demands that every individual should be able to maximise their physical, mental and social capacity in order to gain the greatest personal benefit from their working life and to make a positive contribution to their business and society' (Scottish Executive 2004). The recent HSE *Employers' and managers' guide to managing sickness and recovery of health at work* (HSE 2004) now aims 'to reduce the impact of sickness, injury and disability on your organisation's productivity and the quality of life of its employees'.

Common health problems provide a good example for such a holistic approach. Health care addresses health conditions, but sickness absence and return to work are social activities in the context of the workplace, and also depend on work-related factors and employer attitudes, process and practice. Sickness absence is the outcome of complex interactions among health problems, health care, the balance between physical and mental capacity vs. job demands, and the perceptions, attitudes and behaviour of all the players. Work-related factors are major determinants of job retention and return to work (Fishbain *et al* 1993; Marhold *et al* 2002). There is accumulating evidence that workplace-based interventions are more effective than health care alone for return to work (Krause *et al* 1998, Feuerstein & Zastowny 1999, Brooker *et al* 2000, Staal *et al* 2002). This applies to all health conditions, but most of all to common health problems where there is no absolute health barrier to work.

Given the nature of common health problems, it may be better to address them as matters of health management in the context of 'health at work', which can also be conceptualised as 'recovery at work' (HSE 2004). This shifts the perspective from traditional NHS 'treatment' to a more holistic approach to workers' health. Accepting that symptoms will inevitably occur, good occupational management is about preventing persistent and disabling consequences, which may not be as good as preventing them altogether but is still desirable and more feasible (Frank *et al* 1996, Frank *et al* 1998, Staal *et al* 2003). This may include several overlapping strategies:

- positive health at work strategies

- early detection and treatment of mild to moderate symptoms (whether the worker is absent or not) to promote early recovery and prevent the development of persistent symptoms, progressive disability and long-term incapacity;

- accommodation of temporary functional limitations from recurrent or persistent symptoms (whether at work or returning to work);

- job retention and (early) return to work interventions to minimise sickness absence and promote early return to (sustained) work.

This requires employers, unions and insurers to re-think occupational management for common health problems. The basic aim is to help workers manage these problems better. There is strong evidence that the most effective way of doing so is by addressing all of the health, personal and occupational dimensions of incapacity, identifying obstacles to return to work, and providing support to overcome them (Waddell & Burton 2004b). The same principles are equally applicable to job retention, early return to sustained work and reintegration.

HSE is contributing to that broader and more positive approach to 'health at work' and that shift in thinking, but it still needs to be fully implemented into HSE regulations, informational material and staff activities.

7.4.2 Sickness absence management[135]

Improving health at work must start with organisational policy: the company and organizational characteristics; and the management style and corporate culture (Hunt *et al.* 1993). It depends on the commitment of senior management, who provide top-down support. Implementation depends on the commitment and enthusiasm of line managers and supervisors. Interventions include[136]:

a   health and safety policy and practice (HSE 2000, HSC 2004)

b   sickness absence management (HSE 2004).

Box 18: Key features of effective sickness absence management (James *et al* 2002, 2003, HSE 2004, NAO 2004)

Promotion of a 'health at work' culture

Development of clear corporate policy, processes and responsibilities

Involvement and commitment of senior management

Involvement, training and auditing of supervisors and line managers

Accurate recording and monitoring of sickness absence

Early (and continued) contact with the absent worker

Facilitating access to health care

Access to occupational health services as a source of advice and treatment

Availability of temporary modified work (if required)

Involvement of the absent worker in return to work decisions, planning and process

Involvement of workers, workers representatives and unions in developing policy, and in the return to work process.

Underlying these practical steps, improving health at work depends on a fundamental shift in perceptions and attitudes about common health problems, (in)capacity and work, among both employers and employees. Without this shift in thinking, sickness absence management is likely to have limited impact.

The longer a worker is off work, the harder it is to return and the lower the chance of doing so. The best window of opportunity to prevent chronic disability and long-term incapacity ever developing lies between 1 – 6+ months. Timing is critical and employers, like health professionals, must be aware of the danger of passive inactivity as the weeks and months slip away. A key element of effective management is to shift the company culture from a passive response to longer-term absence to routine proactive management of every case, on an individual basis and with a strong focus on rehabilitation and return to work.

There is now a broad consensus among researchers, employers, unions, government agencies and insurers on the key principles of sickness absence management (Box 18), which is based on a great deal of experience in the real world, even though there is a need for further research to develop a better scientific evidence-base.

A number of practical steps have been described during sickness absence and in the return to work process (HSE 2004, NAO 2004):

• Accurate and timely recording and monitoring of sickness absence

• Keeping in contact with sick employees

• Return to work interviews

- Trigger points for action

- Using professional advice and treatment

- Planning and undertaking workplace controls or adjustments to help workers on sickness absence to return and stay in work

- Agreeing, putting into operation and reviewing a recovery/return to work plan

- Coordinating the return to work process.

The HSE is working with the Institute of Occupational Medicine to develop a sickness absence monitoring tool suitable for Small and Medium sized Enterprises.

Effective strategies depend on cooperation and working together to common goals, rather than confrontation and treating this as a disciplinary matter (TUC 2000, HSE 2004). It is important to 'get the tone right', even if there must inevitably be control measures to prevent abuse. Thus, absence management requires a careful and delicate balance of support and penalties (NAO 2004). Employers should also distinguish health from conduct and performance issues: the sickness route should not be used as a 'easier' option than the disciplinary route.

7.4.3 DDA and work adjustments

Although a lot has been done under the Disability Discrimination Act 1995 and the Disability Discrimination Amendment Act 2005, sick and disabled people still face discrimination in employment (**www.drc.org.uk**). That is particularly true of people with mental health problems (Social Exclusion Unit 2004). Much more still needs to be done to stop discrimination, though that is part of a much larger policy agenda that cannot be covered here (Strategy Unit 2005).

One of the most effective tools to improve health at work and to reduce sickness absence is to manage the demands or 'risks' of work and to make suitable 'adjustments' to accommodate any reduction in capacity due to sickness or disability. Risk assessment (HSC 2000) was originally designed, and is still generally thought of, in terms of prevention of work-related injury or disease - identification of hazards that might potentially cause harm, and reduction of the risk (i.e. the probability) of that harm occurring. Unfortunately, this tends to be a negative approach that often hinders rather than facilitates work with common health problems. For these problems, it may be more appropriate to take a more positive approach to risk management as a tool for accommodating people with common health problems or disabilities. Assuming basic risk is suitably controlled, there is little evidence that most modern work will cause any lasting 'harm' to common health problems. It is more a matter of controlling physical or mental demands to maintain comfortable and productive working conditions. 'Work should be comfortable when we are well, and accommodating when we are ill' (Hadler 1997).

Any perceived 'risk' of work must also be placed in perspective. Most people are going to get some of these symptoms whether or not they are working: the epidemiological evidence shows that the risk is usually little greater at work. Any risk of work must also be balanced against the risks of being out of work. After 4-6 weeks sickness absence with a common health problem, if someone is not allowed to return to work they will then have a 10-20% risk of long-term incapacity. By 12 months, if they are still not allowed to return to work, the *balance of probabilities* is that will condemn them to long-term incapacity for years ahead. The 'risks' of longer-term sickness absence greatly outweigh any risk of returning to work with common health problems, certainly for the individual and probably for the employer also (Waddell & Burton 2000, 2004b).

One of the commonest and most effective elements of sickness absence management (EEF 2004b) is to adjust the demands of work to accommodate temporarily reduced capacity. Adjustments can take many forms. There is considerable (though generally not high quality[137]) scientific evidence that the provision of modified work can reduce by 30-50% the duration of sickness absence and the number of workers who go on to long-term incapacity (Krause *et al* 1998). Indeed, the evidence suggests that such occupational interventions are more effective that any health care intervention for promoting return to work with common health problems.

In conclusion, it is worth repeating that organisational interventions must be underpinned by a fundamental shift in work-place attitudes. Common health problems do not necessarily mean incapacity; and work is generally good for health and well being rather than a 'risk to health'. Common health problems cannot just be left to health care - employers and employees must share responsibility for health at work. The most important message is that employers have a vital role to play in preventing the slide from sickness absence to long-term incapacity.

7.5 Changing the culture

The ultimate aim of benefit reform is a fundamental transformation in the way sick and disabled people see themselves and in the way they are treated by the health care and social security systems. But it is broader even than that. This is a major public health issue that can only be resolved by change in society's and individuals' perceptions and expectations about health and work. Quite simply, we need to transform the culture of sickness and incapacity.

Culture is not just the context in which we lead our lives: it helps to determine how we think and feel and behave. Culture is 'the collective attitudes, beliefs and behaviour that characterise a particular social group over time' (Engel 1977, Waddell 2002, see also Fabrega & Tyma 1976). The 'welfare culture' is the set of ideas, values and basic principles that surround the benefits system and underpin welfare policy, the institutions of the welfare state, and the thinking, feelings and consequent behaviour of the various stakeholders in a given society (developed from Chamberlayne *et al* 1999, Pfau-Effinger 2005). Claimants, health professionals, DWP staff and policy makers may come from different cultures with different assumptions. There may be particular divergence and tension between the 'system' set up by social policy and the bureaucracy that implements it vs. the 'life world' in which individuals live. Understanding culture helps to explain the interaction between the welfare system and its recipients (Chamberlayne *et al* 1999).

At the heart of culture lie beliefs: basic and relatively stable ideas about the nature of reality that mould our perception of our environment and ourselves and shape it's meaning (Fishbein & Ajzen 1975, Lazarus & Folkman 1984). Beliefs drive behaviour, but are in turn modified by experience. But beliefs and culture are not fixed and can change over time. Thus, transforming the culture of incapacity ultimately depends on shifting core beliefs about work, health and sickness (Box 19).

Box 19: The fundamental shift required in thinking about work and health	
Common current beliefs:	**Transform to:**
Work is a 'risk' and (potentially) harmful to physical and mental health.	Work is generally good for physical and mental health.
therefore	*and*
Sickness absence/certification 'protects' the worker/patient from work	Recognise the risks and harm of long term worklessness

Welfare policy is closely linked to a particular social culture but the relationship between them is complex and multi-level (Chamberlayne *et al* 1999, Pfau-Effinger 2005). Policies and legislation are embedded in basic cultural principles and values (Le Grand 2003), which provide their justification and legitimisation. Policy choices are based on ideas, on the one hand, and on the (often conflicting) interests of the various stakeholders, on the other. Political and public debate provides the mediation between (again often contradictory and conflicting) cultural attitudes to welfare and the political and economic realities on which policy decisions must be based. Various stakeholders are involved in this 'policy network' that formulates, implements and delivers policy initiatives. But policy makers and government institutions cannot escape from their own culture of ideologies, paradigms, attitudes and beliefs, missions and institutional memories (Bemelmans-Videc *et al* 1998). Similarly, the social behaviour of individuals is not a simple and logical response to state policy but also depends on the culture in which it occurs. Culture helps to determine how benefit reform will be accepted by the population and its likely impact on claimant behaviour. Thus, IB reform is most likely to produce the desired ends if it is firmly anchored in a corresponding cultural shift.

Social change depends on both structural reform and shifting the underlying culture (Nye 1998, Kendall & Harker 2002). It is much easier to think about changing the benefits structure rather than its culture, particularly to meet the political need for short-term 'progress', but structural reform alone is unlikely to produce real and lasting change. Of course structural reform helps to change the prevailing culture, but policy making must also consider the implementation and delivery of services and how claimants are likely to adapt and change their behaviour in using the service. Benefit reform provides the essential framework for change, but real and lasting change depends on shifting the underlying culture.

Changing the culture of 'incapacity' demands a fundamental transformation in the way society deals with sickness and disability, so that everyone can fulfil their potential and those with the capacity to work are expected, supported and encouraged to do so (while, of course, providing support for those who cannot). That requires a radical re-think of attitudes about sickness and disability and their relation to work among all the key stakeholders –individuals with these problems, health professionals (especially GPs) and employers (Box 19). American experience confirms that changing this culture or mindset requires care, thought and consensus building (Berkowitz & Burkhauser 1996). There is limited empirical evidence on the effectiveness of information and advice as a policy tool and they can have surprising perverse effects. In general, however, they appear to be most effective when they strengthen enlightened self-interest (Bemelmans-Videc *et al* 1998).

The success of any reforms depends ultimately on how future claimants and recipients react and on changing what they do. Organisational, professional and social cultures must also change. It may be objected that such a goal is idealistic and impractical, but it is already happening with disability, even if there is some way to go to translate this fully into practice (DRC 2003a). What is needed now is an equally fundamental shift in the culture of sickness and incapacity. That is not impossible: the present 'epidemic' of incapacity took place within a generation and in principle transforming it again is equally possible (recognising it is not simply a matter of returning to some earlier Eden, and however difficult that may be to engineer).

Back pain (for many years one of the most common causes of long-term incapacity) is an example of how it is possible to transform thinking and management, and to do so surprisingly quickly (Waddell 2004b). The traditional treatment for back pain was rest, but new scientific evidence showed that was ineffective and actually delayed recovery. By contrast, advising and supporting patients to stay active and continue their ordinary activities as normally as possible leads to faster recovery and return to work. Reversing that management strategy involved developing and promulgating the scientific evidence base, new clinical and occupational health guidelines, professional and public education, various occupational and sickness management initiatives, and widespread multi-media publicity. It is difficult to prove which of these was effective and they probably acted in combination, but there is no doubt there has been a complete reversal in clinical management and public beliefs about how to deal with back pain (**www.workingbacksscotland.com**). And the number of new IB claims for back pain, which was rising exponentially up to 1995, has fallen by more than 40% (Waddell *et al* 2002).

Theoretically, policy development progresses from aims to objectives to implementation to pre-determined outcomes (Kendall & Harker 2002, Wistow 2002). In reality, policy-making and implementation are much more messy affairs. Ideally, the process must start by developing a new framework of inter-dependent values, principles and desired goals to provide the driving force and direction for more specific structures and target. In practice, policy-making and implementation are equally important, mutually dependent and need constant revision in response to unpredictable human behaviour, experience and reality. Thus re-structuring benefits is part of this process, but it is not an end in itself nor a panacea for the problems of sickness and disability benefits. Reforms will only have any impact if they can be and are implemented in practice. But the real need is to change what the benefit system, health professionals, employers and sick and disabled people themselves do, to achieve the desired goals. That depends on a comprehensive package of inter-dependent measures.

Such a fundamental change in thinking and behaviour cannot be achieved by benefit reform alone. Indeed, Government cannot do this alone (Halpern *et al* 2004). Implementing new policies and delivery of the desired outcomes depends on the behaviour and cooperation of a number of internal and external stakeholders. Real and lasting change depends on 'getting all players onside' (Frank *et al* 1996, 1998, OECD 2003, Waddell & Burton 2004b, NEP 2005). Front-line DWP staff must be able and committed to put the reforms into practice. GPs and employers are absolutely central: they need to be persuaded to change their approach, and convinced that there are real gains for them too. Government can play a leading role, in cooperation with all the interested parties, to identify and monitor the problem, develop policy, and set the legislative and administrative framework (OECD 2003). Government can encourage and support other players (including health professionals, employers, unions and insurers) to develop, evaluate and support new initiatives, and to identify and disseminate best practice (DWP 2002). IB reform is an essential element, but it can only ever be one part of the wider social and cultural changes that are necessary. Changing culture and practice will depend on a broad-based and comprehensive package of welfare reform, and simultaneous intervention on many levels. And it must be presented in such a way that it gains and retains the support of all the main stakeholders.

In conclusion, real and lasting reversal of benefit trends depends on a fundamental shift in the culture that surrounds sickness, disability, incapacity and work. IB reform should reflect, form part of, and will depend on that cultural change. Thus, IB reform should:

- Address the fundamental problems of IB

- Be integrated with improved clinical and occupational management

- Fit with and contribute to change in the culture that surrounds sickness, disability and incapacity

- Be acceptable to and gain the cooperation of all the main stakeholders.

8 THE DWP GATEWAY TO LONGER-TERM BENEFITS (controlling inflow)

The DWP Gateway is the test for entitlement and the direct control mechanism for inflow to longer-term incapacity benefits. How the above concepts and principles are operationalised in the DWP Gateway is critical, but will depend on the nature of the proposed IB reforms and the structure of any new benefit. All that can be done here is to lay out some basic principles, consider the nature of the available evidence, and look briefly at two examples of how these concepts might be applied – to severe and permanent impairments, and to mild/moderate mental health conditions.

8.1 Basic principles

Government and the DWP are dependent on the other stakeholders for changing the culture of incapacity, for the social gateway to sickness and for reintegration measures. But DWP must take full responsibility for the award of longer-term benefits in the DWP Gateway, though even there it depends on the cooperation of claimants and health professionals to provide the necessary evidence.

The DWP gateway should be based on four principles:

- The DWP Gateway should be the only entry to longer-term benefits and no claimant should receive these benefits before passing this gateway.

- The DWP Gateway should be under the sole control of DWP.

- Decisions should be evidence-based, robust and resistant to drift.

- Award of 'incapacity' benefits should be clearly linked to remaining capacities, rehabilitation and support into work.

If DWP is to achieve full control of the DWP Gateway, then there is a logical argument that no claimant should receive longer-term incapacity benefits before passing the DWP Gateway. Claimants who are employed should be receiving Statutory Sick Pay. Those who are not working or who are already on other benefits (e.g. JSA or IS) will not be suffering any immediate financial loss due to sickness and it may be argued they have no new need for interim benefits before passing the DWP Gateway. Alternatively, any claimants who do have financial loss (actual, not hypothetical) due to sickness could receive a short-term sickness benefit that is clearly distinguished from longer-term incapacity benefits. There is no other financial need for payment of income replacement benefits before entitlement is established in the DWP Gateway. That is in line with most other social security benefits, and justifiable *provided* there is no undue delay in adjudication. It would overcome the problems of having to stop benefits already received (as happens at present with IB) or any question of clawing-back payments. The same principles could apply during appeals, which would remove the financial incentive to unjustified appeals simply to postpone cessation of benefits.

Closely linked to that first principle, the DWP Gateway should be completely under the control of DWP. It should be made absolutely clear to all the stakeholders, especially claimants and doctors, that GPs (and any other treating health professionals) have no role whatsoever in administering the DWP Gateway, in decisions about awarding longer-term benefits, or as 'gatekeepers'. Their only role at this stage should be to provide factual medical evidence, and they should not be asked for nor offer any opinion on long-term functional (in)capacity or (un)fitness for work. Although that is, in principle, the current situation, it is not the perception of many claimants and doctors. This is therefore largely a matter of presentation, but it is very important. If this is handled properly, it could alleviate some of the concerns of GPs about the doctor-patient relationship, gatekeeper vs. caring/advocacy roles, and professional ethics (Chap 3.6) and make them more willing to cooperate in administering the primary social gateway to sickness where their role is indispensable.

The timing of the DWP Gateway will vary according to whether claimants have been on Statutory Sick Pay or are applying directly for the benefit. The fundamental principle, and the goal in practice, is that the DWP Gateway should be delivered within the optimum window of opportunity for effective rehabilitation and reintegration, between about 1-6+ months off work (Waddell & Burton 2004b).

8.2 The evidence base

The DWP Gateway requires several different kinds of evidence, which may be obtained from and cross-checked against different sources (Box 20). A major difficulty in the present system and a key question for future policy is the extent to which entitlement and assessment are or should be based on objective evidence of recognisable medical conditions and impairment vs. claimants' self-report of subjective symptoms and limitations. A secondary question is how these can be balanced and cross-checked against each other.

The primary responsibility for providing or providing access to the necessary evidence lies with the claimant. The initial claim form should provide:

• Basic personal information required to establish entitlement (identification, citizenship, residency, NI, etc).

• Employment (limited information).

Box 20:		
Evidence required	**Possible sources**	
	Claimant	*Independent cross-check*
Factual medical evidence on health condition	Claim form	Health professional(s) Medical records Independent medical assessment
Functional capacity assessment	Self-assessment questionnaire	Medical Adviser scrutiny of evidence Independent medical assessment
Obstacles to rehabilitation and (return to) work Support needs	Self-assessment questionnaire	Independent medical assessment Personal Adviser interview - Employment Focused Assessment

- Basic information about the health condition, history of injury or illness and sickness absence that forms the basis of the claim,

- Sick certificate from GP (or other authorised health professional)

- Agreement to release factual medical evidence and identification of sources where further medical evidence can be obtained if required.

- Any additional factual medical evidence the claimant wishes to be considered (e.g. results of investigations or specialist consultations).

- Informed consent to approach a medical practitioner or any other appropriate source of additional information; and permission to release personal and medical information and records.

- The impact of the health condition on capacity for work.

The present claim form provides the necessary factual medical evidence regarding the claimant's health condition, but the work-related information is very limited and needs to be developed.

The fundamental limitation of self-reports, especially about subjective symptoms and limitations, is that they are open to conscious and unconscious bias and exaggeration (Aylward 2003, Halligan *et al* 2003). Allowing for the frailties of human nature and moral hazard, some form of independent confirmation is essential and medical evidence from health professionals is usually the most appropriate and practical option. Sick certification provides sufficient evidence on fitness for work in the primary social gateway to sickness. When it comes to the

DWP Gateway to longer-term benefits, however, there is a need for better quality medical evidence. At present, there is some confusion about the Med 4-5 and IB113 certificates. In law, they are meant to be a matter of factual medical information rather than opinion or advice, but the forms and the accompanying DWP guidance emphasise 'the disabling effects of the condition', 'incapacity' and advice about 'refraining from work' which are all very much matters of the doctor's judgment and opinion about incapacity, and often based upon the claimant's account of these matters rather than factual medical evidence. Many doctors and claimants believe (and some feel strongly) that these forms allow caring physician to provide evidence on their patient's behalf (Social Security Benefits Agency 1995, Sainsbury & Corden 2004).

There are strong arguments for limiting the role of the GP (and any other health professionals responsible for their patients' health care) to the provision of factual medical evidence about the claimant's health condition, history and prognosis. That is evidence of fact lying within the GP's area of expertise, but excludes hearsay evidence based primarily on the claimant's own account (which is submitted directly in the claim), subjective judgments and advocacy. This would mean redesigning the certificates and the accompanying guidance to make it clear that by this stage they are solely a matter of providing factual medical information about the claimant's health condition. All matters of opinion about 'disabling effects', 'incapacity' and 'risks of work'[138] should be explicitly excluded.

Learning from the insurance industry (and the DTI in handling chronic pulmonary disease claims), access to claimant's GP and hospital records might provide higher quality medical evidence in many cases. The main attractions of accessing claimants' medical records are:

- saving in GPs' time and reduction of form filling, particularly the longer IB113

- providing a better medical evidence base for benefit decisions[139].

GPs' main concerns are about ethics and practicalities:

- patient consent and confidentiality.

- potential risk of loss of or damage to records, or records being away when needed.

DWP pilot studies[140] (Sainsbury *et al* 2003, Marlow & McLaughlin 2003, Sainsbury & Corden 2004) have shown that direct access to GP records is feasible, though the administrative and resource costs are high. GPs, patients and adjudicating doctors who have taken part are generally supportive, though a minority is strongly negative. The standard of GP records varies considerably in quality (content, legibility or abbreviated computer records) and they are not geared towards assessing function. The most useful information generally comes from copies of specialist consultations and results of investigations. Overall, GP records are useful in providing evidence about the diagnosis of health conditions, but less useful for judging (in)capacity, which fits the main purpose now proposed. Pilot studies suggest that direct access to medical records makes no difference to the number of exempt cases, increases the number referred for examination and increases the number of claims disallowed by 3% (Marlow & McLaughlin 2003).

Claimants' agreement is required to access their medical records, and this is already incorporated in the present claim form. This is standard practice for insurance claims and civil litigation, and DWP claimants themselves accept it is entirely reasonable when making a claim (Sainsbury *et al* 2003). If requests were limited to *copies* of GP consultation notes over the past 12-24 months together with relevant specialist consultations and investigations, that might reduce the amount of records required, avoid records being unavailable for clinical care, and let DWP keep key evidence permanently[141]. The onus might be placed on the claimant to obtain copies (if necessary under the Access to Health Records Act 1990) and submit them with the claim for longer-term benefits. Alternatively, experience in the insurance industry suggests there might be potential for developing the capacity of GPs to provide information electronically. There would be a need for delicate discussions with GP representatives to meet likely concerns about confidentiality. Any such approach would also require further piloting and evaluating.

Pragmatically, there would be major advantages to retaining as much as possible of the present IB adjudication process and PCA, but putting it onto a firmer logical basis and integrating it into any reformed benefit structure. That would build upon the extensive developmental work, evidence base, socio-political consensus and Commissioners' decisions that underpin the present system. Much of the argument about the present process is already won, which should make it easier to overcome those parts of any opposition to the proposed reforms. Within that continuing framework, it would then be easier to address anomalies that have developed over the years. Much of the infrastructure and process is already in place, which will minimise the reorganisation, staffing changes and re-training required within DWP and the Medical Services. The recently renewed contract for Medical Services already includes flexibility for IB reform issues.

8.3 Severe and permanent impairments

A critical challenge, in principle and in practice, is how to draw the boundary between claimants who have such severe medical conditions and impairments that they cannot reasonably be expected to work in the foreseeable future vs. those whose health condition is such that they can reasonably be expected to attempt to return to work, if they are given proper opportunity and support. Otherwise, some claimants might be given unconditional benefits when they could actually attempt to work, while others might be required to fulfil benefit conditions that their health condition actually makes unreasonable (Stanley *et al* 2004). The key distinction lies in the permanent nature and severity of the underlying physical or mental condition, i.e. the impairment. It cannot be purely about severity of symptoms, functional limitations, illness or sickness because these cannot be assessed objectively and, however severe or incapacitating they may be *at present*, they are not necessarily permanent. In practice, this depends on evidence:

a   of a physical or mental impairment; *and*

b   that has a severe impact on capacity for work; *and*

c   that this impairment is likely to be permanent.

That may be contrasted with the current Personal Capability Assessment, which focuses mainly on the *effects* of the health condition rather than on the condition itself. Similarly, although the Disability Living Allowance and Disability Working Allowance Act 1991 states that DLA is for people who are 'so severely disabled physically or mentally that (they) require - -', this is operationalised solely in terms of these 'needs' without taking any account of the underlying condition. It may be argued that is why such a large proportion of IB and DLA now go to claimants with longer-term sickness rather than permanent disability.

'Permanent' is clearly defined and understood in normal English usage as 'lasting, intended to last, indefinitely' (OED). In practice, this has become debased over the years into 'long-term'. One of the weaknesses of the Social Security (Incapacity for Work) Act 1994 was that it failed to lay down any criteria for 'long-term' apart from duration of the claim. Schedule 1 of the Disability Discrimination Act 1995 defined a disability as 'long-term' if:

a   it has lasted at least 12 months;

b   the period for which it lasts is likely to be at least 12 months;

or (our emphasis)

c   it is likely to last for the rest of the life of the person affected.

The Treasury Review of ill health retirement in the public sector (HMT 2000) also commented on the wide variation and impact of definitions of 'permanency'.

There is similar difficulty defining severity (Stacey & Short 2000). The Social Security (Incapacity for Work) Act 1994 does not provide any specific legislation on this issue, even though the exempt conditions effectively address it. The Disability Discrimination Act 1995 lays down that the effects of an impairment should be 'substantial' but does not define exactly what this means. In normal English, substantial has a range of meanings from 'considerable amount' to 'actually existing, not illusory' (Oxford English Dictionary). In practice, the term has been expanded by Commissioners' decisions, and the statutory DDA Guidance (DWP 1995) on the definition of disability now explains that the requirement for an adverse effect to be substantial reflects the general understanding of 'disability' as a limitation going beyond the normal differences in ability which may exist among people, and a substantial effect is 'more than minor or trivial'. That last phrase, which has been seized upon by legal representatives, effectively produces a very low threshold. The Treasury Review of ill health retirement in the public sector (HMT 2000) again commented that different schemes focused on the 'medical condition', 'disability', 'incapacity', infirmity' or 'ill health' which affected judgments of severity and permanence.

These current definitions effectively include any sickness that has lasted a specified number of months and/or is likely to last for a further number of months, and whose effects are detectable. That is very different from the normal meaning of 'severe and permanent'. There is clearly a need for any new legislation to provide more specific and meaningful definitions, e.g.:

- *Permanent:* 'the balance of probabilities is that this impairment and its effects will last to retirement age or for the rest of the life of the person affected (whichever is shorter)'. That is consistent with the recommendation of the Treasury Review of ill health retirement in the public sector (HMT 2000) that 'permanence should be defined as being until normal pensionable age'. Permanence cannot be assessed until all reasonable treatment options have been explored and maximum rehabilitation potential has been achieved[142]. That will normally require that the condition has already been present and stable for at least a year. It should be emphasised that it is the underlying physical or mental condition or impairment that is expected to be permanent, not the associated, reported, limitations or restrictions[143].

- *Severe:* 'the nature and severity of impairment is such that it would be unreasonable to expect the person to seek or be available for work'. That definition is clearly focused on incapacity rather than the impairment *per se*.

The closest existing approximation to identifying such severe and permanent impairments is the list of 'exempt conditions' that qualify more or less automatically for IB and are exempt from the PCA (Appendix 2). These exempt conditions have stood the test of time, despite constant lobbying to expand the list[144]. However, that was when they were a purely pragmatic approach to simplifying the administration of the PCA, without any other implications. If such conditions were to be used as the basis for exemption from efforts at rehabilitation and return to work, they would need to be re-defined to serve that new purpose:

- The new list would need to specify (as comprehensively as possible) those severe medical conditions that cause severe physical or mental impairment.
  [The present exempt list is not focused solely on impairment but is also based on various proxies that are assumed to reflect severity (e.g. receipt of various other disability benefits), or on treatment and prognosis.]

- Some of the current categories do not meet the basic evidence requirements of a) impairment, b) that has a severe impact on capacity, and c) is likely to be permanent, so they should be excluded. Other unlisted conditions do meet these basic evidence requirements and should be added.

- There is scope for a little flexibility in this list, which could make it more inclusive without increasing the numbers much, and might help to deflect some political opposition.

Applying these principles would change the list in certain critical respects. The possible revised list given in Appendix 3 retains all of the severe medical conditions and impairments from the original list and makes it more comprehensive by adding a number of comparable though individually rare conditions. It deletes several large categories that fail to fit the definition and are open to most threshold creep. At the same time, it accepts the pragmatic argument that certain well-established categories should be retained. Overall, the resulting list is more logical, robust and defensible yet does not involve any great expansion in the number of claimants who would qualify.

Detailed reasoning for and against all of these revisions is available from the authors, but it may be illustrative to consider one example in detail. Chronic pain and chronic fatigue syndromes have already been proposed for the PCA exempt list, and there are likely to be arguments to include them in any revised list of severe medical conditions. Chronic pain is the most fully debated and representative example, but the arguments are equally relevant to chronic fatigue, fibromyalgia and other similar syndromes[145] (Wessely *et al* 1999). There is a wealth of clinical and epidemiological evidence that chronic pain *can but does not necessarily* cause severe disability and marked life disruption. Chronic pain is extremely common - by some estimates up to 20% of the adult population (Crombie *et al* 1999, British Pain Society 2003) - yet detailed epidemiological studies show that most people with chronic pain lead more or less normal lives, with or without health care (von Korff *et al* 1992, Cassidy *et al* 1997). Pain is ultimately a subjective symptom, so the practical problem is that it can only be assessed on self-report and there is no objective method of assessing its severity or its impact on functional capacity. Moreover, severe and disabling pain may be long-lasting but is not necessarily permanent: in about one third of people it improves within a year (Croft *et al* 1998, Burchardt 2000a). Chronic pain has already been the subject of attempted legislation and legal challenge in North America, with no conclusive answer to these issues (Waddell 2004a). Conceptually, chronic pain, fatigue or comparable syndromes do not meet the criteria of severe and permanent impairments[146]. Pragmatically, it is impossible to set any threshold for severity, while the epidemiology and North American experience shows they could potentially lead to explosive growth. For all of these reasons, we would argue they should not be regarded as severe and permanent impairments, but are better treated, at least initially, as potentially recoverable.

8.4 Mild/moderate mental health conditions

Mental and behavioural disorders now account for 42% of the IB caseload, and if claimants with a secondary mental health diagnosis are included the proportion rises to more than 50%. The vast majority of these recipients have mild/moderate mental health problems. As discussed previously (Chap 4.8), failure to reduce inflow, decreased outflow and increasing caseload reflect a relative failure of control mechanisms (and of reintegration measures – which will be discussed in Chap 9). These trends make it necessary to review the PCA for mild/moderate mental health problems, and it is timely to do this as one part of restructuring incapacity benefits.

Logically, it may be argued there are two inter-related questions:

1   Does this claimant have a mental health condition?

2   Is that mental health condition incapacitating?

The present PCA (and DLA) assessments confuse these issues: Stage 1 - self-report of symptoms and their disabling effects; Stage 2 - medical scrutiny or assessment of whether these symptoms and their impact on functional capacity are 'consistent' with recognised clinical patterns and form a 'reasonable' basis for incapacity. This can become a circular argument in which reported 'effects' become proof of an underlying condition. Mild/moderate mental health conditions clearly can produce disability and incapacity for work. However, mental symptoms are very common in normal people (Table 1) and the difficulty is how and where to draw the boundary between 'ordinary mental symptoms' and 'mental illness' and to set a threshold for when that may reasonably be incapacitating for work.

In personal injury litigation, a plaintiff must establish that he or she has 'not merely grief, distress or any other normal emotion, but a positive psychiatric illness' (Law Commission (England) 1998). The law does not provide compensation for 'ordinary emotions' but only for a 'recognisable psychiatric illness'. Diagnosis of a recognisable psychiatric illness and proof that the plaintiff has such an illness normally depends on factual medical evidence and expert medical opinion. The Law Commission did not consider it would be practical or sensible to attempt a statutory definition. In practice, this is normally based on standard classifications of psychiatric diagnoses in the International Statistical Classification of Diseases and Related Health Problems (ICD-10: WHO 1992-94), or the Diagnostic and Statistical Manual of Mental Disorders (DSM-IV: American Psychiatric Society 1994)[147].

Although not directly relevant, legal debate and case law regarding the DDA raises some important issues (Stacey &Short 2000, Woodhams & Corby 2003). The original DDA did not define 'mental illness' but did stipulate that a mental impairment must be due to 'a clinically recognised illness'. That requirement was intended to exclude claims 'based on obscure conditions unrecognised by reputable clinicians - - (and) moods and mild eccentricities'. The Guidance stated that the illness must be recognised by a respected body of medical opinion and that, in practice, conditions which are specifically mentioned in major classification systems such as ICD-10 or DSM-IV are very likely to be accepted as being 'clinically well recognised'. This requirement has been opposed throughout by the disability lobby, claimants and their legal representatives as being 'too medical' and failing to attach sufficient weight to the individual's own experience. It was finally removed in the Disability Discrimination Amendment Act 2005 though the Explanatory Notes stipulated that 'the removal of this requirement does not affect the need for people with a mental illness to demonstrate that they have an impairment - - -'. Given that impairment is, by definition, objective, it is not clear how it can be based solely on subjective experience and self-report without some form of medical diagnosis.

Logically, diagnosis of a mental health condition should be separated from assessment of its effects on capacity for work:

1   Diagnosis of a mental health condition or impairment.
    The key argument is that diagnosis may establish possible entitlement, but does not assess the level of disability: 'impairment is a necessary but insufficient basis for incapacity'.

2   PCA to assess functional capacity.

In the absence of any objective mental impairment, the closest medical alternative is by diagnosis of a 'recognised mental illness' - well-established and recognisable clinical syndromes with known patterns of symptoms, behaviour and functional restrictions, natural history, response to treatment and prognosis. The only established method of doing this is based on diagnostic classifications such as ICD-10 or DSM-IV, though there is constant pressure from treating health professionals and the disability lobby to expand the list of 'acceptable' diagnoses. The problems are:

•   this is a very 'medical' approach that is resisted by the disability lobby for the reasons discussed earlier,

•   the standard psychiatric classifications become less reliable and valid for less severe mental health conditions (e.g. 'work-related stress' is not included in ICD-10 or DSM-IV)

•   medical assessment of mild/moderate health conditions is itself subjective, with questionable reliability and validity, and open to bias.

Despite these limitations, medical diagnosis of a 'recognised mental illness' may be the closest existing approximation to factual medical evidence[148].

However, that still does not address the second question of how to decide whether a mental health condition is incapacitating. That depends on a more integrated medical and social approach to the boundary between 'ordinary mental symptoms' and 'mental illness' and the threshold when this becomes a 'reasonable' basis for incapacity. Analogous to the development of the original *All Work Test* (Chap 4.6 - Social Security Benefits Agency 1993, 1995), a better mental health section of the PCA would involve an extensive programme of research and development:

- Detailed analysis of DWP administrative data on the existing mental health section of the PCA.

- More specific UK epidemiological surveys of the population prevalence of 'ordinary mental symptoms', the extent of their relationship to self-perceptions of illness and disability, and comparison of working and 'sick' sub-groups.

- Surveys of UK public perceptions about when these constitute a 'mental illness' and the threshold at which they can 'reasonably' form an 'acceptable' basis for sickness absence, long-term incapacity and receipt of social security benefits. (The man on the Clapham omnibus approach.)

- Testing and comparing these population prevalence and public perception data against medical diagnostic criteria for 'recognised mental illness'.

- Testing and comparing these population prevalence and public perception data against confidential, anonymised DWP administrative data from the mental health section of the PCA (in successful and unsuccessful IB claimants with mental health conditions).

- Based on the above evidence, develop key mental health functional areas, descriptors, and scoring systems, and reconsider the non-functional areas.

- Wide consultation from all interested organisations and individuals to obtain a wide range of opinion and comment to assess the strengths and weaknesses of the proposed approach, and to help identify potential difficulties and ways of overcoming them.

- Expert panel(s) drawn from sick and disabled people, those who care for them, their organisations and representatives, doctors and other health professionals from relevant specialties such as general practice, occupational health and mental health, and academics to help develop and refine the mental health functional areas, descriptors, thresholds (at which the condition starts to impact on capacity for work and at which a person cannot reasonably be expected to work) and scores, (and the non-functional areas if it is decided to continue these).

- Large scale evaluation studies to assess the validity and reliability of the test, the effectiveness of the process of assessment and the need for training.

- Consultation on the final version of the proposed test with all the main stakeholders.

Such a programme of research and development would clearly require major investment of time, resources and funding, but in view of the importance and DWP costs of mild/moderate mental health conditions would be worth considering. Ultimately, however, there is no 'medical' or 'scientific' answer: it comes down to a moral, public and political judgment about what mental health symptoms and conditions form an acceptable and reasonable basis for incapacity.

9 SUPPORT INTO WORK (increasing outflow)

9.1 The rationale for support into work

Better rehabilitation, support into work and reintegration measures are the most important elements of any IB reforms (DWP 2002, 2005), on which all else depends.

The basic premise is that many IB recipients have less severe, manageable health conditions and many of them want to work so, *provided* they are given the right support, many of them should be able to (return to) work. However, this support is also likely to be helpful to many recipients with more severe health conditions and impairments, and to promote positive perceptions and expectations it should be equally available to them. So *all* new recipients should be invited to a work-focused interview to discuss their desires and needs, and the options and support available.

This is the area where most needs to be done to develop new, more appropriate and more effective services (Burchardt 2001, DWP 2004, 2005). If these interventions are to be mandatory (even for some recipients) then they must be fully developed, proven effective, and rolled out nationally, *before* they can be made mandatory (DWP 2003c, DRC 2004b, Stanley *et al* 2004, Howard 2004a). In policy terms:

a   Have structural reasonable adjustments been anticipated and made in advance? and

b   Have additional support measures been put in place nationally to enable individuals
     to participate and meet the obligations imposed upon them? (Howard 2004a)

Otherwise, there is a real danger of imposing conditions that some claimants simply cannot meet without help, and further disadvantage those who are already most seriously disadvantaged.

Thus, the key to reform is a strong, integrated support system (Burchardt 2001) (Box 21).

Box 21: a strong support system

- Early intervention

- Better specialist support: - condition management
                                             - employment support

- Investment in staff training, skills and competencies

- Make work pay

- Address benefit weaknesses

- All stakeholders on side   - GPs
                                            - employers

- Changing the culture of incapacity

9.2 The conceptual approach

In a social security context, IB claimants overwhelmingly state that the reason they are not working is because of their sickness or disability. Their prime concern is to obtain financial support to support them (and their dependents) in their everyday life, irrespective of any question of (returning to) work (Davies & Johnson 2001). There is therefore an inherent, initial suspicion and resistance to discussions about work, which must be overcome.

When the *All Work Test* was changed to the Personal Capability Assessment (PCA), the aim was 'so that, as well as determining entitlement to benefit, it also provides information about people's capacities which can be used to help them plan for a return to work: we will change the name of the test so that it reflects this more positive approach' (HM Government 1998b). 'We propose to introduce a new test which provides information about what people can do as well as about their incapacity; assisting those with a long-term illness or disability to understand how they can match their skills and abilities with the range of support that is available to help them into suitable work' (HM Government 1998c). The Capability Report was designed so that the Medical Services doctor who examined claimants could provide work-focused information about the claimant's health condition and capabilities, to assist the Personal Adviser.

Changing from a purely negative view of *in*capacity to a more positive view of *capacity* and providing work-focused medical advice were good in principle, but they did not translate fully into practice. The Capability Report was essentially an attempt to provide a Functional Capacity Evaluation (FCE), based on a medical assessment that functioned primarily as a Gateway to benefits. As noted previously, the PCA never overcame the incompatibility of having to demonstrate incapacity to establish entitlement to benefits and simultaneously try to consider capabilities that might lead to coming off benefits. The Capability Report is supposed to be based on medical evidence only, but many sections are more matters of opinion, and Medical Services doctors sometimes experience conflict between 'being positive' and 'being realistic' about the *prospects* of some claimants returning to work (Legard *et al* 2002). In practice, it is questionable if Medical Services doctors have the necessary occupational health background and focus. More fundamentally, it is doubtful if it is possible to carry out a meaningful FCE by this kind of medical assessment. There are major scientific, legal and practical questions about the validity and practical value of FCE in clinical and administrative settings (King *et al* 1998, Pransky & Dempsey 2004). They depend on valid and reliable measures of worker capabilities and the demands of various jobs: when these assessments are not directly and specifically related to job tasks and performance or when they are dependent on subjective judgments (on both of which the Capability Report falls down), the findings are likely to be invalid.

Even more important conceptually, this is a limited and inadequate – and very negative - approach to rehabilitation and work, particularly for claimants with common health problems. Although the Capability Report was laid out to record what the claimant could and could not do, the emphasis is still on *limitations*. The Capability Report and FCE are essentially methods of 'job matching' claimants' limited capabilities to 'suitable' job demands (Matheson 2000). They reflect a medical model, focus on medical limitations to work capacity, accept these limitations as more or less unchangeable (unless health care can offer a 'cure'), and lead logically to workplace adjustments to accommodate them.

There is certainly a strong case for work adjustments - modifications or adaptations to work to meet an employee's health needs, whether or not they are 'disabled' under the DDA (HSE 2004). However, these are occupational management interventions for workers. Medical advice to return only to modified work may be counter-productive and actually create an obstacle to return to work if modified work is not available (Hall *et al* 1994). Unnecessary or prolonged periods of modified work can have similar adverse effects (Evanoff *et al* 2002, Hiebert *et al* 2003).

For IB recipients who are not employed, however, 'job matching' is a narrow, mechanistic approach that is most appropriate for those with severe and permanent impairments. It is illogical and inappropriate for claimants with 'common health problems', for whom there is limited and contradictory evidence on its effectiveness (Carter & Birrell 2000, Pransky & Dempsey 2004). It is not surprising that Personal Advisers are unsure how they can use the medical advice in the Capability Report (Legard *et al* 2002).

In fairness, DWP has since made efforts to improve the format, content and presentation of the Capability Report and has provided further training for Medical Services doctors and DWP Personal Advisers. However, there is no evidence this has had any significant impact.

Modern concepts of rehabilitation for less severe, physical and mental health conditions (TUC 2000, BSRM 2000, Waddell & Burton 2004b, DWP 2004, DWP 2005) follow a different logic:

- Most common health problems are manageable, and most people should recover, usually quite quickly. There is usually no permanent impairment and long-term incapacity is not inevitable.

- This reverses the question: it is not why some people go on to long-term incapacity, but why these people do not recover as expected.

- There is strong evidence that health-related, personal and social/occupational factors can aggravate and perpetuate incapacity. Crucially, they may continue to act as obstacles or barriers to recovery and return to work.

- Rehabilitation for common health problems should address all of the health-related, personal and social/occupational obstacles and barriers to recovery and return to work.

- Addressing obstacles to recovery and barriers to return to work should be fundamental to all good clinical and occupational management.

This leads to a very different kind of 'rehabilitation' (Box 22) (NIDMAR 2000, OECD 2003, Waddell & Burton 2004b, DWP 2004).

Box 22: Rehabilitation (Waddell & Burton 2004b)	
'Traditional' rehabilitation	**Modern concepts of rehabilitation**
Separate, second stage, after health care is complete.	Principles integrated into: • Clinical management • Occupational management
Overcome, adapt or compensate for permanent impairment.	Address and overcome health-related, personal and social/occupational obstacles or barriers to recovery and return to work.
Restore function, within limits.	Restore normal activity levels and participation.
Retrain and/or re-placement in alternative, suitable work.	Return to full, normal work.
'Medical' or multidisciplinary professional intervention.	Condition management Employment support.
Designed and appropriate for severe medical conditions	Designed and appropriate for common health problems.

It also leads to a more positive and practical approach to identifying and overcoming barriers to return to work (Box 23). Selecting suitable work and temporary work adjustments may form a useful part, but only one part, of this more holistic approach. It lifts the goal from a rather pessimistic accommodation of limitations to more optimistic restoration of full and normal work.

That is much more consistent with the Council of Europe (1996) recommendations on a coherent and global policy for the rehabilitation of people who are disabled or *who are at risk of becoming so* (our emphasis). Some of the key aims and directives include:

• a right to an independent life and full integration into society, and recognizing society's duty to make this possible

• retaining as much personal responsibility as possible in the planning and implementation of rehabilitation and integration processes

• preventing the onset and aggravation of impairment or disability, eliminate or reduce their effects and prevent the occurrence of additional disabilities such as emotional and psychological disorders,

Box 23: Identifying and addressing all of the bio-psycho-social barriers to (return to) work (Adapted from Waddell & Burton 2004b)		
Components of disability	**Barriers to (return to) work**	**Rehabilitation and support into work interventions**
Health-related	Health condition (and health care[149]) Individual capacity vs. job demands[150]	Clinical management Occupational management
Personal / psychological	Motivation and effort Attitudes, beliefs, behaviour Psychosocial aspects of work	Change perceptions, beliefs and behaviour (of all the players)
Social / occupational	Organisational Attitudinal	Health & Safety policy & practice. Sickness absence management
ALLOW FOR INTERACTIONS		

- recognising the need for early intervention,

- draw up in collaboration with the person with a disability and his or her family a rehabilitation programme involving a wide-ranging, continuing and personalised set of services, beginning as soon as an impairment becomes apparent, passing through successive stages to integration in working and community life

- remove wherever possible all obstacles in the environment and in society and make it possible for people with disabilities to play a full role

These recommendations were originally drawn up for people with severe and permanent impairments, but they are equally relevant to support into work for people with common health problems.

This can be operationalised in a DWP context by three mutually dependent elements:

- Employability and Support Assessment,

- Better condition management,

- Better support into work

9.3 Employability and Support Assessment

At least up to the time of *Pathways,* there was evidence that Work Focused Interviews in ONE provided good advice on benefits, but little time was spent on work-related issues and there was no evidence that they had any significant impact on return to work (Loumidis *et al* 2001a, Osgood *et al* 2002, 2003, Green *et al* 2003, Goldstone & Douglas 2003, Kirby & Riley 2004, Watson & Patel 2004). This illustrated the importance of staff training, competencies and commitment for the implementation and delivery of any benefit reforms (Berthoud 1998, Watson & Patel 2004). It is essential to overcome organisational barriers such as poor access, referral and recruitment; lack of time, money, rehabilitation and employment resources; pressures on staff; lack of priority, targets and staff incentives (Goldstone & Douglas 2003, Watson & Patel 2004). Making Work Focused Interviews compulsory without additional support or conditionality might therefore be insufficient to overcome the barriers to work for sick and disabled claimants (Kirby & Riley 2004).

Condition management and employment support must be tailored to meet the individual needs of claimants. This requires detailed assessment of:

- The claimant's health condition and how management can be optimised

- Obstacles and barriers to (return to) work

- Identifying appropriate and effective interventions and support needs to overcome these obstacles and barriers.

This should make it possible to develop an individual Action Plan, including a Health Action Plan and a return to work plan. Assessment and planning are intimately linked and inter-dependent. This is quite different from and must be clearly distinguished from assessment of current functional capacity for entitlement to benefits.

This will require considerable development and improvement of the assessment process[151]. To overcome the inherent tension between demonstrating incapacity and considering capacity, the Employability and Support Assessment (ESA) might be a completely separate, second stage after benefits have been awarded. Some basic personal information and factual medical evidence will be common to both stages and need not be repeated, but the employment support elements of the ESA should be completely separate and (for reasons discussed further below) largely performed by different people.

Basic information about claimants' own perspectives on their health condition, capacities and limitations can be obtained most efficiently and cost-effectively by self-report questionnaires, cross-checked against factual medical evidence from medical certificates and/or records.

DWP has extensive experience of screening[152] to identify claimants at risk of long-term incapacity (Waddell *et al* 2003, Bryson & Kasparova 2003, Watson & Patel 2004), with continuing debate about its accuracy, utility and cost-effectiveness (Wells 2004). The practical limitation is that screening generally cannot achieve more than about 70-80% accuracy[153]. However, by the DWP Gateway, *all* claimants have at least a 30-40% risk of going on to long-term incapacity. There is therefore no need to 'screen' to identify who is at risk: the purpose of assessment now is to decide what kind of support might be appropriate and helpful (Waddell *et al* 2003).

Pragmatically, claimants fall into three broad groups, which are somewhat similar to the psychological model of 'stages of change', in which different patients are at different stages in moving towards readiness to undertake self-management of their condition[154] (Proschaska & DiClemente 1983, Proshaska *et al* 1991, Kerns *et al* 1997):

1   Some are nearly ready to return to work, are likely to return to work within the foreseeable future, and need minimal help. The *Pathways* approach is likely to be highly successful with these claimants, at very little individual cost, but with significant deadweight[155].

2   Some are thinking about or ready to think about return to work, but are unlikely to manage to overcome the barriers on their own without help. *Pathways* is designed for these people: these are the ones who need and who are most likely to benefit from condition management programmes and employment support.

3   Some are not able or prepared to even think about return to work. That may be because of the nature and severity of their health condition, or more a matter of attitudes, perceptions and expectations (which may or may not be accurate, and however these have developed). In essence, it is a question of what the claimant cannot do vs. what they will not do. The former cannot reasonably be pushed into work *at this point in time*: any support at present can only be to prepare the ground for some future time when they will be ready to consider work, and is likely to be minimal. The latter present the most difficult challenge to *Pathways*. Any progress will depend on personal change: Condition Management Programmes may attempt to shift claimants' attitudes and beliefs about their health condition; employment support may attempt to shift their attitudes and beliefs about work. It remains to be seen whether or to what extent *Pathways* can be effective with this group, and conditionality may also be a necessary ingredient. This group are the main reason why *Pathways* alone is unlikely to completely solve the IB problem and why benefits reform is also necessary.

That broad framework may be helpful for considering the likely reactions of different claimants to *Pathways* but considerable work is still needed to develop any practical method of classifying claimants to different levels of support (Bryson & Kasparova 2003, Dickens *et al* 2004a).

However, this kind of assessment must be used positively to improve understanding of claimants' attitudes, and of their individual barriers and support needs for return to work. In earlier studies of ONE, Corden & Sainsbury (2001) found that Personal Advisers failed to refer patients because they (the PAs) thought they were 'not ready' for work focused activity. In common health problems, that is rarely justified and must not become a reason for inactivity.

Claimants being considered for support into work need more detailed assessment to determine the kind and amount of support they require. This requires much more comprehensive assessment than what is needed to determine entitlement to benefits. This is new and additional information, and will mean the development of new and specific protocols, recording forms and decision-making. This will require a great deal of development work and piloting, but the preliminary results of *Pathways* show it is feasible. It is also critical that the process is designed and resourced to obtain the necessary information quickly and efficiently, so that condition management and support into work interventions can begin without delay.

The factual medical evidence provides the basis of medical advice about the health condition, the nature and severity of any physical or mental impairment, and whether this is likely to be permanent. However, an objective basis for such medical advice is only present in 25-30% of claimants. For less severe, common health problems, neither the factual medical evidence nor the PCA of *current* capabilities provides an adequate basis for assessing future clinical progress and capacity for work, potential for rehabilitation, or support needs. The Medical Services doctor's *opinion* on these matters is unfounded, of limited value and can be counter-productive (Legard *et al* 2002)[156].

The primary function of Medical Services doctors will always be to assess the factual medical evidence, current functional capacity and entitlement to benefits. Medical Services doctors' contribution to the Employability and Support Assessment should:

- Work within the constraints of a single interview with the primary role of assessment for entitlement (and the potential conflict that generates), these doctors' professional characteristics and skills, and Medical Services resources (which places strict limitations on any significant increase in the workload)

- Provide the maximum possible useful contribution to developing an Action Plan (which discussions show Medical Services doctors are keen to do)

- With the major and over-riding caveat that any medical contribution must not be counter-productive.

The doctor's most important and unique contribution is medical advice about the factual medical evidence: permanent impairment and any direct consequences on functional capacity for work; any substantial and specific 'risks' to work; and any specific medical needs or contraindications to rehabilitation. In common health problems, where there is limited factual medical evidence on any of these issues, the doctor should simply state that there is *no* objective physical or mental health barrier to rehabilitation or (return to) work. They should provide a medical perspective on health-related obstacles to return to work and any health care action that is likely to overcome them. They might usefully draw attention to any other obstacles identified during the medical assessment that need to be considered further. In common health problems, that should be the limit of the Medical Adviser's contribution: rehabilitation potential and support needs are non-medical matters that are better left to other members of the team. That demands a paradigm shift in the doctors' thinking and professional practice. It will also require the development of a new section of structured interview, a replacement for the PCA form, and specific professional education and training.

In most less severe health conditions, the claimant's own report of their limitations and capabilities, for all its subjective limitations and potential bias, is the most appropriate and relevant starting point. Whether or not claimants' perceptions are an accurate reflection of their health condition, their attitudes, beliefs and expectations are central to rehabilitation and return to work. The claimant's own view of obstacles to returning to work is likely to identify those most important to him or her. The claimant might even be able to suggest possible personalised solutions that are best suited to his or her particular context. It is insufficient to claim simply that he or she is 'too sick or disabled to (consider) work'. Obtaining this kind of information will require the development and piloting of completely new assessment protocols covering the claimant's own ideas on:

- his or her remaining capabilities, realistic goals and what would need to change to achieve them

- where they are in terms of 'stages of change' (Kerns *et al* 1997)

- health-related, personal and social/occupational obstacles to (return to) work (Chapter 3.4)

- health-related, personal and social/occupational interventions that might help to overcome these obstacles (Waddell & Burton 2004b)

- support needed to achieve this (DWP 2002, 2004a, 2005).

Some of this information could be obtained by questionnaire, but by its nature that is standardized and passive. Much of it will need to be obtained by one-to-one interview, which allows more open-ended exploration of individual and personal issues, developing a common understanding and rapport, and active involvement of the claimant. The two might usefully be combined, using a questionnaire to collect preliminary information and start the claimant thinking, and then using the completed questionnaire as the starting point for exploring these and other issues at interview. It would be better if this were completely separated from the PCA (to avoid the conflicts noted earlier) and presented as a second stage with a positive focus on support and reintegration. Some of the health-related aspects are better addressed by a non-medical health professional with a particular focus on condition management, but many of the work-related aspects would be better addressed by a skilled Personal Adviser. Whatever the exact division of labour, it is essential these two work closely together. Both will require special training and a high level of skills and competencies. All of the questionnaires, interview protocols and recording forms will require extensive development and piloting. Crucially, however, this is not just a matter of staff 'obtaining' information from a passive claimant and then planning how to help. It depends on the claimant being actively involved, and on claimant and staff working together to analyse the problem and develop solutions. Building rapport and a working partnership are essential first steps to both condition management and employment support.

Whatever the input to the ESA, legislation will require that any final decisions on action or conditionality must be made (or negotiated with the claimant) by a statutory authority, i.e. a DWP employee, most likely the Personal Adviser.

9.4 Job Retention and Rehabilitation Pilots (JRRPs)

The JRRPs are designed to help people in the early stages of illness or disability, who have been off work 6-26 weeks but who are still employed, before they become long-term incapacitated. The goal is to reduce the number moving on to incapacity benefits.

The JRRPs are sponsored jointly by DWP and the Health Departments and are an example of joint working by DWP and the NHS. A randomised controlled design is comparing the relative value of an individualised health care intervention and a workplace intervention, separately and in combination, against 'usual care'. The pilots are also testing several delivery models.

Live service delivery began on 1 April 2003 in six areas of the country. Recruitment ended in December 2004, by which time 2951 subjects had been randomised. Service delivery ended on 31 March 2005, and follow-up will continue for 6 months. The context of the JRRPs is described in two research reports on employers' (Nice & Thornton 2004) and GPs' (Mowlam & Lewis 2005) management of sickness absence. No results of the RCT are available at the time of writing, but the evaluation should be published in Winter 2005:

- Evaluation database: individual data from baseline to follow-up, including personal, family and financial circumstances, and detailed records of the health condition, treatment and management received.

- Effectiveness of screening tool to identify those at risk of long-term incapacity.

- Outcome data: length of sickness absence, labour market outcomes, health outcomes

- Process evaluation: qualitative studies of recipients, DWP staff, health professionals and employers.

- Cost benefit analysis

9.5 Pathways to Work Pilots

9.5.1 *The Pathways package: Condition management and Employment support*

The *Pathways* pilots are the culmination and test of some of the support into work ideas discussed in this review.

Pathways is an integrated package of support specifically designed to help IB recipients to manage their health problems and get back to work (NIDMAR 2000, OECD 2003, Waddell & Burton 2004b, DWP 2004). It is particularly appropriate for those with common health problems, e.g. mild/moderate mental illness or musculoskeletal pain. Although initially for new claimants (inflow) it is gradually being extended to existing recipients (stock). It combines a balanced package of rights and responsibilities, and targets a number of the health-related, personal and occupational barriers to return to work. The NHS and Jobcentre Plus work closely together to help people manage their health problem (through innovative NHS 'condition management programmes') and to get back to work (through Jobcentre Plus employment support). *Pathways* is another large scale initiative with joint working between the two organisations and is an example for future partnership working. It has placed UK at the forefront of the developed world in actively engaging with this client group.

In policy terms, Pathways has five main strands:

- A new and much more intensive framework of early and sustained work-related responsibilities delivered by specially trained Personal Advisers

- A tight gateway applied in a timely manner to ensure those who are not entitled leave IB as quickly as possible

- Better access to existing return to work support and entirely new NHS support to manage health conditions

- Improved financial and non-financial incentives to prepare for and find work

- Work to change prevailing attitudes held towards this client group amongst other key stakeholders - particularly GPs and employers.

Pathways embodies a fundamental philosophical shift in the services provided for sick and disabled people. Traditionally, their service needs were perceived to be primarily for health *care*, led by and provided by health professionals, supported secondarily by rehabilitation and employment services. *Pathways* reverses that, based on three grounds:

- That traditional approach has not worked for people with common health problems who reach the stage of moving on to IB[157].

- Changing concepts of disability, the modern disability role and disability rights.

- A more pro-active DWP approach to providing positive support.

Pathways is primarily a social rather than a health care intervention, about financial, rehabilitation and employment *support*, led by DWP and supported by health condition management. *Pathways* is largely provided in a DWP, home and work setting, rather than in a health care setting, in a deliberate attempt to de-medicalise the process.[158]

Practically, *Pathways* tailors support to meet individual needs, through a Choices package:

- A new Return to Work Credit of £40 per week tax free

- Earlier access to Adviser Discretionary Fund

- Access to new condition management programmes run jointly with local NHS providers

- Immediate access to Jobcentre Plus New Deals and the national network of Job Brokers who work closely with employers to secure sustainable employment for sick and disabled people.

- Access to current 'Permitted Work' arrangements

- Existing help such as Job Grant, Travel to Interview Scheme, Access to Work[159], Job Introduction Scheme, Work based learning for Adults and Training for Work, Work Trials, Work Preparation and WORKSTEP.

Condition Management Programmes (CMPs) are short-term, work-focused interventions aimed at helping claimants understand and manage their health conditions better, particularly in a working context. They cover the common health problems that are the main causes of incapacity – e.g. mild/moderate mental health or musculoskeletal conditions - but there is a lot of commonality and CMPs are generally not condition-specific. When necessary, arrangements can be made to expedite 'treatment' if that is appropriate, e.g. a specialist opinion, physiotherapy or formal counselling. However, CMPs are not primarily about 'treatment': they are generally more about encouraging and supporting the development of self-management strategies, with elements of self-help (Newman *et al* 2004) and expert patient programmes (Dept of Health 2002b & c), so that claimants are enabled to manage their health condition better and return to work. CMPs are based on cognitive behavioural principles, but they are not formal psychological interventions and might be described better as advisory or 'talking' therapies. They are about engagement, enablement and empowerment, and the key word is 'support' rather than 'care'.

The main aims of CMPs are:

- To help participants to understand and manage their health condition better, particularly in a working context.

- To reduce fears about health and work and to help participants feel more confident and better able to cope, particularly for returning to work.

- To enable participants who return to work to be more 'expert' in managing their health condition and in its occupational management.

Boxes 24 and 25 summarise some of the practical details of CMPs.

Box 24: Practical elements of Conditional Management Programmes (after N Bennie)
• Address the main health conditions identified
• Have a clear work focus with vocational goals and outcome measures
• Address biological, psychological and social components of disability
• Identify and address obstacles to return to work
• Increase activity levels and restore function
• Attempt to shift beliefs and behaviour using cognitive-behavioural techniques
• Close working partnership with Personal Advisers to facilitate return to work

CMPs can be placed in the context of the *NHS Improvement Plan* (Dept of Health 2002a), which aims to support people to improve their own health, to enable social and economic independence, and to tackle continuing inequalities of health. Such an approach reflects current evidence on best clinical practice for these conditions, where increasing activity levels and returning to normal life, including work, are seen as key elements of good clinical management. It is also consistent with modern principles of rehabilitation and participation. Within this broad framework, the NHS has considerable flexibility to develop the CMPs in ways that suit local needs and available resources. For example, the Gateshead and South Tyneside pilot offers a selection of modules (Box 26).

Box 25: CMP – Developing fitness for work (after N Bennie)

- Information and advice about health condition

- Identify and address health-related barriers to work

- Challenge perceptions regarding health and work

- Increase awareness of the benefits of increased activity, including work

- Agree activity goals

- Pacing of activities to increase general fitness and well being

- Introduction of relaxation techniques

- Action plan to develop fitness for work

- Develop self-help and support strategies

- Agreed outcome(s) achieved

- Readiness for work: coordinate with Personal Adviser on return to work plan

Box 26: Condition Management modules in the Gateshead and South Tyneside Pathways Pilot (after T Webb)

- Making sense of your condition

- Overcoming stress and anxiety

- Learning to be assertive

- Promoting emotional/physical well-being

- Living with fatigue

- Living with pain

Patients have detailed psychosocial assessment including barriers to return to work by a senior health care professional (occupational nurse or therapist, or psychologist), and then receive an appropriate selection of modules. 49% of patients in this CMP have a primary and a further 39% have a secondary mental health diagnosis.

Employment support is provided by specially trained Personal Advisers who carry out mandatory work-focused interviews (Box 27) every month for the first 6 months of the claim. Timing of this intervention is important (SSAC 2003, Watson & Patel 2004) and reflects a balance between:

Box 27: The content of work-focused interviews (adapted from DWP 2002)

Engaging and Understanding:
- Help claimants understand the nature of the benefits and the medical tests that underpin them.

- Encourage access to appropriate services, e.g. Choices or NDDP.

- Identify any problems with basic skills and encourage take-up of appropriate help or training.

- Explain the range of financial support available to help 'make work pay'.

Develop positive expectations:
- Help build self-confidence and positive attitudes to health and work. Reinforce the message that most claimants are still able to do some work.

- Explore options for work-focused activity, including: help with clarifying work goals; developing job seeking and job retention skills; encouraging transitions back to work through trial work, the permitted work rules, training or voluntary work

Implementation:
- Facilitate and negotiate return to work, where possible with the previous employer, or into alternative employment.

- Claimants and advisers jointly draw up and agree an Action Plan for return to work, which includes (SSAC 2003):
  - basic employment related information
  - the client's job goals and steps they agree to take towards work
  - the support the Personal Adviser agrees to undertake to help the client get back to work and to support them after they return to work
  - agreed future Work Focused Interviews

- Close liaison with Condition Management Programmes.

- Continued support in work

Particular consideration needs to be given to the impact of WFI on claimants with mental health conditions (Seebohm & Scott 2004).

- It should be clearly separate from and *after* decisions on award of benefits (to avoid uncertainty, ambiguity and conflicts of purpose – as discussed above)

- It should be after the acute stage of illness, once the health condition / disability has stabilised to some extent (by which time many claimants will have or clearly soon will return to work, hence reducing deadweight), but before the situation becomes irretrievable

- The strong evidence that the optimum window of opportunity for effective intervention is between 1-6+ months off work.

Pathways has currently struck the balance by carrying out the WFI about 8 weeks after the point of claim.

Mandatory involvement, face-to face contact and making support available can, in themselves, have a surprising impact on claimant attitudes and behaviour (Box 28).

Box 28: The Irish Renaissance Project: Preventing chronic disability from low back pain (Leech 2004, 2005)

- Implementation of clinical and occupational health guidelines in a social security setting.

- Early intervention at 4-6 weeks from claim

- Approved Medical Advisers given specific training in diagnostic triage and workplace issues to determine fitness to work.

- *The Back Book*[160] provided free to claimants.

- On receipt of invitation for assessment, 62% of claimants came off benefit and returned to work.

- 64% of back pain cases declared fit for work compared with ~20% previously.

- Fewer appeals and lower success rate of appeals.

- Reduced duration of claims and reduced benefit expenditure.

- These results have been maintained on further follow-up.

For those who need more support, Personal Advisers play a key role in case management: 'a collaborative process which assesses, plans, implements, coordinates, monitors and evaluates the options and services required to meet an individual's health care, educational and employment needs, using communication and available resources to promote quality, cost-effective outcomes, (Case Management Society of UK – **www.cmsuk.org**). PAs have close contact with the therapists providing condition management programmes, enabling both to work together to make sure that health and occupational management are closely integrated to meet individual claimant's needs. There are strong local partnerships with the New Deal for Disabled People – voluntary and private sector employment advisers. There is also pro-active contact with local employers and GPs, in a conscious and deliberate attempt to change the local culture and attitudes towards IB recipients.

The *Pathways to Work* pilot schemes cover 9% of the national inflow to IB in 7 Jobcentre Plus districts across the country. The first wave of three (Derby in England, Bridgend in Wales and Renfrewshire in Scotland,) was launched in October 2003. and the second wave of four (Essex, Gateshead & S. Tyneside, Somerset and E. Lancs) in April 2004. Starting from October 2005, *Pathways* will be extended to a third of the country, covering the most disadvantaged areas and local authority areas with the greatest concentration of IB claimants (HMT 2004). There will be increasing extension to more, longer-term recipients (stock). Including the existing pilots, the area covered by *Pathways* will have 900,000 IB recipients. Assuming the results are maintained, national roll-out could take place by 2008, though that will obviously depend on budgeting and has major implications for staff resources and training.

9.5.2 Preliminary results of Pathways pilots

The *Pathways* pilots are being evaluated by a consortium of companies, headed by the Policy Studies Institute, and will include[161]:

- Administrative process data

- Health and labour market outcomes

- Perceptions and experiences – of claimants, Personal Advisers, health professionals and employers

- Responses from key stakeholders

- Effectiveness of particular elements (e.g. condition management programmes, various employment support interventions) and of DWP / NHS cooperation

- Areas that could be improved in future.

In-house analysis of DWP Administrative data shows that over 58,000 IB claimants had entered the pilots by August 2004. Starts have now achieved a steady state of around 3,000 – 3,500 per month in the Wave 1 Districts and around 4,500 per month in the Wave 2 districts. About 10% of those taking part are long-term recipients who have been on IB more than 12 months and have volunteered to participate. These take-up rates are higher than expected and much higher than the usual 3-6% achieved in previous social security pilot studies with this client group, both in UK and internationally (Waddell *et al* 2002).

Early benefit outcomes are encouraging, with an 8-10% increase in the six-month IB outflow rate in the pilot areas compared with non-pilot areas (Figure 12). At the time of writing, results in the first wave had been maintained for seven months and initial results in the second wave pilots are similar. These results are better than predicted and well over the calculated threshold for cost-effectiveness.

Figure 12: IB outflow in *Pathways* pilot districts compared with non-*Pathway* districts.

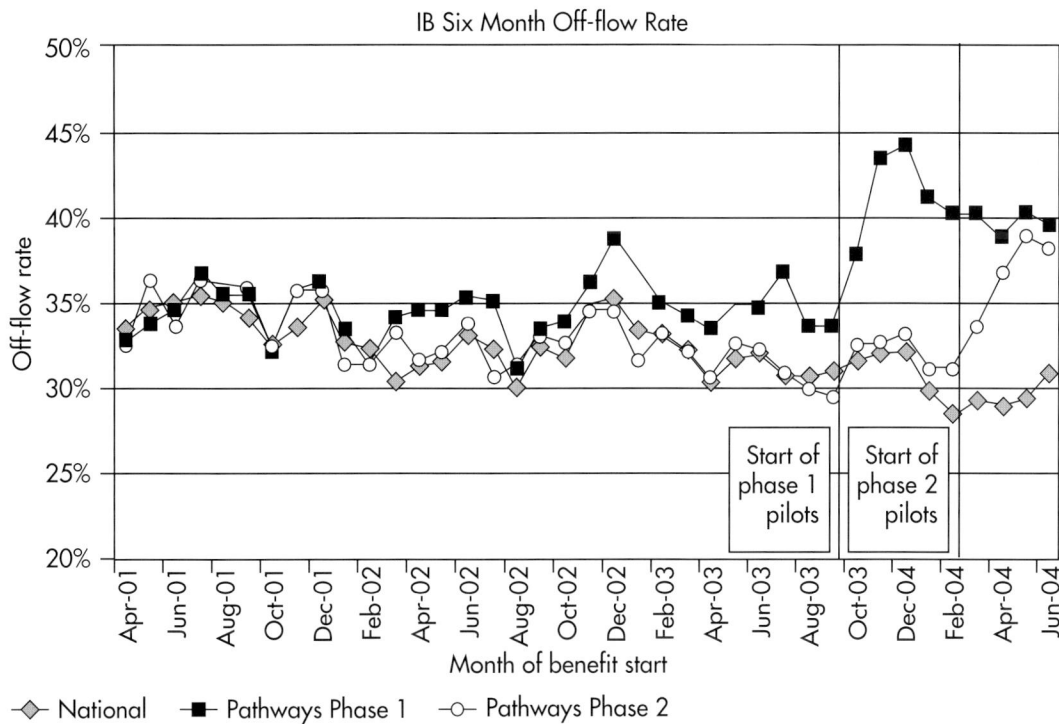

These are the numbers coming off benefits: there is no direct evidence on whether they have all returned to work, though there is circumstantial evidence that most have done so. Other data show no increase in the numbers moving on to other benefits. Following the initial Work Focused Interview, 15-20% of claimants take up elements of the Choices Package, with over 10% joining New Deal for Disabled People in the *Pathways* areas compared to 4% joining NDDP in Jobcentre Plus Pathfinder offices and 2% nationally. Separate data show that the number of sick and disabled claimants entering work has doubled in the *Pathways* areas compared to the same period the previous year (Figure 13). Significantly, 18% of recorded job entries are longer-term benefit recipients.

Qualitative studies have looked at the perceptions and experiences of claimants and Personal Advisers (Dickens et al 2004a & b). Interviews were carried out at an early stage before the pilot studies were fully bedded down and are best regarded as initial reactions.

Claimants' reactions:

• Claimants largely welcomed the new environment – even those who did not want to use it at present.

• Claimants made a clear link between the Jobcentre and the concept of work, and expected that the purpose of the Work Focused Interview (WFI) was to discuss work.

Figure 13: Sick and Disabled job entries in Pathways Pilot Districts: year-on-year comparison.

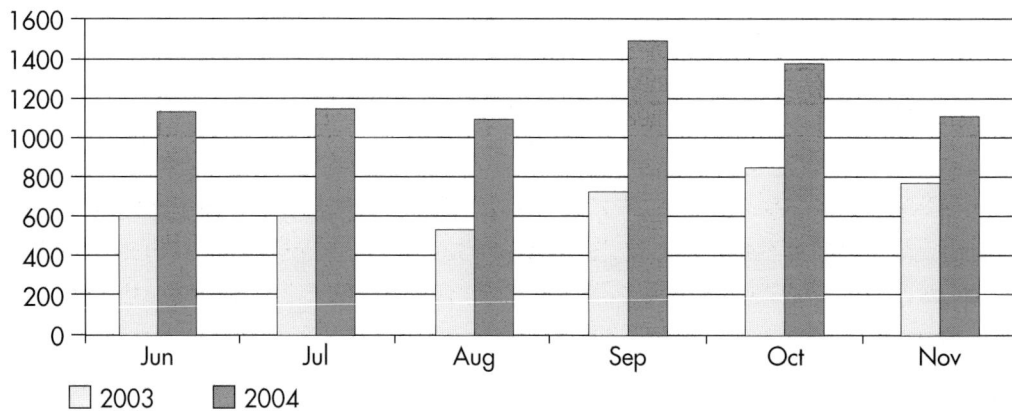

- Some claimants experienced practical problems attending WFIs, including difficulties with fluctuating health, transport and access, and privacy.

- Claimants' reactions to the content of early WFIs varied. One key group expressed clear interest in 'moving on' from their current situation and tended to be positive in principle about the idea of attending WFIs once they had understood their purpose. A second group were adamant at this stage that they did not need or want help to move towards work or training. These customers tended to be negative about their experience of the WFI, feeling that there had been too much emphasis on returning to work, and that the inappropriateness (as they saw it) of their attendance at WFIs had not been acknowledged.

- Claimants found the Condition Management Programmes and the Return To Work Credits particularly valuable.

Personal Advisers felt their management of the Work Focused Interview process was critical to the success of the IB Reforms. They recognised that their main role was to provide tailored, individualised, packages of support to help claimants overcome barriers to returning to work. They typically felt that helping claimants to overcome key barriers was just as important and valid as moving them immediately into work. Within this process, Personal Advisers felt that they had the flexibility and resources (via the Choices Package) to be responsive to individual claimants' needs in determining when and how the issue of returning to work was raised and the pattern and timing of interviews. Typically, claimants with the most serious or severe conditions had their interview waived and claimants who were undergoing treatment, awaiting results or had a temporary health condition would have their interview deferred. Personal Advisers felt their new role was rewarding, though it also raised significant challenges: it could be emotionally draining and they could feel out of their depth at times.

Specific reactions from Personal Advisers included:

- In an earlier in-house study, Personal Advisers reacted very positively to the intensive training they received. The felt that it had resulted in: improved interviewing skills, greater confidence to work with IB customers, the ability to introduce the reforms and the concept of work in a positive way.

- Personal Advisers described how they could often overcome initially negative reactions from customers through direct contact prior to the Work Focused Interview.

- Where Personal Advisers had been in contact with customers attending the Condition Management Programme (CMP) the feedback had been encouraging, with Personal Advisers finding these customers more talkative in interviews and more confident about their future.

- Personal Advisers felt they were increasingly knowledgeable about and confident in referring claimants to the CMP. A regular CMP presence in Jobcentres seemed to be effective in building links and allowing opportunities to jointly discuss cases and determine the suitability of the programme for individual customers. Personal Adviser confidence increased through training and links with local CMP providers.

- Personal Advisers unanimously reported a positive reaction to the Return to Work Credit.

- However, some Personal Advisers said that there were some claimants they had not been able to move forward at all.

These reactions clearly show that many claimants, health professionals and Personal Advisers involved in *Pathways* like the approach. However, there is still no direct evidence on the process, effectiveness or health-related outcomes of the Condition Management Programmes. These will be the subject of a current Department of Health Call for Research Proposals to evaluate:

- The nature and operation of the different CMPs.

- The impact of the CMPs

- The impact on local health services.

When these policies were set out in the Green Paper (DWP 2002), they received almost unanimous support from all the key stakeholders (DWP 2003c)[162]. Responses to the 5-year plan (DWP 2005) are broadly supportive of *Pathways*, though there are more mixed reactions to the IB reform package as a whole[163]:

Disability Rights Commission: Together, these new proposals and the roll-out of the new Jobcentre Plus services offer huge potential for creating a new and more positive balance between a 'rights-based' delivery of state support and the responsibilities Government s seeking to confer on individuals requiring such support.

DRC welcomes the Government's announcement today that those who are able to, and want to, will be supported into work. The changes introduced today will mean that disabled people will be able to make a positive contribution. But for these measures to work, high quality support will be needed from assessment of those deemed able to work, right through to finding and maintaining opportunities to work.

Child Poverty Action Group: CPAG praised the Pathways to Work pilots, and urged more investment in projects to support Incapacity Benefit claimants who want and are able to do so to move towards a return to work. Support and not threats are clearly the way forward.

Citizens' Advice: The Pathways to Work scheme - - - provides a much more positive approach, involving interviews with specially trained personal advisers, NHS rehabilitation support, and a £40 a week return to work credit. All this is welcome, but it is resource intensive.

Leonard Cheshire: We will need to hear much more detail about how this will work in practice – staff must be fully trained to be able to deal with the complex new demands that will be placed on them. - - If the new proposals are implemented with sensitivity to the individual then there is much that will be welcomed in today's announcement. The system needs to be able to deal with the complexities of disability such as fluctuating and progressive conditions – a 'one size fits all' approach would have the potential to be very damaging for disabled people.

Institute of Directors: The fact that so many people actually want to engage in employment but for one reason or another have not been able to, means that action is needed. This would not only benefit individuals, but also business and the economy as a whole.

National Employment Panel, Employer's Working Group: We feel that the Pathways pilots are a practical, broad-based approach to moving people from IB into work.

TUC: The Government's Pathways to Work pilots have been remarkably successful in helping people find work.

The main concerns were around decisions about who was fit to consider work:

Disability Alliance: We are deeply concerned about the amount of power that could be given to officials in Jobcentre Plus offices. Is the DWP seriously suggesting that junior Jobcentre Plus staff are to decide whether or not someone who's had a mental breakdown is ready to start looking for work? - - - We are appalled at the idea that people in this position would be penalised by having their benefit (cut) - -

Disability Benefits Consortium: This could give a dangerous amount of discretion to Jobcentre Plus staff who would have to make judgments about whether or not someone is too ill to fulfil the work conditions. Claimants already have to pass an exacting medical test of incapacity and should not be treated like jobseekers and forced to work with a personal adviser and undertake compulsory work-focused activities.

9.5.3 Future Challenges to Pathways

Extrapolating from the present results, DWP estimates that if these preliminary results were maintained, national roll-out of *Pathways* to all IB recipients (including the existing stock) might help up to 100,000 people into work each year. There are widely varying estimates of the likely impact on the long-term caseload, depending on a number of uncertain assumptions. It does appear likely that *Pathways* would pay for itself. However, national roll-out would involve some major challenges:

- National roll-out would require major expenditure, which is only likely if there is strong evidence that it would be cost-effective.

- These preliminary results need to be confirmed on a national scale and over the longer term, with a particular focus on sustained work outcomes.

- *Pathways* is resource intensive and demands a high level of staff skills and competencies, both for the Condition Management Programmes and for specialist Personal Advisers. This would require major investment in staff recruitment and training. There must still be some question whether this can be delivered effectively on a national scale.

- Although the *Pathways* package appears to be effective, there are still major questions about the effectiveness of different Condition Management Programmes, Employment Support interventions, and delivery models. This will involve detailed analysis of the pilot studies and further research and development over several years.

- All previous evidence suggests it is unlikely that *Pathways* will be as acceptable or effective with the existing stock, particularly those who are aged > 50 years and/or have been on benefits for more than 1-2 years. A number of longer-term recipients in the pilot areas are taking part voluntarily and successfully re-entering work, which is encouraging. However, extending *Pathways* on a mandatory basis to all suitable longer-term recipients raises a number of additional questions and challenges and would require considerable further research and development, and evidence of its effectiveness and cost-effectiveness.

- Personal Advisers recognise a group of claimants whom they have not been able to move forward. Qualitative studies identify a group of claimants who are adamant that they are 'too ill to work' or even to consider work or to cooperate with work-focused interviews. Certain lobby groups appear strongly resistant to certain categories of sick people being expected or put under any pressure to undertake work-focused activities. It is not clear to what extent these are the same groups of recipients. There are clearly some sick or disabled claimants who are unfit to undertake work focused activities at a given point in time. However, the entire analysis presented in this review, and some of the examples given in the lobby submissions, suggest that for many it is as much a matter of perceptions and expectations as of impairment or incapacity[164]. There is a battle still to be won over this issue, though that may be a broader political battle over IB reform and the culture of sickness and incapacity. *Pathways* cannot resolve that on its own: demonstrable success of *Pathways* will contribute to that battle; but lasting success of *Pathways* is also likely to depend on winning that larger battle.

- Supply side interventions (e.g. *Pathways*, benefit conditionality and making work pay) must be balanced by demand side interventions (e.g. job availability, stopping employer discrimination).

9.5.4 Preliminary Conclusions of Pathways Pilots

These are preliminary results but, despite all the caveats, it is important to recognise what has been achieved so far. These are very large-scale pilot studies covering a significant portion of the caseload and country. Very few social security interventions in the world have ever achieved such take-up rates, enthusiasm and labour market outcomes with this client group (Corden & Thornton 2002). These results stand in marked contrast to the long history of failed international efforts to address the problem of long-term incapacity (Waddell *et al* 2002).

Provided the success of *Pathways* is maintained, it will provide a promising basis for IB reform. Most important, the consensus and support that *Pathways* has already generated across the employment, medical and disability lobbies is something that DWP will give up at its peril.

10 CONDITIONALITY

'Conditionality' is simply the terms and conditions of the welfare contract – the individual responsibilities that must be accepted in return for social rights. There have always been conditions attached to receipt of social security benefits, the primary purpose of which is to influence the behaviour of claimants and recipients (Field 1997, White 2004a, Stanley *et al* 2004). So one side of the welfare contract is that society provides financial and other support to sick and disabled people who need it, but the other side is that recipients must meet certain obligations and responsibilities, and must not take unfair advantage[165]. As a condition for providing benefits, the state may legitimately demand and enforce these responsibilities. This does not undermine citizenship: mutual responsibilities and reciprocity express and support the ethic of solidarity on which social democracy rests. It is also essential to maintain the legitimacy of sickness and disability benefits and the willingness of the taxpayer/voter to fund them. There is an intrinsic moral attraction (Blair 1999, Goodin 2002) and strong public support for this concept of 'mutual obligation' (Williams 1999, Dwyer 2000, OECD 2003).

There are philosophical arguments for and against conditionality (Dwyer 2000, Collins & Rossiter 2004). The arguments for conditionality (Deacon 2004) include:

1 The contractual argument: social rights are balanced by individual obligations.

2 The reciprocity argument: mutual obligations between citizens, irrespective of claims on the state.

3 The paternalistic argument: it is in the best interests of claimants themselves. Participation is the main route to social inclusion and integration. From a policy perspective, increasing participation is the key strategy to reducing social disadvantage, marginalisation and poverty.

The arguments against (White 2004a, 2004b) are that conditionality is unfair because:

4 Welfare is a human and social right of citizenship that should be unconditional.

5 It is contrary to liberal principles.

6 It is inequitable to impose special conditions on selected benefit recipients.

7 Because it burdens those who are already unjustly disadvantaged.

After laying out the pros and cons of each argument, all of these authors concluded that conditionality can be philosophically and morally justified on arguments 1-6, *provided* care is taken to avoid 7 (Rawls 1999, White 2004b)[166].

Sickness and disability lead to different rights and obligations, but they do not give exemption from the social contract or from personal responsibility to fulfil individual obligations (Duckworth 2001, OECD 2003). Equal citizenship does not necessarily mean treating everyone exactly the same; it may be reasonable to treat disabled people differently in order to achieve equal outcomes (Howard 2004a). For sickness and disability benefits, the key obligations include (Box 10):

- Recognise that symptoms, feeling unwell, sickness and incapacity are not the same.

- Accept an appropriate share of responsibility for managing one's health condition, rehabilitation and return to work.

- Central to the economic contract with society, return to work when reasonably able to, even if still with some symptoms.

- The greater the subjectivity and the personal/psychological element in incapacity, the greater the degree of personal responsibility.

This is very similar to the legal principle in personal injury litigation, that claimants must 'mitigate the loss', i.e. do all that they can to recover from their injuries so as to minimise the need for compensation (Council of Europe 2002).

Many benefit recipients (Dwyer 1998, 2002, Saunders 2002) agree that the imposition of conditions and therefore the exclusion of certain individuals from welfare rights can be legitimate, even though the extent to which they agree depends on the context. Perhaps unexpectedly, Dwyer found that disabled recipients were most likely to agree that compulsory work/training was reasonable and might help people to re-enter the labour market and develop 'a totally new outlook' on life.[167]

White (2004b) suggested three philosophical tests of any conditionality policy[168]:

1 *The basic rationale test:* Does the policy have a clear rationale in terms of social democratic values?

2 *The evidence test:* Is there evidence that the policy (is likely to) produce(s) the desired change in behaviour?

3 *The unfair side effects test:* Together with other relevant policies, is the conditionality fair?

   a *The inequity test:* Does the conditionality rule generate objectionable inequity in the enforcement of social duties?

   b *The harm test:* Does the conditionality rule generate unacceptable harm to society's most disadvantaged group or groups?[169]

Collins & Rossiter (2004) suggested three further practical tests for sanctions[170]:

The clarity condition: The policy must have a definite and unchanging point at which the behavioural sanction is applied and the nature of this sanction must be unambiguously clear.

The principal condition: the sanction must be targeted at the person who is accused of non-compliance and not at a third party (e.g. dependent children).

The capability condition: The person sanctioned must be capable of changing their behaviour.

Howard (2004a) identified specific concerns about how conditionality might be unfair to disabled people:

- People should not be forced into activities they are not able to do because of their impairment or health condition;

- Mandatory activity will not be effective unless appropriate, high-quality support is provided;

- Increasing pressure cannot make people (return to) work if the labour market does not make suitable jobs available;

- Sanctions could have very negative effects on incomes, health and confidence;

- There are still many external barriers which make it difficult for sick and disabled people to work;

- Focusing on the individual is unfair when employers can still discriminate against disabled people;

- In summary, conditionality is only fair if there is a real rather than theoretical prospect of suitable work[171].

Fairness also demands that mutual obligations work both ways. Thus, a fair welfare contract places the onus on society to provide the necessary opportunities, support and incentives *before* imposing conditionality on benefit recipients (Kuptsch & Zeitzer 2001, White 2003, 2004b, Deacon 2004, Howard 2004a). Rather than rights being conditional on meeting responsibilities, additional needs must be identified and met first (rather than the other way round). In employment terms, this means considering the nature of work-related 'responsibility' (rather than exempting people from it) and also the support required for claimants to meet it. For sickness and disability benefits, the key elements are (Stanley *et al* 2004, Howard 2004a):

- Providing better health care and condition management (especially for common health problems).

- Providing better support into work, and demonstrating that these interventions are effective.

- Making sure that work is available, stopping employer discrimination against sick and disabled people (especially those with mental health conditions), and ensuring that work is suitable, of decent 'human' quality, financially rewarding and secure.

Providing society fulfils these obligations, it is then legitimate for DWP to stipulate that provision of sickness and disability benefits is conditional on recipients fulfilling their obligations. The goal is to create the right combination of rights, conditionality and support to encourage and enable them to do so, in a way that is fair and just and also practical.

- *Provided* the nature and severity of the health condition is manageable and allows some capacity for work –
  and
  provided society gives the necessary opportunity, support and incentives to (return to) work -

- *then* receipt of (particular elements of) benefits should be conditional upon:
  participation in and active cooperation with condition management, rehabilitation and return to work initiatives,
  and
  demonstrating motivation and effort to rehabilitate, restore functional capacity as far as practical, and return to work.

Fair implementation depends on striking a balance between specifying and if necessary enforcing some minimum requirements, creating the broader culture of expectations and behaviour, and providing genuine flexibility to recognise and respond to individual capacities and circumstances (FACS 2002).

A workable system of conditionality would require all of the following elements:

- Identify a reasonable level of job preparation requirement based on the individual's health condition or impairment

- Properly impose such a requirement

- Offer effective support and interventions to help the claimant meet these requirements

- Monitor compliance

- Apply sanctions and be prepared to defend them when challenged

- Ensure claimants can find suitable work

- Make sure work pays.

The practicality and impact of conditionality depends on the level of Job Preparation that is set:

- Attendance and participation in regular interviews with a Personal Adviser.

- Attendance and participation in assessment with a Condition Management therapist.

- Development of and agreement to an Action Plan (both for condition management and a return to work plan).

- Participation in and active cooperation with a Condition Management Programme (if that is agreed in the Action Plan).

- Participation in and active cooperation with return to work efforts (if that is agreed in the Action Plan) – and various levels of job preparation, job search and job trials.

The closer the claimant is to the job market, the higher the level of Job Preparation activity that could reasonably be set. The more fundamental question is what to do if recipients fail to return to work. The principle of 'Progressive Engagement' would mean that the longer the claimant was off work the higher the level of Job Preparation activity demanded. However, the TUC argue the opposite – that the longer the claimant is off work, the lower the chances and expectations of return to work, and hence the *lower* the demands should be regarding Job Preparation activity. The problem is that would seriously weaken the principle of conditionality and effectively mean there was no ultimate sanction.

The Job Preparation Premium in the Pathways pilot areas from February 2005 could serve as the starting point and should provide emerging evidence. This is likely to require further consultation, piloting and political debate.

It is important to be realistic about the goals and likely outcomes of conditionality. The goal is to change behaviour, which may be achieved either by measures to make the desired behaviour more attractive, or to make that behaviour a requirement for receipt of some benefit (Hoskins *et al* 2001). Both ultimately appeal to self-interest. Human nature being what it is, positive incentives for desired behaviour are likely to be more effective than negative disincentives for undesired behaviour (Halpern *et al* 2004): though the problem is that the withdrawal of incentives can then become a disincentive. Thus, the ultimate sanction on failure to comply with obligations is to withdraw (parts or particular elements of) benefits. However, there is limited and conflicting evidence on the effectiveness of sanctions (Mead 1997a & b, Deacon 1997, Gardiner 1997, Walker 1998, Stanley *et al* 2004). Most of the evidence is from the United States, which has been a world leader in developing conditionality, but most of that evidence is related to poverty, lone parents and unemployment benefits, while disabled people have traditionally been regarded as exempt from any conditionality about work, even in the US. Nor is it clear how far American evidence can be applied to the different social security, political and cultural context of UK. There are reasonable grounds to suppose that conditionality can change behaviour, but it is notoriously difficult for state agencies to enforce sanctions with any sensitivity. There is little empirical evidence of any direct effect of sanctions on behaviour or outcomes, but even the main American advocate of conditionality concluded that 'heavy-handed use of benefit sanctions can be counter-productive' (Mead 1997b).

However, conditionality can have more subtle and indirect effects on changing attitudes and behaviours (Halpern *et al* 2004). It represents a fundamental political and psychological shift from receipt of benefits as an entitlement to receipt based on meeting certain criteria, obligations and behaviour (Hoskins *et al* 2001). So the real question should be how to make sure conditionality and sanctions deliver the correct messages and influence behaviour to the desired ends. Mead (1997a) concluded that: 'The purpose of sanctions is to clarify what is expected (of claimants) - - sanctions can act as a motivational tool rather than a means of coercion.' Indeed, the 'toughest' American conditionality programmes that were most effective at getting people back to work actually had much lower rates of imposing the final sanctions of benefit cuts (Mead 1997b). Used sensitively, benefit sanctions may be better seen as a motivational tool rather than a means of coercion. The goal is to encourage or 'push' people into work, so positive incentives are more effective than compulsion, which is liable to create unwilling and uncooperative 'conscripts' who will exit at the first opportunity. That approach is also more consistent with public opinion that people should be helped, encouraged and supported rather than compelled into work (Willams *et al* 1999, Saunders 2002). In principle, conditionality is likely to be most effective when it provides the framework within which Personal Advisers can work together with claimants to provide positive support into work.

However it is argued and presented, conditionality is likely to face fierce political opposition, as illustrated by experience in the Netherlands. The Donner Commission[172] was set up to develop a cross-party political consensus on options for reform and reported in 2001. They recommended restructuring social security benefits for incapacity, with some similarities to recent UK proposals (DWP 2005). They proposed two new benefits. Claimants with severe physical impairments or 'anyone whose psychological difficulties were judged to render them permanently unsuitable for work' would be categorised as totally incapable of any work (100%) and receive a full disability benefit (possibly enhanced) until retirement age. The Commission estimated that about 70% of current recipients might be eligible for this full 'ill health retirement pension'. All other beneficiaries would be categorised as partially disabled and receive a different new benefit at a lower rate, which would only be payable for 2 years. During this period, the employee would be under stronger pressure for rehabilitation and return to work, while employers would also be under stronger pressure to help re-integration. After 2 years recipients would be re-categorised as unemployed. These proposals led to fierce political opposition from various stakeholders, they became bogged down in the pluralistic and 'pillarised' Dutch political system, and there was not the political will to push them through.

In the UK about 2002-03, the Disability Rights Commission (DRC 2003b) argued that participation in work-focused activities should not be mandatory, but should be voluntary and based largely on claimants' own perceptions of their health condition and when they were ready. It argued that effective support systems would attract claimants (many of whom want to work), that voluntary participation and motivation have been central to the success of *Pathways*, and that mandatory participation might undermine that success. However, there is now greater concern that some people might be written off by not having Work Focused Interviews. It is certainly true that sanctions should be used as little as possible, only as a last resort, and in a sense are an admission that the process has failed. But human nature requires the presence of some kind of ultimate sanction to set the limit on acceptable behaviour. Otherwise, any benefit reform would be meaningless beyond the provision of *Pathways*. The question has also been raised whether participation in work-focused activities might be 'based more on the social model of disability, rather than the medical model' - which would presumably mean that exemption from work-focused activities should be based on the extent of the external barriers to work. However, that would effectively return to incapacity benefits largely determined by socio-demographic, labour market and regional circumstances. It is also illogical to deny WFIs, which are designed to provide help and support to overcome these barriers, to the very people who need it most!

Box 29: The argument for conditionality

Many benefit recipients with less severe health conditions do not have any absolute physical or mental barrier to work.

Personal / psychological factors are central to incapacity associated with common health problems.

The individual has personal responsibility for his or her actions.

The sick role embodies a social contract between the citizen and the welfare state, with a balance between social rights and individual obligations

Sickness and disability benefits are given on condition that the recipient meets these obligations.

The central obligation is to (return to) work when the claimant is reasonably able to.

There must be safeguards to make sure this does not further disadvantage those who are already the most disadvantaged.

10.2 Recipients with longer-term sickness who fail to return to work after rehabilitation / support into work interventions.

At the end of the whole process, there will undoubtedly be some recipients with less severe health problems, who receive Condition Management / support into work interventions, but who do not return to work. They need repeat medical assessment (e.g. at 1 year +/-) to check for any change in their medical condition: some may no longer be incapacitated so their benefits might be stopped and some may have developed impairment that entitles them to longer-term incapacity benefits. The difficult and probably the largest group will be those who remain unfit for work at present but still suitable for support into work. They might continue to 'engage' in Job Preparation activities indefinitely, but that would increasingly be a matter of repeating interventions that had already failed, with diminishing chance of achieving anything, and no realistic likelihood of returning to work (Waddell & Burton 2004b). Options for these recipients include:

- Simply continue incapacity benefits (indefinitely?) – as occurs at present with IB. However, that would mean there was ultimately no sanction, so conditionality would effectively be meaningless. That would fail to resolve one of the major problems with the present system.

- Use failure to improve with time and optimal treatment by an appropriate specialist (e.g. over 2 years) as evidence of severe and permanent incapacity, even if there is no evidence of permanent impairment, and effectively give them permanent incapacity benefits. This is a pragmatic (rather than a principled) approach that acknowledges the reality that these claimants are very unlikely ever to come off benefits or return to work. This approach is used by the insurance industry for 'total and permanent disability'[173]. This option is likely to gain considerable political support but would effectively mean there was no ultimate sanction. It would not only fail to resolve the problem with the present system, but could provide a perverse incentive for recipients to remain on benefits till they had 'proven' that they were severely and 'permanently' incapacitated.

- Continue incapacity benefits indefinitely, but with flexibility to increase or decrease the level of conditionality over time according to change in the claimant's health condition, change in their employability, the likely effectiveness of appropriate Condition Management Programmes or support into work interventions, or the *likelihood* of the recipient actually returning to work. Some flexibility is essential to tailor support and conditionality to the individual's health condition and needs. However, depending on how it was applied, this option would risk meaning there was no ultimate sanction, with similar potential consequences to the previous two options.

- Only continue any rehabilitation element of incapacity benefits for as long as realistic rehabilitation/reintegration activities are taking place, after which recipients might revert to a lower benefit rate. If the policy goal is to provide incentive and support for vocational rehabilitation, then when barriers to return to work have been addressed and/or meaningful rehabilitation ceases, there is no logical basis for continuing any premium (Levine 1997). The problem would be how to define that point. It could be a matter of clinical judgement about 'completing treatment' or reaching 'maximal medical improvement' (AMA 2000), though that is a subjective judgment that is likely to be disputed. Alternatively, it could be argued that condition management programmes and support into work are likely to demonstrate any effect within 6 months (though that time limit could be debated and there is some room for negotiation) and there is then no point in continuing. That could raise the arguments about arbitrary time-limits, but it could be countered that the decision is based on the demonstrated outcome of the individual case. In either event, it would need robust decision-making processes based on the principles of consistency and consensus (Aylward & LoCascio 1995). *

- After a set period, e.g. 1 year, give a smaller 'permanent disability pension' for life or a lump sum payment in final settlement and stop incapacity benefits. (There are precedents for this in IIDB, the insurance industry, civil litigation and North American Workers Compensation systems.)*

- For people approaching retirement (e.g. > 55-60 years) after a set period (e.g. 1 year) give an actuarially reduced pension. *

* These options are each open to the potential problem of re-cycling, i.e. resubmitting a new claim either after some time and/or with a new diagnosis. Follow-up of claimants leaving IB suggests this could be anything from <10% to nearly one third (Dorsett *et al* 1998, Bowling *et al* 2004), but it is unclear how common this problem is likely to be under the new structure. Consideration might be given to some form of linking rules either to confer positive advantages (as under the present linking rules) or to block fresh claims. However, that would seriously disadvantage some claimants with 'genuine' new medical conditions, it could be difficult to operationalise and is likely to face political opposition. It is unclear whether such measures would be effective or cost-effective.

There is an important caveat. Discussion of rights and responsibilities and conditionality may lead to 'help for those who help themselves'. That may be most effective for those who are closest to the labour market. However, it must be acknowledged that some recipients are 'hard to help'. This approach may fail the most disadvantaged and marginalized members of society - those who are incapable of grasping the opportunity or who simply cannot meet the increasingly complex demands of the modern labour market (Hattersley 1998). There is no evidence whether stricter conditionality will be effective for these people (Gilbert 2000). Society – and the benefits system – must make due allowance and provide additional help for 'the deprived, the disadvantaged and the excluded' (Hadler 1996b).

There is another, final caveat. The focus of this section has been on the rights and responsibilities of the individual, but that is only one side of the story. They must always be balanced by the duties and responsibilities of society, Government and the social security system. There are also corresponding duties and responsibilities on employers, which are beyond the scope of this review (Stanley & Regan 2003, DRC 2003b).

11 CONCLUSION

11.1 Basic concepts and principles

This review provides a very broad evidence-base and a compelling theoretical argument for IB reform. Whatever the future direction of reform, it should take account of these basic concepts and principles, though its impact will also depend critically on how the principles are implemented and delivered in practice.

IB recipients include very diverse groups of people, with different kinds of problems, in widely differing circumstances. IB is often used to provide more generous support for unemployment, (early) retirement and poverty: these should be 'unbundled' and incapacity benefits should focus on providing income replacement for people who have financial loss (actual, not hypothetical) due to incapacity (and not to supplement Income Support, unemployment benefits or early retirement). However, that depends on adequate provision being made for these other contingencies. Any reform must provide fairly and equitably for all IB recipients, taking particular care not to further disadvantage those who are already among the most disadvantaged members of society.

It is important to distinguish basic concepts of sickness and disability, which are often confused and obscure the welfare debate. Rational policy and legislation depends on clear definitions and precise usage:

Disease is objective, medically diagnosed, pathology.

Impairment is significant, demonstrable, deviation or loss of body structure or function.

Symptoms are bothersome bodily or mental sensations.

Illness is the subjective feeling of being unwell.

Disability is limitation of activities and restriction of participation.

Sickness is a social status granted to the ill person by society.

Incapacity is inability to work associated with sickness or disability.

However, these are not inevitable consequences of disease or injury, and the correlation between the elements is poor. In particular:

- The main problem now is 'longer-term sickness' (>50% of IB recipients regard themselves as sick rather than disabled).

- Sickness and disability do not necessarily mean incapacity (50% of 'disabled' people are working).

There is a tension between the traditional sick role which is about the right *not* to work and the modern disability role which is about the right *to work*. Sickness and disability benefits are based on citizenship - a social contract between individuals, employers and Government, with a balance of rights and responsibilities on all sides. There is a pressing need for a new and more explicit welfare contract, more appropriate to today's problems, and in which rights and responsibilities are clearly defined.

Social security systems for sickness and disability were designed primarily for people with severe medical conditions and objective evidence of permanent impairment, e.g. blindness, severe neurological disease, or psychoses. These are still the public image of 'disabled people' and the examples used in welfare debates. However, such severe medical conditions only account for about a quarter of the current IB caseload. Most IB recipients now have less severe 'common health problems': 42% mental health conditions; 21% musculoskeletal conditions; 11% cardio-respiratory conditions. Since the late 90s, there has been a dramatic increase in the proportion with mild/moderate mental health conditions. However, many of these common health problems should be manageable and long-term incapacity is not inevitable. *Provided* these people are given the right opportunities, support and incentives, many of them should be able to (return to) work.

Many factors influence whether or not a health condition leads to incapacity for work. Health usually comes high on the list. But incapacity associated with common health problems depends on interactions between health-related, personal *and* social factors. Moreover, recognition of the complex factors influencing incapacity must not obscure free will and personal responsibility for one's actions. The less severe and more subjective the health condition, the more important the role of personal factors (motivation and effort, attitudes and beliefs, behaviour, functioning and participation). That does not mean these people are all 'malingerers': all the evidence is that outright fraud accounts for <1% of incapacity and disability benefits. But it is entirely appropriate to question whether all IB recipients are completely incapacitated for work and to suggest that claimants must bear some responsibility for their own health management, rehabilitation and return to work.

It is also important to understand the predicament that many IB recipients are in. There are close links between poor health, disability, social and regional disadvantage, unemployment and poverty. Many IB recipients have multiple disadvantages and face multiple barriers to work: age (half are aged > 50 years), poor work history (1/3rd of new recipients have already been out of work for > 2 years), low skills (40% have no qualifications, 15% have basic skills problems), local labour markets and high local unemployment rates (with ten-fold variation in IB rates between the best and worst local authority areas), and employer discrimination. Even if the health condition itself is not totally incapacitating, it is confounded by these other disadvantages.

Uncertainty is a key issue: about whether they will be fit to work regularly, about the risk of losing benefits or getting back on to benefits if the need arises, and about the financial consequences of coming off benefits.

A major difficulty in the present system and a key question for future policy is the extent to which entitlement and assessment are based on objective evidence of recognisable medical conditions and impairment vs. claimants' self-report of subjective symptoms and limitations.

The threshold for incapacity depends on when sickness or disability make it unreasonable to expect the claimant to attempt or make efforts to (return to) work. In many common health problems this is ultimately a social rather than a medical judgment.

'Incapacity' benefits contain a fundamental paradox: claimants must demonstrate their *in*capacity for work to establish and maintain entitlement to benefits, but obtaining/returning to work depends on their *capacity* for work. Too often, long-term IB wrote people off, created negative expectations and welfare dependency, and trapped people on benefits till retirement age. The benefit should be re-structured and re-branded to get away from the image, culture and expectancy of 'incapacity'.

Historically, social security in UK was about passive benefits and failed to provide any active support into work. To achieve political consensus, gain the essential cooperation of all the key stakeholders, and deliver real and lasting change, benefit reform should be led by much more active support into work, tailored to suit individual needs and providing help to overcome the health-related, personal and social barriers to work. Three key elements underpin IB reform:

- Better clinical and occupational management, particularly of common health problems (Waddell & Burton 2004b).

- Re-structuring and re-naming the benefit to 'unbundle' sickness, disability and incapacity for work (OECD 2003).

- A much stronger focus on providing opportunities, a new system of support (*Pathways*), and incentives to promote 'work for those who can' (DWP 2002, 2005).

That positive lead should provide the moral and political justification for a more fundamental debate about 'incapacity', entitlement, Gateways to benefits, rights and responsibilities, conditionality and control mechanisms. That could potentially have much greater impact on benefit trends than any direct effect of *Pathways* in returning benefit recipients to work.

DWP cannot do this alone (Halpern *et al* 2004). Benefit trends represent the sum of millions of individual decisions and behaviours, by sick and disabled people, their GPs and employers, and

DWP staff. DWP has no direct involvement in the primary social gateway to sickness, but it can influence attitudes and behaviour. Real and lasting reversal of current trends depends on getting enough of these people to change what they do. That will only happen if there is a fundamental shift in the culture of health and work, sickness and 'incapacity', and that in turn depends on getting all of these key stakeholders on side. This is not just a pious hope but involves some very practical steps (Box 30). It is also not enough in itself (Scheel *et al* 2002): action depends on actually working together according to a shared agenda to the desired ends. Crucially, that depends on reforms being perceived as positive and in everyone's best interests, and avoiding antagonistic approaches and confrontation.

Box 30: Government sets policy; implementation and delivery depends on the cooperation of all the key stakeholders	
All players onside	*Essential practicalities*
• Individuals	• Communication
• Health professionals	• Common language
• Employers	• Common understanding
• DWP staff	• Common goals

Real and lasting change also depends on a coherent and comprehensive social policy for sickness, disability and work, of which benefit restructuring is only one, albeit an important, element (Box 31). Every one of these elements must be in place and acting in a fully coordinated manner. Otherwise, benefit reform alone is unlikely to have any real impact and could even be counter-productive.

Box 31: DWP 5-year plan on IB reform (DWP 2005):
• No automatic assumption that sick or disabled people are incapable of doing any sort of work.
• More active GP and NHS management – empowering the health professions.
• Reforming the benefit – focusing on what claimants can do and how to help them do it, not on what they can't do.
• Comprehensive support to overcome obstacles and barriers and to return to work.
• Healthier workplaces.
• Employers' role and responsibilities.
• Disability rights.

11.2 A vision for the future

More than three-fold increase since 1979 in the number of people on longer-term incapacity benefits was a tragedy – for the country, for the economy, but most of all for these people and their families. The real tragedy was that so much of it should have been avoidable. Of course there are people with severe and permanent impairments who cannot reasonably be expected to work and who should receive appropriate and adequate support from society. But many IB recipients have less severe health problems that should be manageable, if they are given the right support. The real failure lay in giving the wrong kind of support, effectively condemning many people to a lifetime on benefits instead of providing better help to manage their health conditions and get on with their lives.

Since the IB reforms in 1994-95, inflow has fallen by 30% and the apparently inexorable rise in caseload has been stopped. That is better than any other country has achieved. But more still needs to be done to improve the situation. The goals now are to help more people to return to work (improve outflow) and to reduce the number of people on longer-term benefits. If we achieve even part of these goals it will be the first time any country has managed to do so. But the vision of the reforms considered in this paper goes much deeper than that:

- A fundamental transformation in the way sick and disabled people see themselves and are treated by the health care and social security systems.

- Ensuring that each person on sickness and disability benefits receives the most appropriate kind of help and support to meet their individual needs.

- Better support for people with severe and permanent impairments who cannot reasonably be expected to work.

- Better clinical, occupational and social management of less severe health conditions, so that everyone with the capacity to (return to) work is given the opportunity, support and incentives to do so.

- A better balance between social protection and social integration.

- A balanced approach to reform of the gateways to benefits, the benefit structure, condition management and support into work.

- Getting all stakeholders on side: particularly sick and disabled people themselves, GPs, employers and DWP Personal Advisers.

Real social security means much more than a benefits system: it is about citizenship, responsibilities and mutual obligations. All of this depends on a fundamental shift in the culture that surrounds health, sickness, disability, incapacity and work. Reform of incapacity benefits should reflect and will depend on that cultural change, and form part of the change, rather than expecting it to be the sole or even the primary driver of change. But the situation is eminently changeable with the right policy focus across central Government and other key players such as employers and GPs. It could potentially deliver huge gains for society, employers, DWP, the NHS and, most important, for sick and disabled people themselves and their families.

The challenge of changing the culture of sickness, disability and incapacity for work should not be underestimated, but neither should the prize: a world where sick and disabled people are given the opportunities, support and incentives they need to fulfil their potential, and are empowered to participate in and contribute to society. That is a world worth striving for.

Reducing long-term worklessness and the ill health that goes with it is potentially one of the most potent policy interventions to improve physical and mental health, and to reduce social disadvantage and poverty. The kind of fundamental cultural shift envisaged here could reduce much preventable ill health and lead directly to major health improvements. Social security is not just about passive support for people with poor health outcomes. Social security should provide active support for sick and disabled people and work closely with the NHS to improve health and social outcomes. This is not just a matter of benefits and costs: it is about improving health and about citizenship, social justice and fairness.

REFERENCES

Abberley P 1991 Handicapped by numbers: a critique of the OPCS disability surveys. Occasional Papers in Sociology No. 9 Bristol Polytechnic, Bristol www.leeds.ac.uk/disability-studies

Abel-Smith B, Titmuss K (Eds) 1987 The philosophy of welfare: selected writings of Richard M Titmuss. Allen & Unwin, London.

ABI/TUC 2002 Getting back to work: a rehabilitation discussion paper. Association of British Insurers/Trades Union Congress, London.

Acheson D 1998 Inequalities in Health Report. The Stationary Office, London

Alcock P Beatty C Fothergill S Macmillan R Yeandle S 2003 Work to welfare: how men become detached from the labour market. Cambridge University Press, Cambridge

Alexanderson K Norlund A (Eds) 2004 Sickness absence – causes, consequences, and physicians' sickness certification practice. A systematic literature review by the Swedish Council on Technology Assessment in Health Care. Scand J Public Health Suppl 63: 1-263

AMA 2000 Guides to the evaluation of permanent impairment. Eds: Cocchiarella L Andersson GBJ. Chicago, Ill: American Medical Association. Fifth Edition.

American Psychiatric Association 1994 Diagnostic and Statistical Manual of Mental Disorders. 4th Edition. (DSM-IV) American Psychiatric Association, Washington, DC

Anema JR van der Giezen AM Buijs PC van Mechelen W 2002 Ineffective disability management by doctors is an obstacle for return-to-work: a cohort study on low back pain patients sicklisted for 3-4 months. Occupational and Environmental Medicine 59:729-733.

Arluke A Kennedy L Kessler RC 1979 Re-examining the sick role concept: an empirical assessment. J Health & Social Behavior 20:30-36

Armitage P Berry G 1994 Statistical methods in medical research. Blackwell Science, Oxford.

Arrelov B Borgquist L Ljungberg D Scardsudd K 2003 The influence of changes of legislation concerning sickness absence on physicians' performance as certifiers. A population based study. Health Policy 63(3):259-268

Arskey H Thornton P Williams J 2002 Mapping employment focused services for disabled people. DWP In House Report 93. Dept for Work and Pensions, London

Arthur S Corden A Green A et al 1999 New Deal for Disabled People: Early Implementation. Department of Social Security Research Report No 106. The Stationary Office, London

Ashworth K Hartfree Y Stephenson A 2001 Well enough to work? Department of Social Security Research Report No 145 Corporate Document Services, Leeds

Aylward M 2003 Origins, practice and limitations of disability assessment medicine. In Halligan PW Bass C (Eds) Malingering and illness deception. Oxford University Press, Oxford. Chapter 22 pp 287-300

Aylward M 1999 Chronic fatigue and its syndromes: historical perspectives. www.eumass.com

Aylward M Locascio JJ 1995 Problems in the assessment of psychosomatic conditions in social security benefits and related commercial schemes. J Psychosomatic Res 39:755-765

Aylward M Sawney P 1999 Disability assessment medicine. BMJ 318:2-3

Bajekal M 2005 Healthy life expectancy by area deprivation: magnitude and trends in England, 1994-1999. Health Statistics Quarterly No 25:18-27

Bajekal M Harries T Bremun R Woodfield K 2004 Review of disability estimates and definitions. DWP In-house Report 128

Bane MJ Ellwood DT 1994 Welfare realities: from rhetoric to reform. Harvard University Press, Cambridge, Mass.

Barnes C 1991 Disabled people and discrimination: a case for anti-discrimination legislation. Hurst & Co, London

Barnes C Mercer G (Eds) 1995 Exploring the divide: illness and disability. The Disability Press, Leeds www.leeds.ac.uk/disability-studies

Barnes C Mercer G (Eds) 2004a Implementing the social model of disability: theory and research. The Disability Press, Leeds

Barnes C Mercer G (Eds) 2004b Disability Policy & practice: applying the social model of disability. The Disability Press, Leeds

Barnes H Baldwin S 1999 Social security, poverty and disability. In Ditch J (Ed) Introduction to social security: Policies, benefits and poverty. Routledge, London & New York. Chap 7 56-176

Barsky AJ 1988 The paradox of health. New Eng J Med 318:414-418

Barsky AJ Borus JF 1999 Functional somatic syndromes. Ann Intern Med 130:910-921

Bartley M Sacker A Schoon I Kelly MP Carmona C 2005 Work, non-work, job satisfaction and psychological health. NHS Health Development Agency, Sheffield.

Beatty C Fothergill S 2004 The diversion from 'unemployment' to 'sickness' across British regions and districts. Centre for Regional Economic and Social Research, Sheffield Hallam University, Sheffield.

Beaumont DG 2003a Rehabilitation and retention in the workplace - the interaction between general practitioners and occupational health professionals: a consensus statement. Occupational Medicine 3:254-255.

Beaumont DG 2003b The interaction between general practitioners and occupational health professionals in relation to rehabilitation for work: a Delphi study. Occupational Medicine 3:249-253.

Bemelmans-Videc M Rist R Vedung E (Eds) 1998 Carrots, Sticks, and Sermons: Policy Instruments and their Evaluation, Transaction Publishers, New Brunswick NJ.

Berglind H Gerner U 2002 Motivation and return to work among the long-term sicklisted: an action theory perspective. Disability and Rehabilitation 24:719-726

Berkowitz ED Burkhauser RV 1996 A United States perspective on disability programs. In Aarts LJM Burkhauser RV de Jong PR (Eds) 1996 Curing the Dutch disease: an international perspective on disability policy reform. Avebury, Aldershot Chap 4 pp 71-91

Berthoud R 1998 Disability benefits: a review of the issues and options for reform. Joseph Rowntree Foundation, York

Berthoud R 2003 Multiple disadvantage in employment. Joseph Rowntree Foundation, London

Berthoud R 2004 The profile of exits from incapacity related benefits over time. Version 1: July 2004 DWP internal document.

Bevan S Hayday S 2001 Costing sickness absence in the UK. Report 382. Institute for Employment Studies, Brighton.

Beveridge W 1942 Social Insurance and Allied Services. Cmd 6404 HMSO, London

Bickenbach J Chatterji S Badley EM Ustun TB 1999 Models of disablement, universalism and the international classification of impairments, disabilities and handicaps. Social Science and Medicine 48:1173-1187

Biklen D 1988 The myth of clinical judgment Journal of Social Issues;44:127

Blair T 1995 The rights we enjoy reflect the duties we owe. The Spectator lecture 22.3.95 In: Blair T New Britain: my vision of a young country. Fourth Estate, London 1996

Blair T 1996 New Britain: my vision of a young country. Fourth Estate, London

Blair T 1997 'The 21st Century Welfare State'. Social Policy and Economic Performance Conference. Rijksmuseum, Amsterdam 24 January 1997

Blair T 1999 Beveridge revisited: a welfare state for the 21st century. In R Walker (Ed) Ending child poverty: popular welfare for the 21st century? The Policy Press, Bristol pp7-18

Blair T 2004 Reforming the welfare state. IPPR Speech 11 October 2004

Bogduk N 2000 Editorial What's in a name? The labelling of back pain. Medical Journal of Australia 173: 400-401

Bolderson H 1991 Social Security, Disability and Rehabilitation: Conflicts in the Development of Social Policy 1914-1946. Jessica Kingsley Publishers, London

Bolderson H Mabbett D Hvinda B et al 2002 Social security and social integration. Definition of disability in Europe: a comparative analysis. European Commission: Employment and Social Affairs, Brussels.

Bowling J Coleman N Wapshott J Carpenter H 2004 Destination of benefit leavers. DWP In House Research Report 132. HMSO, London.

Boyd KM 2000 Disease, illness, sickness, health, healing and wholeness: exploring some elusive concepts. Med Humanit 26(1):9-17

Brage S 2005 Preliminary results of Norwegian study of GP sick certification. Presented to Fit for Work International Research Conference, Liverpool, March 2005

Briner RB 1996 Absence from work. Brit Med J 313:874-877.

British Pain Society 2003 Pain in Europe 2003. www.britishpainsociety.org

Brooker A-S Clarke J Sinclair S Pennick V Hogg-Johnson S 2000 Effective disability management and return-to-work practices. In Sullivan T (Ed) Injury and the new world of work: pp246-261, University of British Columbia Press, Vancouver

Bruyere SM Golden TB Zeitzer I 2003 What works and looking ahead: U.S. Policies and Practices Facilitating Return to Work for Social Security Beneficiaries. Paper prepared for UK/US Pathways to Work in the 21st Century Seminar and Workshop, May 1-2, 2003 Washington, DC

Bryson A Kasparova D 2003 Profiling benefit claimants in Britain: a feasibility study. Dept for Work and Pensions Research Report 196 Corporate Document Services, Leeds

BSRM 2000 Vocational rehabilitation. The way forward. British Society of Rehabilitation Medicine, London

BSRM 2004 Musculoskeletal rehabilitation. British Society of Rehabilitation Medicine, London

Burchardt T 1999 The Evolution of Disability Benefits in the UK: Re-weighting the basket", CASEpaper 26, London School of Economics, London.

Burchardt T 2000a The dynamics of being disabled. Journal of Social Policy 29:645-668

Burchardt T 2000b Enduring economic exclusion: disabled people, income and work. Joseph Rowntree Foundation, York.

Burchardt T 2001 Lessons for employment policy. Joseph Rowntree Foundation, York.

Burchardt T 2003a Employment retention and the onset of sickness or disability: evidence from the Labour Force Survey longitudinal datasets. DWP In House Research Report 109. Dept for Work and Pensions, London

Burchardt T 2003b Disability, capability and social exclusion. In Millar J (Ed) Understanding social security: issues for policy and practice. The Policy Press, Bristol Chap 8 pp145-165

Burdorf A van Duijn M Koes B 2002 The natural course of sickness absence due to low-back pain and prognostic factors for return to work among occupational populations. (unpublished work)

Burton AK, Main CJ. 2000. Obstacles to recovery from work-related musculoskeletal disorders. In Karwowski W (Ed) International encyclopaedia of ergonomics and human factors. Taylor & Francis, London. pp1542-1544

Burton C 2003 Beyond somatisation: a review of the understanding and treatment of medically unexplained physical symptoms (MUPS). British Journal of General Practice 53:231-239.

Bury M 2000 A comment on the ICIDH2. Disability & Society 15:1073-7

Cardol M Schellevis FG Spreeuwenberg P van de Lisdonk EH 2005 Changes in patients' attitudes towards the management of minor ailments. Brit J Gen Prac 55:516-521

Carson AJ Best S Postma K Stone J Warlow C Sharpe M 2003 The outcome of neurology outpatients with medically unexplained symptoms: a prospective cohort study. Journal of Neurology Neurosurgery and Psychiatry 74:897-900.

Carson AJ Ringbauer B MacKenzie L Warlow C Sharpe M 2000a Neurological disease, emotional disorder, and disability: they are related: a study of 300 consecutive new referrals to a neurology outpatient department. Journal of Neurology Neurosurgery and Psychiatry 68:202-6.

Carson AJ Ringbauer B Stone J McKenzie L Warlow C Sharpe M 2000b Do medically unexplained symptoms matter? A prospective cohort study of 300 new referrals to neurology outpatient clinics. Journal of Neurology Neurosurgery and Psychiatry 68:207-10

Carter JT Birrell LN 2000 Occupational health guidelines for the management of low back pain at work - principal recommendations. Faculty of Occupational Medicine, London www.facoccmed.ac.uk

Cassidy JD Carroll L Cote P Senthilselvan A 1997 The prevalence of graded chronic low back pain severity and its effect on general health: a population based study. Presented to the International Society for the Study of the Lumbar Spine, Singapore

CBI 2000 Their health in your hands. Focus on occupational health partnerships. Confederation of British Industry, London

CBI 2003 Absence and labour turnover 2003. The lost billions: addressing the cost of absence. Confederation of British Industry, London.

CBI 2004 Room for improvement: CBI absence and labour turnover 2004. Confederation of British Industry, London. www.cipd.org.uk

Cedraschi C Nordin M Nachemson AL Vischer TL 1998 Health care providers should use a common language in relation to low back pain patients. In Nordin M Cedraschi C Vischer TL (Eds) New approaches to the low back pain patient. Bailleire's Clinical Rheumatology. Bailliere Tindall, London 12:1-15

Chamberlayne P Cooper A Freeman R Rustin M 1999 Welfare and culture in Europe. Jessica Kingsley Publishers, London

CIPD Employee Absence 2004. Chartered Institute of Personnel and Development, London. July 2004 www.cipd.org.uk

Clark DM 2005 Cognitive Behavioural Therapy: the evidence. Presentation to Cabinet Office Strategy Unit seminar, Whitehall 20 January 2005

CMG 2004a A guide for registered medical practitioners IB204 Section 3 Advice to patients regarding fitness for work. Department for Work and Pensions, Corporate Medical Group, London.

CMG 2004b Patients: their employment and their health. Desk aid and educational DVD. Department for Work and Pensions, Corporate Medical Group, London

Coetzer P 2001 Assessing impairment and disability for syndromes presenting with chronic fatigue. J Insur Med 33:170-182

Collins P Rossiter A (Eds) 2004 On condition. Social Market Foundation, London

Commission on Social Justice. 1994 Strategies for national renewal. IPPR, London

Corden A Sainsbury R 2001 Incapacity benefits and work incentives. DSS Research Report No 141. Her Majesty's Stationery Office, London.

Corden A Thornton P 2002 Employment programmes for disabled people: Lessons from research evaluations. DWP In-House Report 90 Department for Work and Pensions, London.

COST Action B13. 2003 Low back pain: guidelines for its management. European Commission Research Directorate General. www.backpaineurope.org

Council of Europe 1996 Recommendation No R(92)6 of the Committee of Ministers to Member States on a Coherent policy for people with disabilities (adopted by the Committee of Ministers on 9 April 1992 at the 474th meeting of the Ministers' Deputies)

Council of Europe 2002 Assessing Disability in Europe – similarities and differences. Report of a Working Party. Council of Europe Publishing, Strasbourg

Council of Europe 2003a Recommendation 1592 Towards full social inclusion of people with disabilities.

Council of Europe 2003b Rehabilitation and integration of people with disabilities: policy and legislation. Council of Europe Publishing, Strasbourg

Cox RH 1998 The consequences of welfare reform: how conceptions of social rights are changing. Journal of Social Policy 27:1-16

CPAG 2001 Welfare Benefits Handbook. 3rd Edition. Child Poverty Action Group, London

CPAG 2004 Poverty: the facts (summary). Child Poverty Action Group, London.

Croft PR Macfarlane GF Papageorgiou AC Thomas E Silman AJ 1998 Outcome of low back pain in general practice: a prospective study. British Medical Journal 16:1356-1359

Crombie IK Croft PR Linton SJ LeResche L Von Korff M 1999 Epidemiology of Pain: International Association for the Study of Pain Task Force on Epidemiology. IASP Press, Seattle

CSAG 1994 Report on back pain. Clinical Standards Advisory Group. HMSO, London

Davies V Johnson C 2001 Moving towards work: The short-term impact of ONE, DSS Research Report No. 140. Dept of Social Security, London.

de Boer WEL Brenninkmeijer V Zuidam W 2004 Long-term disability arrangements: a comparative study of assessment and quality control. TNO Report. The Netherlands Organisation for Applied Scientific Research, Hoofddorp, the Netherlands.

de Bont A 2005 Guidelines as policy instruments. Presented to 'Cost of Vagueness' - International Social Policy Seminar, Amsterdam, The Netherlands. 8 April 2005

de Jong PR 2003 Disability and disability insurance. In: Prinz C (Ed.) European Disability Pension Policies. 11 Country Trends 1970-2002, Ashgate, Aldershot/Brookfield. Chap 2 pp77-106

Deacon A 1994 Justifying workfare: the historical context of the workfare debates. In White M (Ed) Unemployment and public policy in a changing labour market. Policy Studies Institute, London

Deacon A 1996 Commentary: welfare and character. In Field F Stakeholder welfare. Institute of Economic Affairs Health & Welfare Unit, London. Choice in Welfare No. 32 pp60-73

Deacon A 1997 From welfare to work: lessons from America. Institute of Economic Affairs, Health & Welfare Unit, London

Deacon A 1998 The Green Paper on welfare reform: a case for enlightened self-interest? Political Quarterly 69:306-311

Deacon A 2004 Can conditionality be justified? In Collins P Rossiter A (Eds) On condition. Social Market Foundation, London

Deal M 2003 Disabled people's attitudes toward other impairment groups: a hierarchy of impairments. Disability & Society 18:897-910

Dean H 2003 Re-conceptualising welfare-to-work for people with multiple problems and needs. J Social Policy 32:441-459

Dennett D 2003 Freedom evolves. Viking Press, New York

Dept of Health 2002a Improvement, expansion and reform: the next 3 years: priorities and planning framework 2003 – 2006. www.dh.gov.uk

Dept of Health 2002b The expert patient: a new approach to chronic disease management in the 21st century. Dept of Health, London www.dh.gov.uk

Dept of Health 2002c NHS Expert Patients Programme. Self-management of long-term health conditions: a handbook for people with chronic disease. The Stationery Office, London

Dept of Health 2004a Public Health White Paper. Choosing health: making healthier choices easier. Cm 6374 Chap 7 Work and health.

Dept of Health 2004b Improving Chronic Disease Management. www.dh.gov.uk

Dept of Health/DRC 2004 Framework for Partnership Action on Disability 2004/05. Dept of Health and the Disability Rights Commission (www.dh.gov.uk/assetRoot/04/08/35/05/04083505)

Deyo RA Battie M Beurskens AJ et al 1998 Outcome measures for low back pain research. A proposal for standardized use. Spine 23:2003-13.

DHSS 1985a Severe Disablement Allowance Handbook for Adjudicating Medical Authorities. Dept of Health and Social Security, London

DHSS 1985b Green Paper. Reform of Social Security. Cmnd 9517 HMSO, London

DHSS 1985c White Paper. Reform of Social Security Cmnd 9691 London, HMSO

DHSS 1986 Industrial Injuries Handbook for Adjudicating Medical Authorities. Dept of Health and Social Security, London

Dickens S Mowlam A Woodfield K 2004a Incapacity Benefit Reforms – early findings from qualitative research. DWP Research Report No. 202.

Dickens S Mowlam A Woodfield K 2004b Incapacity Benefit Reforms - the Personal Adviser Role & Practices. National Centre for Social Research Report prepared for the Dept for Work and Pensions

Disability Rights Task Force 1998 Working Group on defining disability discrimination. 23 October 1998.

Donoghue C 2003 Challenging the authority of the medical definition of disability: an analysis of the resistance to the social constructionist paradigm. Disability & Society 18:199-208

Doran T Drever F Whitehead M 2004 Is there a north-south divide in social class inequalities in health in Great Britain? Cross sectional study using data from the 2001 census. BMJ 328:1043-5

Dorsett R Finlayson L Ford R Marsh A White M Zarb G 1998 Leaving Incapacity Benefit. Department of Social Security Research Report No 86. The Stationary Office, London

Drake R 1999 Understanding disability policies. Macmillan, Basingstoke

DRC 2003a The DRC 2003 attitudes and awareness study. Disability Rights Commission, London. www.drc-gb.org

DRC 2003b Response to the DWP Consultation Document, 'Pathways to Work, Helping People'. Disability Rights Commission, London. www.drc-gb.org

DRC 2004a Disability Briefing. Disability Rights Commission, London. December www.drc-gb.org

DRC 2004b Conditions for conditionality. Disability Rights Commission, London. www.drc-gb.org

DRC 2004c Disability Rights Commission Strategic Plan 2004-2007. Disability Rights Commission, London. www.drc-gb.org

DSS 1993 The growth of social security. Dept of Social Security, London

DSS 1994 The medical assessment for Incapacity Benefit. Dept of Social Security, London

DSS 1996 The government's expenditure plans 1996-97 to 1998-99. Departmental Report, Department of Social Security. Cm 3213. HMSO, London

Duckworth S 2001 The disabled person's perspective. In New beginnings: A symposium on disability. UNUM, London.

Duncan SS Edwards R 1998 Lone mothers and paid work: discourses, contexts and actions. Macmillan, London

Dunnell K 1995 Population review (2): are we healthier? Population Trends 82:12-18

DWP 1995 Guidance on matters to be taken into account in determining questions relating to the definition of disability
http://www.direct.gov.uk/DisabledPeople/RightsAndObligations/YourRights/YourRightsArticles/fs/en?CONTENT_ID=4001069&chk=Bjab3%2B

DWP 2000 Incapacity Benefit Handbook for Medical Services Doctors. Department for Work and Pensions, London

DWP 2002 Pathways to work: Helping people into employment. Department for Work and Pensions Cm 5690. London: HMSO

DWP 2003a Review of Employers' Liability Compulsory Insurance. First stage report. Department for Work and Pensions, London www.dwp.gov.uk

DWP 2003b Review of Employers' Liability Compulsory Insurance. Second stage report. Department for Work and Pensions, London www.dwp.gov.uk

DWP 2003c Pathways to work: helping people into employment - the government's response and action plan. Cm 5830. Department for Work and Pensions. HMSO, London

DWP 2004 Building capacity for work: a UK framework for vocational rehabilitation. Department for Work and Pensions, London

DWP 2005 Department for Work and Pensions Five Year Strategy: Opportunity and security throughout life. Department for Work and Pensions, London.

DWP/HSE 2004 Managing sickness absence in the public sector. A joint review by the Ministerial Task Force for Health, Safety and Productivity and the Cabinet Office.

Dwyer P 1998 Conditional citizens? Welfare rights ad responsibilities in the late 1990s. Critical Social Policy 18:493-517

Dwyer P 2000 Welfare rights and responsibilities: contesting social citizenship. Policy Press, Bristol.

Dwyer P 2002 Making sense of social citizenship: some user views on welfare rights and responsibilities. Critical Social Policy 22:273-299

EEF 2004a Managing long-term sickness absence and rehabilitation: summary of the EEF/IRS survey. www.eef.co.uk Also published as Silcox S Managing long-term sickness absence and rehabilitation. Part 1: IRS Employment Review 2004;794:18-24. Part 2: IRS Employment Review 2004;796:18-24.

EEF 2004b Fit for work: the complete guide to managing sickness absence and rehabilitation. www.eef.co.uk

Einerhand M Nekkers G 2004 Modernizing social security: changing responsibilities and individual choice. International Social Security Review 57:25-43

Elwan A 1999 Poverty and disability: A survey of the literature. Social Protection Discussion Paper No. 9932. Social Protection Unit, The World Bank; Washington DC.

Engel GL 1997 The need for a new medical model: a challenge for biomedicine. Science 196:129-136.

Englund L Tibblin G Svardsudd K 2000 Effects on physicians' sick-listing practice of an administrative reform narrowing sick-listing benefits. Scand J Prim Health Care 18:215-9

Epstein M Mendelson G Strauss N 1998 Clinical Guideline to the rating of psychiatric impairment. Victoria Government Gazettte No S87 Melbourne, Australia. 28 August 1998

Eriksen HR, Svendsrod R, Ursin G, Ursin H. 1998 Prevalence of subjective health complaints in the Nordic European countries in 1993. Eur J Public Health 8: 294-298

Euzeby C 2004 Rethinking social security in the European Union: extending fundamental universal rights. International Social Security Review 57:85-103

Evanoff B Abedin S Grayson D Dale AM Wolf L Bohr P 2002 Is disability under-reported following work injury? Journal of Occupational Rehabilitation 12:139-150.

Fabrega H, Tyma S. 1976 Language and cultural influences in the description of pain. British Journal of Medical Psychology 49:349-371

FACS 2002 Participation support for a more equitable society: Final report of the reference group on welfare reform. Australian Department of Family and Community Services, Canberra. www.facs.gov.au

Faculty of Occupational Medicine 2004 Position paper on age and employment. Faculty of Occupational Medicine, London

Feuerstein M Zastowny TR 1999 Occupational rehabilitation: Multidisciplinary management of work-related musculoskeletal pain and disability. In: Gatchel RJ, Turk DC (Eds) 1999 Psychological approaches to pain management. A practitioners' handbook. The Guilford Press, London. pp 458-485

Feuerstein MA 1991 A multidisciplinary approach to the prevention, evaluation and management of work disability. J Occup Rehab 1:5-12.

Field F 1996 Stakeholder welfare. Institute of Economic Affairs Health & Welfare Unit, London. Choice in Welfare No. 32

Field F 1997 Reforming welfare. The Social Market Foundation, London

Field F 1998 Reflections on welfare reform. The Social Market Foundation London

Finerman R Bennet LA 1995 Overview: guilt, blame and shame in sickness. Soc Sci Med 40:1-3

Finkelstein V 1980 Attitudes and Disabled People. World Rehabilitation Fund, Geneva

Finkelstein V French S 1993 Towards a psychology of disability. In Swain J Finkelstein V French S Oliver M (Eds) Disabling barriers – enabling environments. SAGE Publications, London Chap 1.3 pp 26-33

Fishbain DA Cole B Cutler R Lewis J Rosomoff HL Rosomoff RS 2003 A structured, evidence-based review of the meaning of nonorganic physical signs: Waddell signs. Pain Medicine 4:141-181

Fishbain DA Rosomoff HL Goldberg M et al. 1993 The prediction of return to the workplace after multidisciplinary pain center treatment. Clinical Journal of Pain 9:3-15.

Fishbein M Ajzen I 1975 Belief, attitude, intention and behavior: an introduction to theory and research. Addison-Wesley, Reading MA

Fordyce WE 1995 Back pain in the workplace. Report of an IASP Task Force. IASP Press, Seattle.

Foucault M 1973 The birth of the clinic: an archaeology of medical perception. Tavistock, London

Frank J Brooker A-S DeMaio SE et al. 1996 Disability resulting from occupational low back pain. Part II: What do we know about secondary prevention? A review of the scientific evidence on prevention after disability begins. Spine 21:2918-2929.

Frank J Sinclair S Hogg-Johnson S et al 1998 Preventing disability from work-related low-back pain. New evidence gives new hope - if we can just get all the players onside. Canadian Medical Association Journal 158:1625-1631.

French S 1993 Disability, impairment or something in between? In Swain J Finkelstein V French S Oliver M (Eds) Disabling barriers – enabling environments. SAGE Publications, London Chap 1.2 pp 17-25

Gallacher EB 1976 Lines of reconstruction and extension in the Parsonian sociology of illness. Soc Sci Med 10:207-218

Gardiner J 1997 Bridges from benefit to work: a review. Joseph Rowntree Foundation, York www.jrf.org.uk/knowledge/findings/socialpolicy/sp130.asp

Gatchel R, Turk DC 2002 Psychological approaches to pain management. Guildford Press, New York.

Geisser ME Robinson ME Miller QL Bade SM 2003 Psychosocial factors and functional capacity evaluation among persons with chronic pain. J Occup Rehabil 13(4):259-276

Gilbert N (Ed) 2000 Targeting social benefits: international perspectives and trends. International Social Security Series Volume 1. Transaction Publishers, New Brunswick NJ.

Gilbert N Van Voorhis RA (Eds) 2003 Changing patterns of social protection. International Social Security Series Volume 9. Transaction Publishers, New Brunswick NJ.

Gimeno D Benavides FG Benach J Amick BC 2004 Distribution of sickness absence in the European Union countries. Occup Environ Med 61:867-9

Glenton C 2003 Chronic back pain sufferers – striving for the sick role. Soc Sci Med 57:2243-2252

Glouberman S 2001 Towards a New Perspective on Health Policy. Canadian Policy Research Networks Study No H|03 http://www.cprn.org/cprn.htm

Glouberman S Kisilevsky S Groff P Nicholson C 2000 Towards a New Concept of Health: Three Discussion Papers. Canadian Policy Research Networks Study No H|03 http://www.cprn.org/cprn.htm

GMC 1998 Good Medical Practice: the duties and responsibilities of a doctor. General Medical Council, London

Goldstone C Douglas L 2003 Pathways to Work from Incapacity Benefits: A pre-pilot exploration of staff and customer attitudes. Report prepared for DWP. Department for Work and Pensions, London

Goodin RE 2002 Structures of mutual obligation. J Social Policy 31:579-596

Gordon GH 1978 The criminal law of Scotland. 2nd Edition. The Scottish Universities Law Institute, Edinburgh. (3rd edition Edited by MGA Christie 2000)

Graham H 2004 Tackling inequalities in health in England: remedying health disadvantages, narrowing health gaps or reducing health gradients. J Social Policy 33:115-131

Green H Marsh A Connolly H Payne J 2003 Final Effects of ONE. Part 1: The medium-term effects of compulsory participation in ONE. DWP Research Report 183 Dept for Work and Pensions, London

Green H, Smith A, Lilly R, Marsh Johnson C, Fielding S. 2000 First Effects of ONE. Department of Social Security Research Report No 126. The Stationary Office, London

Green P 2003 The patient seemed to be making an effort but the results were not valid. The Canadian Neuropsychologist. The Canadian Psychological Association Section 23 Clinical Neuropsychology Newsletter, May 2003, 6-12

Greenhalgh T 1997 Personal view: I need you to sign this, doctor. BMJ 314:80

Grewal I Joy S Lewis J Swales K Woodfield K 2002 Disabled for life? Attitudes towards, and experiences of, disability in Britain. DWP Research Report 173. Department for Work and Pensions, London.

Grewal I McManus S Arthur S Reith L 2004. Making transition: addressing barriers in services for disabled people, Department of Work and Pensions Research Report No. 204, Corporate Document Services, Leeds.

Griffiths J 1969 Memory. JM Dent, London

Grundy E Ahlburg D Ali M Breeze E Sloggett A 1999 Disability in Great Britain: Results from the 1996/97 Disability Follow-up to the Family Resources Survey. DWP Research Report No. 94. Department for Work and Pensions, London.

Gureje O Simon GE Ustun TB et al 1997 Somatization in cross-cultural perspective: a World Health Organisation study in primary care. Am J Psychiatry 154:989-995

Hadler NM 1995 The disabling backache: an international perspective. Spine 20:640-649

Hadler NM 1996a If you have to prove you are ill, you can't get well: the object lesson of fibromyalgia. Spine 21:2397-2400

Hadler NM 1996b The disabled, the disallowed, the disaffected and the disavowed. J Occup Environ Med 38:247-254

Hadler NM 1997 Workers with disabling back pain. New Eng J Med 337:341-343

Halderson EMH Brages S Johannessen TS Telines G Ursin H 1996 Musculoskeletal pain: concepts of disease, illness and sick certification in health professionals in Norway. Scand J Rheumatol 25:224

Hall H McIntosh G Melles T Holowachuk B Wai E 1994 Effect of discharge recommendations on outcome. Spine 18:2033-2037.

Halligan PW Bass C Oakley DA (Eds) 2003 Malingering and illness deception. Oxford, Oxford University Press

Halpern D Bates C Beales G Heathfield A 2004 Personal Responsibility and Changing Behaviour: the state of knowledge and its implications for public policy. Issue Paper. Cabinet Office: Prime Minister's Strategy Unit, London.

Harris AI Cox E Smith CRW 1971 Handicapped and impaired in Great Britain. Office of Population Censuses and Surveys, Social Survey Division. HMSO: London

Harris J 1999 Beveridge and the Beveridge Report – life, ideas, influence. In R Walker (Ed) Ending child poverty: popular welfare for the 21st century? The Policy Press, Bristol pp 21-27

Hattersley R 1998 Speech to the National Local Government Forum Against Poverty conference on Welfare Reform, Stirling. 29 May 1998

Haug TT Mykletun A Dahl AA 2004 The Association Between Anxiety, Depression, and Somatic Symptoms in a Large Population: The HUNT-II Study. Psychosomatic Medicine 66:845–851

Hayden C Boaz A Taylor F 1999 Attitudes and Aspirations of Older People: A Qualitative Study. DSS Research Report No 102. The Stationary Office, London

Haynes R Bentham G Lovett A Eimermann J 1997 Effect of labour market conditions on reporting of limiting long term illness and permanent sickness in England and Wales, J Epidemiol Community Health 51:283-288

Hiebert R Skovron ML Nordin M Crane M 2003 Work restrictions and outcome of nonspecific low back pain. Spine 28:722-728.

Hill M 1990 Social Security Policy in Britain. Edward Elgar, Aldershot

Hills J Ditch J Glennerster (Eds) 1994 Beveridge and social security: An international retrospective. Clarendon Press, Oxford

Hills J Gardiner K 1997 The future of welfare: a guide to the debate. Joseph Rowntree Foundation, London. Revised edition

Hirsch D 2003 Crossroads after 50: improving choices in work and retirement. Joseph Rowntree Foundation, York.

Hiscock J Ritchie J 2001 The role of GPs in sickness certification. Dept for Work and Pensions Research Report No 148 The Stationery Office, London

HM Government 1944 Disabled Persons (Employment) Act 1944

HM Government 1946 National Insurance (Industrial Injuries) Act 1946

HM Government 1976 Social Security (Medical Evidence) Regulations 1976 (as amended)

HM Government 1990 Access to Health Records Act 1990

HM Government 1991 Disability Living Allowance and Disability Working Allowance Act 1991

HM Government 1992 Social Security Contributions and Benefits Act 1992

HM Government 1994 Social Security (Incapacity for Work) Act 1994 Chapter 18

HM Government 1995a Disability Discrimination Act 1995

HM Government 1995b Social Security (Incapacity for Work) (General) Regulations

HM Government 1998a New Ambitions for Our Country: A New Contract for Welfare. Cm 3805. London: HMSO

HM Government 1998b A New Contract for Welfare: Principles into Practice. Cm 4101. London: HMSO

HM Government 1998c A New Contract for Welfare: Support for Disabled People. Cm 4103. London: HMSO

HM Government 1999 Welfare Reform and Pensions Act 1999

HM Government 2005 Disability Discrimination Amendment Act 2005

HMT 2000 Review of ill health retirement in the public sector. Her Majesty's Treasury, London. www.hm-treasury.gov.uk

HMT 2003 Full employment in every region. Her Majesty's Treasury, London. www.hm-treasury.gov.uk

HMT 2004 Pre Budget Report. Opportunity for all: the strength to take the long-term decisions for Britain. Her Majesty's Treasury, London. www.hm-treasury.gov.uk

Hofman B 2002 On the triad disease, illness and sickness. J Med Philosophy 27(6):651-673

Holland-Elliott K 2004 Occupational health perspective. In Holland-Elliott K (Ed) What about the workers? Proceedings of an RSM Symposium, London, 30 March 2004. Royal Society of Medicine Press, London. Chap 8 pp 32-34

Hoskins DB Dobbernack D Kuptsch C (Eds) 2001 Social security at the dawn of the 21st century. Social Security Series Volume 2. Transaction Publishers, New Brunswick NJ.

Howard M 2003 An interactionist perspective on barriers and bridges to work for disabled people. IPPR Research paper. Institute for Public Policy Research, London. (www.ippr.org)

Howard M 2004a Equal citizenship and Incapacity Benefit reform. Paper to IPPR seminar on the future of incapacity benefits. London 28 October 2004. Disability Rights Commission, London. www.drc-gb.org

Howard M 2004b Definitions from disability programmes in other countries. Paper to the discussion forum on the definition of disability. Social Security Advisory Board.

HSC 2000 Management of health and safety at work. Management of Health and Safety at Work Regulations 1999. Approved Code of Practice. HSE Books, Sudbury.

HSC 2004 A strategy for workplace health and safety in Great Britain to 2010 and beyond. Health and Safety Commission, London. www.hse.gov.uk/aboutus/strategy2010.pdf

HSE 2000 Securing health together. HSE Books, Sudbury.

HSE 2002 Survey of use of Occupational Health Support. Health & Safety Executive, London. Contract Research Report 445/2002.

HSE 2004 Managing sickness absence and return to work: an employers' and managers' guide. HSE Books, London

HSE 2005 Description of the Service: Evaluation of Workplace Health Direct. www.hse.gov.uk HSE 6141/R56.114

Huddleston T 2000 Explaining the growth in the number of people claiming incapacity benefits. DWP Internal paper

Hume D 1748 Of the original contract.

Humphrey A Costigan P Pickering K Stratford N Barnes M 2002 Factors affecting the labour market participation of older workers. DWP Research Report N0. 200 Corporate Document Services, Leeds.

Hurst R 2000 To revise or not to revise? Disability & Society 15:1083-7

Hussey S Hoddinott P Wilson P Dowell J Barbour R 2004 Sickness certification system in the United Kingdom: qualitative study of the views of general practitioners in Scotland. BMJ 328:88-91

IIAC 2004 Stress at work as a prescribed disease and post-traumatic stress disorder. Position Paper 13. Industrial Injuries Advisory Council, London.

ISSA 1996 Social protection in Europe: outline of social security programmes 1996. International Social Security Association, Geneva.

James P, Cunningham I, Dibben P. 2002 Absence management and the issues of job retention and return to work. Human Resource Management Journal 12:82-94.

James P, Cunningham I, Dibben P. 2003 Job retention and vocational rehabilitation: The development and evaluation of a conceptual framework. Research Report 106. Her Majesty's Stationery Office, London.

Jenkins SP Rigg JA 2004 Disability and disadvantage: selection, onset and duration effects. J Social Policy 33:479-501

Jones P Cullis J 2000 'Individual failure' and the analytics of social policy. J Soc Policy 29:73-93

Kendall L Harker L (Eds) 2002 From welfare to wellbeing: the future of social care. Institute for Public Policy Research, London

Kerns RD Rosenberg R Jamison RN Caudill MA Haythornewaite JA 1997 Readiness to adopt a self-management approach to chronic pain: the Pain Stages of Change Questionnaire (PSOCQ). Pain 72:227-234

King D Wickham-Jones M 1999 From Clinton to Blair: the Democratic (Party) origins of welfare to work. Political Quarterly 70:62-74

King PM Tuckwell N Barrett TE 1998 A critical review of functional capacity evaluations. Physical Therapy 78:852-866

Kingson ER Schulz JH (Eds) 1997 Social Security in the 21st Century. Oxford University Press, New York.

Kirby S Riley R 2004 Compulsory work-focused interviews for inactive benefit claimants: an evaluation of the British ONE pilots. Labour Economics 11:415-429

Kitchen R 2003 Investigating benefit fraud and illness deception in the United Kingdom. In Halligan PW Bass C Oakley DA Malingering and illness deception. Oxford, Oxford University Press chap 24:313-322

Kleinman A 1988 The illness narratives: suffering, health and the human condition Basic Books

Krause N Dasinger LK Neuhauser F 1998 Modified work and return to work: a review of the literature. J Occup Rehabil 8: 113-139.

Krause N Frank JW Dasinger LK Sullican TJ Sinclair SJ 2001 Determinants of duration of disability and return to work after work-related injury and illness: challenges for future research. Am J Ind Med 40(4):464-484

Kroenke K Mangelsdorff D 1989 Common symptoms in ambulatory care: incidence, evaluation, therapy and outcome. Amer J Med 86:262-6.

Kuptsch C Zeitzer IR 2001 Public disability programs under new complex pressures. In Hoskins DB Dobbernack D Kuptsch C (Eds) Social security at the dawn of the 21st century. Transaction Publishers, New Brunswick NJ. Chap 8 pp 205-230

Law Commission (England) 1998 Liability for psychiatric illness. LAW COMM No 249

Layard R 2004 Mental health: Britain's biggest social problem. Cabinet Office Prime Minister's Strategy Unit, London

Lazarus RA Folkman S 1984 Stress, appraisal and coping. Springer, New York

Le Grand J 1997 Knights, knaves or pawns? Human behaviour and social policy. Journal of Social Policy 26:149-169

Le Grand J 2003 Motivation, agenda and public policy: of knights and knaves, pawns and queens. Oxford University Press, Oxford.

Leech C 2004 Renaissance project: preventing chronic disability from low back pain. Irish Department of Social & Family Affairs, Dublin.

Leech C 2005 Preventing chronic disability from low back pain: Ireland's Renaissance Project. Disability Medicine 5:15-25

Legard R Lewis J Hiscock J Scott J 2002 Evaluation of the Capability Report: identifying the work-related capabilities of incapacity benefits claimants. DWP Research Report No. 162. Dept for Work and Pensions, London.

Leonard NH Beauvais LL Scholl RW 1995 A self-concept model of work motivation. Paper presented to the Annual Meeting of the Academy of Management. http://www.cba.uri.edu/Scholl/Papers/Self_Concept_Motivation.htm

Levine D 1997 Reinventing disability policy. Working Paper No. 65, Institute of Industrial Relations, Berkeley.

LFS Labour Force Survey. Spring 2004. Office of National Statistics, London www.statistics.gov.uk Quarterly Supplement. London: The Stationary Office

Lilley P 1993 Benefits and costs: securing the future of social security. The 1993 Mais Lecture by the Secretary of State for Social Security. 23 June 1993 DSS Press Release 93/114

Lilley P 1995 winning the welfare debate. Social Market Foundation, London

Linton SJ 2002 New avenues for the prevention of chronic musculoskeletal pain and disability. Elsevier Science B.V., Amsterdam

Locke J 1690 An essay concerning the true, original extent and end of civil government.

Loeser JD Henderlite SE Conrad DA 1995 Incentive effects of workers' compensation benefits: a literature synthesis. Medical Care Research and Review 52:34-59

Lonsdale S 1993 Invalidity Benefit: an international comparison. Dept of Social Security In-House Report No. 1 DSS, London

Lonsdale S Aylward MA 1996 United Kingdom perspective on disability policy. In Aarts LJM, Burkhauser RV, de Jong PR Curing the Dutch disease: an international perspective on disability policy reform. Avebury, Aldershot. Chap 5 pp 93-115

Loumidis J Stafford B Youngs R et al 2001a Evaluation of the New Deal for Disabled People Personal Adviser Service pilot. DWP Research Report No 144. Corporate Document Services, Leeds.

Loumidis J Youngs R Lessof C Stafford B 2001b New deal for disabled people: national survey of incapacity benefit claimants. DWP Research Report No 160 Corporate Document Services, Leeds

Lund B 1999 Ask not what your community can do for you: obligations, New Labour and welfare reform. Critical Social Policy 19:447-462

Luz J Green MS 1997 Sickness absenteeism from work – a critical review of the literature. Public Health Rev 25(2):89-122

Mackay S Rowlingson R 1999 Social security in Britain. Macmillan Press, Basingstoke

Main CJ 1983 The modified somatic perception questionnaire. Journal of Psychosomatic Research 27:503-514

Main CJ Burton AK 2000 Economic and occupational influences on pain and disability. In Main CJ Spanswick CC (Eds) Pain management. An interdisciplinary approach. Churchill Livingstone, Edinburgh. Chap 4 pp63-87

Main CJ Spanswick CC 2000 Pain Management: An Interdisciplinary Approach. Churchill Livingstone, Edinburgh

Marhold C Linton SJ Melin L 2002 Identification of obstacles for chronic pain patients to return to work: evaluation of a questionnaire. Journal of Occupational Rehabilitation 12:65-75.

Marin B 2003 Transforming disability welfare policy: completing a paradigm shift. In Prinz C (Ed.) European Disability Pension Policies. 11 Country Trends 1970-2002, Ashgate, Aldershot/Brookfield. Chap 1 pp23-76

Marlow S McLaughlin J 2003 Evidence gathering pilot: quantitative analysis. DWP In-House Report No 119. DWP, London

Marmot M 2004 Status Syndrome. Bloomsbury, London.

Marshall TH 1950 Citizenship and Social Class and Other Essays. Cambridge University Press, Cambridge

Mashaw JL Reno VP (Eds) 1996 Balancing security and opportunity: the challenge of disability income policy. Summary and Overview Report of the Disability Policy Panel National Academy of Social Insurance, Washington DC

Matheson LN 2000 Job analysis, job matching, and vocational intervention. In: Mayer TG Gatchel RJ Polatin PB (Eds) 2000 Occupational Musculoskeletal Disorders. Function, Outcomes and Evidence. Lippincott Williams & Wilkins, Philadelphia. Chap 34 pp609-627

Mayhew H 1861-62 London labour and the London poor. Griffin, Bohn & Co, London. Dover Publications, New York 1968.

Mclean C Carmona C Francis S Wohlgemuth C Mulvihill C 2005 Worklessness and health: what do we know about the causal relationship? NHS Health Development Agency, Sheffield.

Mead LM (Ed) 1997a The new paternalism: supervisory approaches to poverty. Brookings Institute Press, Washington DC

Mead LM 1997b From Welfare to Work: Lessons from America. In Deacon A (Ed) From welfare to work: lessons from America. Institute of Economic Affairs, Health & Welfare Unit, London pp 1-55

Meager N Bates P Dench S Honey S Williams M 1998 Employment of disabled people: assessing the extent of participation. Institute for Employment Studies, Brighton.

Mechanic D 1968 Medical Sociology. Free Press, New York.

Mendelson G 2004 Survey of methods for the rating of psychiatric impairment in Australia. J Law Med 11(4):446-481

Mill JS 1859 On liberty. Penguin Books, London 1974

MISSOC 1996 Social Protection in the Member States of the Union: Situation on July 1st 1996 and Evolution. European Commission Directorate-General Employment, Industrial Relations and Social Affairs, Brussels

MISSOC 2001 Attitudes Of Europeans To Disability: Eurobarometer 54.2 A Report prepared by the European Opinion Research Group (EORG) for the Education and Culture Directorate-General. European Commission, Brussels

Morley S Eccleston C Williams A 1999 Systematic review and meta-analysis of randomized controlled trials of cognitive behaviour therapy and behaviour therapy for chronic pain in adults, excluding headache. Pain 80: 1-13

Morris DB 1998 Illness and culture in the post-modern age. University of California Press, Berkeley Ca.

Moss N Arrowsmith J 2003 A review of 'what works' for clients over age 50. DWP Research Management, Sheffield.

Mowlam A Lewis J 2005 Exploring how general practitioners work with patients on sickness absence. DWP Research Report In press

Nagi S 1969 Disability and rehabilitation: legal, clinical and self-concepts of measurement. Ohio State University Press, Columbus, OH

NAO 1989 National Audit Office Report on Invalidity Benefit. London, HMSO

NAO 2004 Current thinking on managing attendance: A short guide for HR professionals. National Audit Office Research Paper. Institute for Employment Studies & Institute of Work Psychology.

National Statistics 2005 Client Group Analysis: Quarterly bulletin on the population of working age on key benefits – February 2005. IAD150605-QBWA-Jun05 http://www.dwp.gov.uk/asd/cga.asp

NEP 2005 Able to work. Report of the National Employment Panel's employer's working group on disability. (Chair M Thompson). National Employment Panel, London

New B 1999 Paternalism and public policy. Economics & Philosophy 15:63-83

Newman S Steed L Mulligan K 2004 Self-management interventions for chronic illness. Lancet 364:1523-37

Newton M Waddell G 1993 Trunk strength testing with iso-machines. Part 1: Review of a decade of scientific evidence. Spine 18(7):801-11.

NHS 2004 The National Health Service (General Medical Services Contracts) Regulations. www.opsi.gov.uk/si/si2004/20040291.htm

Nice K Thornton P 2004 Job Retention and Rehabilitation Pilot: Employers' management of long-term sickness absence. Department for Work and Pensions Research Report No 227. Corporate Document Services, Leeds.

NIDMAR 2000 Code of practice for disability management. National Institute of Disability Management and Research, Ottowa, Canada.

Nimnuan C Hotopf M Wessely S 2001 Medically unexplained symptoms: an epidemiological study in seven specialties. J Psychosomatic Research 51:361-7

Niven K 2005 The potential for certification of incapacity for work by non-medical healthcare professionals. DWP Research Report 225. Department for Work and Pensions, London

Noah L 1999 Pigeonholing illness: Medical diagnosis as a legal construct. Hastings Law Journal 50:241-307.

Nocon A Baldwin S 1998 Trends in rehabilitation policy. a review of the literature. Kings Fund, London.

Nordenfelt L 2003 Action theory, disability and ICF. Disabil Rehabil 25:1075-9

Nye R (Ed) 1998 The future of welfare. The Social Market Foundation, London

OECD 2003 Transforming disability into ability. Policies to promote work and income security for disabled people. The Organisation for Economic Co-operation and Development, Paris.

Oliver M 1983 Social work with disabled people. Macmillan, Basingstoke.

Oliver M 1990 The politics of disablement. Macmillan, Basingstoke.

Oliver M 1993 Disability and dependency: a creation of industrial societies? In Swain J Finkelstein V French S Oliver M (Eds) Disabling barriers – enabling environments. SAGE Publications, London Chap 1.6 pp49-60

Oliver M 1995 Defining impairment and disability: issues at stake. In Barnes C Mercer G (Eds) Exploring the divide: illness and disability. The Disability Press, Leeds Chapter 3 pp 29-54 www.leeds.ac.uk/disability-studies

Oliver M 2004 The social model in action: if I had a hammer. In Barnes C Mercer G (Eds) Implementing the social model of disability: theory and research. The Disability Press, Leeds Chap 2 pp 18-31

Oliver M Barnes C 1998 Disabled people and social policy: from exclusion to inclusion. Longman, London & New York

ONS 2000 Psychiatric morbidity among adults. Office of National Statistics, London

ONS 2001 Fraud and error in claims to Incapacity Benefits: The results of the Benefit Review of Incapacity Benefit. Office of National Statistics and Dept for Work & Pensions Analytical Services Division. HMSO, London

ONS 2003 Better or worse: a longitudinal study of the mental health of adults living in private households in Great Britain. Office of National Statistics, London.

OPCS 1985-1988 Disability Surveys. Office of Population Censuses and Surveys, Social Survey Division. HMSO: London

Osgood J Stone V Thomas A 2002 Delivering a work-focused service: the views and experiences of clients. DWP Research Report 167 Dept for Work and Pensions, London

Osgood J Stone V Thomas A Dempsey S Jones G Solon R. 2003 ONE Evaluation: Summary of service delivery findings. DWP In House Report No. 108. Department for Work and Pensions, London.

Oxman AD Thomson MA Davis DA Haynes RB 1995 No magic bullets: a systematic review of 102 trials of interventions to improve professional practice. Canadian Medical Association Journal 153:1423-31.

Page LA Wessely S 2003 Medically unexplained symptoms: exacerbating factors in the doctor-patient encounter. Journal of the Royal Society of Medicine 96:223-227

Palme J 2003 Foundations and guarantees of social security rights at the beginning of the 21st century. Findings & Opinions No. 8 International Social Security Association, Geneva

Parsons T. 1951 The social system. New York: Free Press.

Peace R 2001 Social exclusion: a concept in need of definition. Social Policy Journal of New Zealand 16:17-35

Pfau-Effinger B 2005 Culture and welfare state policies: reflections on a complex interrelation. J Social Policy 34:3-20

Pfeiffer D 1998 The ICIDH and the need for its revision. Disability & Society 13:503-523

Pfeiffer D 2000 The devils are in the details: the ICIDH2 and the disability movement. Disability & Society 15:1079-1082

Phillips M 1996 Commentary: Welfare and the common good. In Field F Stakeholder welfare. Institute of Economic Affairs Health & Welfare Unit, London. Choice in Welfare No. 32 pp97-106

Piachaud D 1997 Social security and dependence. International Social Security Review 50:41-55

Ploug N Kvist J (Eds) 1996 Recent Trends in Cash Benefits in Europe. Danish Institute of Social Research, Copenhagen.

Powell M 2000 New Labour and the third way in the British welfare state: a new and distinctive approach? Critical Social Policy 20:39-60

Pransky G Katz JN Benjamin K Himmelstein J 2002 Improving the physician role in evaluating work ability and managing disability: a survey of primary care practitioners. Disability and Rehabilitation 24:867-874

Pransky GS Dempsey PG 2004 Practical aspects of Functional Capacity Evaluation. J Occup Rehabil 14:217-229

Priestley M 2000 Adults only: Disability, social policy and the life course. Journal of Social Policy 29:421-439.

Prins R Bloch FS 2001 Social security, work incapacity and reintegration. In Bloch FS Prins R (Eds) Who returns to work and why: a six-country study on work incapacity and reintegration. International Social Security Series Vol 5. Transaction Publishers, New Brunswick. Chap 2 pp 9-26

Prinz C (Ed) 2003 European Disability Pension Policies. 11 Country Trends 1970-2002. Ashgate, Aldershot/Brookfield.

Prior L Wood F 2003 Characteristics of the sick role. In Halligan PW Bass C Oakley DA (Eds) Malingering and illness deception. Oxford, Oxford University Press. Chap 9 pp122-131

Prochaska JO DiClemente CC 1983 Stages and processes of self-change in smoking: toward an integrative model of change. J Consult Clin Psychol 51:390-5

Prochaska JO Rossi JS Wilcox NS 1991 Change process and psychotherapy outcome in integrative case research. J Psychother Integr 1:103-120

Rawls J 1999 A theory of justice. (Revised Edition) Oxford University Press, Oxford

Reeve D 2004 Psycho-emotional dimensions of disability and the social model. In Barnes C Mercer G (Eds) Implementing the social model of disability: theory and research. The Disability Press, Leeds. Chap 6 pp 83-100

Reno V Mashaw J Gradison B (Eds) 1997 Disability: Challenges for Social Insurance, Health Care Financing and Labor Market Policy. National Academy of Social Insurance, Washington DC.

Ritchie H Casebourne J Rick J 2005 Understanding workless people and communities: a literature review. Institute for Employment Studies. DWP Research Report Draft, in press. Dept for Work & Pensions, London

Ritchie J Ward K Duldig WA 1993 Qualitative Study of the Role of GPs in the Award of Invalidity Benefit. Department of Social Security. Research Report No 18. HMSO, London.

Roland M Waddell G Klaber-Moffett J Burton K Main C 2002 The Back Book Second Edition. The Stationery Office, Norwich.

Ross JF 1995 Where do real dangers lie? Smithsonian Nov, 42-53

Rousseau J-J 1762 The social contract.

Rowlingson K Berthoud R 1996 Disability, Benefits and Employment. Department of Social Security Research Report No 54. HMSO, London.

Royal College of Psychiatrists 2002 Employment opportunities and psychiatric disability. Council Report CR111. Royal College of Psychiatrists, London.

Rupp K Stapleton D (Eds) 1998 Growth in disability benefits: Explanations and policy implications. W.E. Upjohn Institute for Employment Research, Kalamazoo, Michigan.

Rupp K Stapleton D 1995 Determinants of the growth in the Social Security Administration's disability programs - an overview. Soc Security Bull 58:43-64

Sainsbury R Corden A 2004 Medical evidence and Incapacity Benefit appeals: evaluation of a pilot study. In House Report No.129. Dept for Work and Pensions, London

Sainsbury R Corden A Finch N 2003 Medical evidence and IB: evaluation of a pilot study. Dept for Work and Pensions Research Report No. 189. Corporate Document Services, Leeds.

Saunders P 2002 Mutual obligation, participation and popularity: Social security reform in Australia. Journal of Social Policy 31:21-38

Sawney P 2002 Current issues in fitness for work certification. Brit J Gen Prac 52:217-222

Sawney P Challenor J 2003. Poor communication between health professionals is a barrier to rehabilitation. Occupational Medicine 53: 246-248.

Scales J Scase J 2000 Fit and Fifty? A report prepared for the Economic and Social Research Council. University of Essex: Institute for Social and Economic Research. pp 1-59.

Scheel IB Hagen KB Oxman AD 2002 Active sick leave for back pain patients: all the players on side, but still no action. Spine 27:654-659

Schneider J Heyman A Turton N 2003 Employment for people with mental health problems: Expert briefing. National Institute for Mental Health in England, London www.nimhe.org.uk/whatshapp/item_display_publications.asp?id=324

Schuster 1914 Report of the Departmental Committee on Sickness Claims under the National Insurance Act. Cd 7687 HMSO, London

Scottish Executive 2004 Healthy Working Lives: a plan for action. Strategy paper. Scottish Executive, Edinburgh.

Seebohm P Scott J 2004 Addressing disincentives to work associated with the welfare benefits system in the UK and abroad. Research paper for Social Enterprise Partnership, London.

Sharpe M Carson A 2001 "Unexplained" somatic symptoms, functional syndromes, and somatization: do we need a paradigm shift? Ann Int Med 134:926-30

Shilling C 2002 Culture, the 'sick role' and the consumption of health. Brit J Sociol 53:621-638

Sigerist H 1929 The special position of the sick. (Transl R Connell) In: MI Roemer E Henry (Eds) 1929 Sigerist on the sociology of medicine. MD Publications, New York

Sirvastava S Chamberlain AM 2005 Factors determining job retention and return to work for disabled employees: a questionnaire study of opinions of disabled people's organizations in the UK. J Rehabil Med 37:17-22

Sivaraman Nair KP 2003 Life goals: the concept and its relevance to rehabilitation. Clinical Rehabilitation 17:192-202.

Smith N Middleton S Ashton-Brooks K Cos L Dobson B Reith L 2004 Disabled people's costs of living: more than you would think. Joseph Rowntree Foundation, York.

Social Exclusion Unit 2004 Mental health and social exclusion. Office of the Deputy Prime Minister, London.

Social Security Benefits Agency 1993 A consultation on the medical assessment for Incapacity Benefit. Internal DSS Report

Social Security Benefits Agency 1995 The Medical Assessment for Incapacity Benefit. Internal DSS Report

Soderberg E Alexanderson K 2003 Sickness certification practices of physicians: a review of the literature. Scand J Public Health 31(6):460-474

SSA 2001 Social Security Handbook. US Social Security Administration, Washington, DC.

SSAC 1988 Benefits for disabled people: a strategy for change. Social Security Advisory Committee. London: Her Majesty's Stationery Office

SSAC 2002 Social Security Advisory Committee Fifteenth Report April 2001-March 2002. Social Security Advisory Committee, London. www.ssac.org.uk

SSAC 2003 The Social Security (Incapacity Benefit Work-Focused Interviews) Regulations (Explanatory Memorandum)

Staal JB Hlobil H van Tulder MW Köke AJA Smid T van Mechelen W 2002 Return-to-work interventions for low back pain. A descriptive review of contents and concepts of working mechanisms. Sports Med 32:251-267.

Staal JB, Hlobil H, van Tulder MW et al 2003 Occupational health guidelines for the management of low back pain: an international comparison. Occupational and Environmental Medicine 60:618-626.

Stacey M Short A 2000 Challenging disability discrimination at work.
Institute of Employment Rights, London

Stafford B 1998 National Insurance and the Contributory Principle. Department of Social Security In-house Report 39. Department of Social Security, London.

Stanley K Lohde LA White S 2004 Sanctions and sweeteners: rights and responsibilities in the benefits system. Institute for Public Policy Research, London

Stanley K Maxwell D 2004 Fit for purpose: the reform of Incapacity Benefit.
Institute for Public Policy Research: London

Stanley K Regan S 2003 The missing million: supporting disabled people into work.
Institute for Public Policy Research: London

Strategy Unit 2005 Improving the life chances of disabled people. (final report) Cabinet Office, Prime Minister's Strategy Unit, London www.strategy.gov.uk

Stuart N Watson A Williams J Meager N Lain D 2002 How employers and service providers are responding to the Disability Discrimination Act 1995. DWP In-House Report 96 Dept for Work and Pensions, London.

Susser M 1990 Disease, illness, sickness; impairment, disability and handicap.
Psychol Med 20(3):471-3

Swain J Finkelstein V French S Oliver M (Eds) 1993 Disabling barriers – enabling environments.
SAGE Publications, London

Tawney RH 1931 Equality. (1964 Edition) Unwin Books, London

Telles JL Pollack MH 1981 Feeling sick: the experience and legitimation of illness.
Soc Sci Med 15A:243-251

Tibble M 2004 User's guide to disability estimates and definitions.
Dept for Work and Pensions, London.

Titmuss R 1956 The social division of welfare: some reflections on the search for equity.
Eleanor Rathbone Lecture. In Abel-Smith B, Titmuss K (Eds) 1987 The philosophy of welfare: selected writings of Richard M Titmuss. London: Allen & Unwin. pp 39-59.

Tomlinson J 1998 Why so austere? The British welfare state of the 1940s.
Journal of Social Policy 27:63-77

Toon PD 1992 Ethical aspects of medical certification by general practitioners.
Brit J Gen Practice 42:486-8

TUC 2000 Consultation document on rehabilitation. Getting better at getting back.
Trades Union Congress, London.

TUC 2002 Rehabilitation and retention - what works is what matters.
Trades Union Congress, London.

TUC 2004 Defending Incapacity Benefit. Trades Union Congress, Economic and Social Affairs: London.

Tuomi K Ilmarinen J Jahkola A Katajarinne L Tulkki A 1998 Work ability index.
Finnish Institute of Occupational Health, Helsinki.

Tuomi K Ilmarinen J Seitsamo J et al 1997 Summary of the Finnish research project (1981-1992) to promote the health and work ability of aging workers. Scand J Work Environ Health 23: 66-71.

Twaddle A Nordenfelt L (Eds) 1994 Disease, illness and Sickness: Three Central Concepts in the Theory of Health. Studies on Health and Society, Linkoping 18.

Twaddle AC 1972 The concepts of the sick role and illness behavior. Adv Psychosom Med 8:162-179

United Nations 1948 Universal Declaration of Human Rights. General Assembly Resolution 217A(III) Adopted 10 December 1948. www.unhchr.ch/udhr/lang/eng.htm

United Nations 1975 General Assembly Resolution 34/47 Adopted 9 December 1975.
Declaration on the Rights of Disabled Persons http://www.ohchr.org/english/law/res3447.htm

Unwin C Blatchley N Coker W et al 1999 The health of United Kingdom Servicemen who served in the Persian Gulf War. Lancet 353: 169-178.

UPIAS 1976 Fundamental principles of disability.
Union of Physically Impaired Against Segregation, London.

Upmark M Lundberg I Sadigh J Bigert C 2001 Conditions during childhood and adolescence as explanations of social class differences in disability pension among young men.
Scand J Public Health 29(2):96-103

Ursin H 1997 Sensitization, somatization, and subjective health complaints: A review.
Internat J Behav Med 4:105-116

Ursin H 2004 Demographics of subjective health complaints. Presented to Pathways to work: enabling rehabilitation. Royal Society of Medicine, London. 18 October 2004

Ustun TB 2000 Creating a common language for disability: ICIDH-2. Presented to Back pain and disability - unravelling the puzzle. New York, Nov 30-Dec 2, 2000.

Ustun TB Bickenbach JE Badley E Chatterji S 1998 A reply to David Pfeiffer 'The ICIDH and the need for its revision'. Disability & Society 13:829-831

Vives JL 1526 De Subventione Pauperum. Bruges. In Salter FR (Ed) Some early tracts on poor relief. Methuen, London 1926

von Korff M Ormel J Keefe F Dworkin SF 1992 Grading the severity of chronic pain. Pain 50: 133–149

Waddell G 2002 Models of disability: using low back pain as an example.
Royal Society of Medicine Press, London.

Waddell G 2004a Compensation for chronic pain. The Stationery Office, London

Waddell G 2004b The back pain revolution. Churchill Livingstone, Edinburgh. Second Edition

Waddell G Aylward M Sawney P 2002 Back pain, incapacity for work and social security benefits: an international literature review and analysis. Royal Society of Medicine Press, London

Waddell G Burton AK 2000 Occupational health guidelines for the management of low back pain at work. Faculty of Occupational Medicine, London www.facoccmed.ac.uk

Waddell G Burton AK 2004a Information and advice for patients. In: Waddell G The back pain revolution. Churchill Livingstone, Edinburgh. Second Edition Chap 16, pp323-342.

Waddell G Burton AK 2004b Concepts of rehabilitation for the management of common health problems. The Stationery Office, London

Waddell G Burton AK Bartys S 2004 Concepts of rehabilitation for the management of common health problems: Evidence Base. (Appendices & Tables of Evidence) www.dwp.gov.uk/medical

Waddell G Burton AK Main CJ 2003 Screening to identify people at risk of long-term incapacity for work. Royal Society of Medicine Press, London www.rsmpress.co.uk/bkwaddell2.htm

Waddell G Norlund A 2000 Review of social security systems. In: Nachemson A, Jonsson E (Eds) 2000 Neck and Back Pain: The Scientific Evidence of Causes, Diagnosis and Treatment. Lippincott, Williams & Wilkins, Philadelphia. Chap 21 pp427-471

Waddell G Pilowksy I Bond MR 1989 Clinical assessment and interpretation of abnormal illness behavior in low back pain. Pain 39:41-53

Waddell G Waddell H 2000 Social influences on neck and back pain and disability. In: Nachemson A, Jonsson E (Eds) Neck and Back Pain: The Scientific Evidence of Causes, Diagnosis and Treatment. Philadelphia: Lippincott, Williams & Wilkins. Chap 2, pp13-55

Wade DT Halligan PW 2004 Do biomedical models of illness make for good healthcare systems? Brit Med J 329:1398-1401

Wainwright D 2004 The benefits of incapacity. In O'Donnell M (Ed) Beyond understanding? Getting to the root causes of ill health. Chief Medical Officer's Report UNUMProvident, Dorking pp36-40

Wainwright D Calnan M 2002 Work and stress: the making of a modern epidemic. Open University Press, Buckingham.

Walker R 1998 Does work work? J Social Policy 27:533-542

Walker R 2003 Employment, support and security: balancing the needs of disabled people. IPPR research paper. Institute for Public Policy Research, London. (www.ippr.org).

Walker R Howard M 2000 The making of a welfare class? Benefits receipt in Britain. The Policy Press, Bristol.

Walley J 1972 Social Security – another British failure? Chas Knight & Co, London.

Watson PJ Patel S 2004 The barriers and bridges to work in unemployed people with chronic pain. Report to DWP Research and Evaluation Dept, Sheffield.

WCBA 2004 Workers Compensation Board of Alberta Policy: 03-01 Part II Chapter: Injuries Application 7: Chronic pain / chronic pain syndrome. http://www.wcb.ab.ca/policy/manual/0301p2a7.asp

Weiner B 1993 On sin versus sickness. A theory of perceived responsibility and social motivation. Am Psychol 48(9):957-965

Wells B 2004 The profile from incapacity related benefits over time: Comments by Bill Wells. DWP internal document.

Welsh Assembly 2005 Design for Living. Welsh Assembly, Cardiff

Welsh Office 1997 Annual Report of the Chief Medical Officer 1996. HMSO, Norwich.

Wessely S 2004 Mental health issues. In Holland-Elliott K (Ed) What about the workers? Royal Society of Medicine Press, London.

Wessely S Chalder T Hirsch S et al 1996 Psychological symptoms, somatic symptoms and psychiatric disorder in chronic fatigue and chronic fatigue syndrome: a prospective study in primary care. American Journal of Psychiatry 153:1050-1059.

Wessely S Nimnuan C Sharpe M 1999 Functional somatic syndromes: one or many? Lancet 354:936-939

White S 2000 Social rights and the social contract: political theory and the new welfare politics. Brit J Political Science 30:507-532

White S 2003 The civic minimum. Oxford University Press, Oxford

White S 2004a Is conditionality unfair? In Collins P Rossiter A (Eds) On condition. Social Market Foundation, London.

White S 2004b A social democratic framework for benefit conditionality. In Stanley K Lohde LA White S Sanctions and sweeteners: rights and responsibilities in the benefits system. Institute for Public Policy Research, London

Whitehead M Drever S Doran T 2005 Is the health of the long term unemployed better or worse in high unemployment areas? Health Statistics Quarterly Spring No 25:12-17

Whiteside N 1996 Creating the welfare state in Britain, 1945-1960. J Social Policy 25:83-103

WHO 1948 Preamble to the Constitution of the World Health Organisation. World Health Organisation, Geneva. www.who.int/en

WHO 1980 International Classification of Impairments, Disabilities and Handicaps (ICIDH). World Health Organisation, Geneva.

WHO 1992-94 International Classification of Diseases Tenth Revision (ICD-10) World Health Organisation, Geneva. www.who.int/classifications/icd/en

WHO 2000 Global burden of disease study. World Health Organisation, Geneva.

WHO 2001 International classification of functioning, disability and health. World Health Organisation, Geneva www.who.int/entity/classifications/icf/en

WHO 2003 The burden of musculoskeletal conditions at the start of the new millennium. (WHO Technical Report Series 919). World Health Organisation, Geneva.

WHO 2004 Family of International Classifications: definition, scope and purpose. Revised: August 2004 World Health Organisation, Geneva. http://www.who.int/classifications/icd/docs/en/WHOFICFamily.pdf

Williams R Hill M Davies R 1999 Attitudes to the welfare state and the response to reform. DSS Research Report No. 88. Corporate Document Services, Leeds.

Wistow G 2002 The future aims and objectives of social care. In Kendall L Harker L (Eds) From welfare to wellbeing: the future of social care. Institute for Public Policy Research, London. Chap 3, pp 38-67.

Woodhams C Corby S 2003 Defining disability in theory and practice: a critique of the British Disability Discrimination Act 1999. J Social Policy 32:159-178

Woodward C Kazimirski A Shaw A Pires C 2003 Interim Report, New Deal for Disabled People: Evaluation Eligible Population Survey: Wave One. WAE170. Department for Work and Pensions, London.

Wynn PA Williams N Snashall D Aw TC. 2003 Undergraduate occupational health teaching in medical schools - not enough of a good thing? Occupational Medicine 53:347-348.

Zadek S Scott-Parker S. 2001 Unlocking the evidence: the new disability business case. Employers' Forum on Disability, London. www.employers-forum.co.uk

Zola I 1989 Toward the necessary universalising of a disability policy. The Millbank Quarterly 67:401

APPENDIX 1: LITERATURE REVIEW

This is a review of concepts, goals and political practicalities, which has drawn on as broad an intellectual base as possible. To that end, selection and extraction of the included material was qualitative rather than quantitative. The inclusion criteria were deliberately broad to retrieve all relevant background material on social support for sickness and disability. The main limitations were:

a   A focus on adults of working age (18-65 years)

b   Material published in English (with a few key exceptions).

The starting points were MA and GW personal bibliographies. Four areas of literature were then searched for relevant material. To reflect current thinking, electronic searches focused on material published from 1990 to early 2005, but key earlier material was identified from published reviews and citation tracking.

1   *The medical literature:*

The main focus was on theoretical and conceptual papers, reviews, editorial and discussion papers, rather than evidence on effectiveness of interventions. Serial MEDLINE searches of the biomedical literature used appropriate MESH terms (chronic disease, sick leave, disability evaluation, social security, insurance benefits, pensions and insurance disability) and free text terms (sickness, disability, incapacity, sick role, illness behaviour, functional capacity evaluation, pension). These were supplemented by detailed electronic searching of the British Medical Journal since 1994, citation tracking and searches for Related Articles and published work of leading international experts.

2   *The social policy literature and policy think tanks:*

Relevant international and UK political philosophy literature was reviewed from Plato to Field. The current social policy literature was searched via SOSIG (Social Science Information Gateway **www.sosig.ac.uk**). This was supplemented by hand searches of Social Science and Medicine (2000-4), the Journal of Social Policy (1992-2004), Critical Social Policy (1998-2004), the International Social Security Review (1994-2004) and the Social Security Bulletin (1998-2004).

Additional internet sources included:

International Social Security Association (ISSA) (**www.issa.int/engl/homef.htm**)

European Union of Medicine in Assurance and Social Security (EUMASS) (**www.eumass.com**)

Organisation for Economic Cooperation and Development (OECD) (**www.oecd.org**)

Council of Europe (**www.europa.eu.int**)

Mutual Information System on Social Protection in the member States of the European Union (MISSOC) (**www.europa.eu.int**)

The main UK policy 'think-tanks' were searched electronically and in hard copy, as appropriate. These included:

The Joseph Rowantree Foundation (**www.jrf.org.uk**),

The Institute for Public Policy Research (**www.ippr.org**),

The Social Market Foundation (**www.smf.co.uk**)

The Adam Smith Institute (**www.adamsmith.org**)

3 *UK disability literature:*

The UK disability literature was searched through the Disability Rights Commission website (**www.drc.gov.uk**) and all linked sites, and the Leeds University Centre for Disability Studies (**www.leeds.ac.uk/disability-studies**). This was supplemented by hand searches of Disability and Society from 1998-2004.

Google searches under 'disability' and 'incapacity' provided additional material.

4 *DWP material:*

Relevant Legislation and Regulations.

DWP Reports, Research Reports and In House Research Reports (**www.dwp.gov.uk/asd/asd5**)

Unpublished Government policy papers from 1992-April 2005.

DWP administrative data (Analytical Services Division).

DWP educational material for doctors (**www.dwp.gov.uk/medical**)

APPENDIX 2: Current 'exempt conditions'

that qualify for IB with exemption from the Personal Capability Assessment.

The following categories are listed in Regulation 10 of the Social Security (Incapacity for Work) (General) Regulations 1995 [SI 1995 No 311] (as amended) and can be determined by a Decision-Maker, with or without advice from an approved Medical Adviser:

1   People suffering from the following severe medical conditions:
    tetraplegia;
    paraplegia (or uncontrollable involuntary movements or ataxia which effectively renders the sufferer functionally paraplegic);
    persistent vegetative state;
    dementia.

2   People who are registered blind – defined as on the appropriate register.

3   People who are terminally ill – defined as suffering from a progressive disease and death in consequence of that disease can reasonably be expected within six months.

4   People who are assessed at 80% disablement for war pension, industrial injury or Severe Disablement Allowance.

5   People who are receiving the highest rate care component of DLA; an increase of disablement pension under section 104 of the Contributions and Benefits Act; or a Constant Attendance Allowance.

The following additional categories require the Decision-Maker to consider advice from an approved Medical Adviser on whether the claimant is suffering from the condition:

6   severe mental illness – defined for this purpose as the presence of mental disease which severely and adversely affects a person's mood and behaviour, and which severely affects his social functioning, or his awareness of his immediate environment.

7   severe learning disability – defined as a condition which results from the arrested or incomplete physical development of the brain, or severe damage to the brain, and which involves severe impairment of intelligence and social functioning.

8   severe and progressive neurological or muscle-wasting diseases.

9   active and progressive forms of inflammatory polyarthritis.

10 progressive impairment of cardio-respiratory function which severely and persistently limits effort tolerance.

11 dense paralysis of the upper limb, trunk and lower limb on one side of the body.

12 multiple effects of impairment of function of the brain or nervous system causing severe and irreversible motor, sensory and intellectual deficits.

13 manifestations of severe and progressive immune deficiency states characterised by the occurrence of severe constitutional illness of opportunistic infections or tumour formation (including but not limited to AIDS or HIV related conditions).

The Incapacity Benefits Handbook (DWP 2000) gives more comprehensive descriptions and examples.

APPENDIX 3: Possible revised list of severe & permanent impairments

1 People with the following severe medical conditions:

   - tetraplegia;
   - paraplegia (or uncontrollable involuntary movements or ataxia which effectively renders the person functionally paraplegic);
   - persistent vegetative state;
   - severe and progressive neurological or muscle-wasting diseases
   - active and progressive forms of inflammatory polyarthritis
   - progressive impairment of the cardio-respiratory function which severely and persistently limits effort tolerance
   - dense paralysis of the upper limb, trunk and lower limb on one side of the body
   - severe and progressive immune deficiency states characterised by the occurrence of severe constitutional illness of opportunistic infections or tumour formation (AIDS, etc).
   - systemic genetic, congenital or developmental abnormalities causing severe or multiple structural abnormalities or deformities
   - physical, thermal or radiation injuries and scarring causing severe and multiple deformities or structural abnormalities.
   - amputations of both hands at or above the level of the carpo-metacarpal joints. (This level effectively renders the hands functionless for all dextrous manipulation).
   - severe tissue damage and scarring of both hands, caused by crushing, ischaemia, burns or irradiation, which renders the hands functionless for all dextrous manipulation and is functionally equivalent to amputation.
   - amputation of a hand and a foot.
   - end-stage renal failure requiring regular and continuing haemo-dialysis
   - severe liver failure
   - severe, life-threatening physical or mental disease that remains uncontrolled or uncontrollable and has unpredictable manifestations with substantial risk for causing substantial danger to the individual, co-workers or the public.

2 People with severe mental illness:

   - organic brain disorders (due to arrested or incomplete development of the brain, physical brain damage or degenerative brain disease), which include all dementias and severe learning disabilities
   - psychoses (schizophrenia, paranoid psychosis and depression with psychotic features, but excluding alcohol or drug induced psychoses) with objectively demonstrable mental impairment and incapacity
   - severe mental impairment with disruptive and dangerous behavioural problems, such that throughout the day or night he requires from another person frequent and prolonged (i) attention in connection with his bodily functions, or (ii) supervision in order to avoid substantial danger to himself or others.

3   People who are registered blind.

4   People with severe hearing and speech impairments, who are unable to communicate effectively beyond family and close friends.

5   People who are terminally ill.

GLOSSARY

Adjustment: any modification or adaptation to work to meet an employee's health needs, whether or not they are disabled (HSE 2004)

Approved doctor: A specially trained doctor who is approved by the Secretary of State for Work and Pensions to provide advice and undertake examinations of Incapacity Benefit claimants.

Biomedical conditions: medical diagnoses based on demonstrable disease and pathology. (See also **Disease**)

Capability Report: Report designed to provide information on the work-related capabilities of IB claimants, which is completed by an approved doctor at the same time as the Incapacity Report, and provided to DWP Personal Advisers (Legard *et al* 2002).

Case management: a collaborative process which assesses, plans, implements, coordinates, monitors and evaluates the options and services required to meet an individual's health care, educational and employment needs, using communication and available resources to promote quality, cost-effective outcomes (Case Management Society of UK – **www.cmsuk.org**).

Common health problems: less severe health conditions, consisting mainly of symptoms and often with limited evidence of objective disease or impairment: e.g. many mental health, musculo-skeletal and cardio-respiratory conditions. These are essentially whole people, any incapacity is relative and a matter of judgment, and the conditions are potentially remediable.

Conditionality: receipt of certain benefits (e.g. Incapacity Benefit for common health problems) might be conditional upon certain personal actions (e.g. participation in a rehabilitation programme) (Halpern *et al* 2004).

Culture: is 'the collective attitudes, beliefs and behaviour that characterise a particular social group over time' (Engel 1977; Waddell 2002, See also Fabrega & Tyma 1976). The social group may range from 'western society', to a social class, a locality, or a particular work force. (See also **welfare culture**.)

Dependency: implies the inability to do things for oneself and consequently the reliance on others to do things or to help. The term is often used in two ways: firstly, the ways in which welfare states have created classes of people who become dependent on the state for services and particularly financial support; secondly, the inability of some individuals or groups to provide self-care because of their functional limitations or impairments (Adapted from Oliver 1993).

Disability and incapacity benefits (UK) currently include Statutory Sick Pay, Incapacity Benefit, Severe Disablement Allowance, Attendance Allowance, Disability Living Allowance, disability premiums to Income Support, Industrial Injuries Disablement Benefit, War Disablement Pension and Invalid Care Allowance.

Disability: in the most basic and general sense, is altered functioning - limitation of activities and restriction of participation in life situations (WHO 2001) – associated with a physical and/or mental condition. Under the Disability Discrimination Act 1995, a disabled person is anyone with 'a physical or mental impairment which has a substantial and long-term adverse effect on his or her ability to carry out normal day-to-day activities'. (See also *Models of disability*.)

Disablement: The overall effect of permanent medical condition(s) or impairment(s) on functional capacity for the normal activities of life and work.

Disease: is a disorder of structure or function of the human organism that deviates from the biological norm, and is associated with mobilisation of the organism's defences and coping mechanisms. It includes biochemical, physiological or anatomical abnormalities which can result from congenital, traumatic, infective, inflammatory, degenerative or other pathological processes. The key features are that it is objective, at an organic level, in the individual, and a matter of medical diagnosis (WHO 1980, Boyd 2000).

Exempt conditions: qualify automatically for disability and incapacity benefits and are exempt from assessment under the DWP Personal Capability Assessment. A full list of the exempt conditions is given in Appendix 2. Furthermore, claimants identified as having a severe psychiatric illness are exempt from filling in the PCA questionnaire and from medical assessment.

Expert Patient Programme: is a DH initiative to help people with long-term conditions maintain their health and improve their quality of life (Dept of Health 2002b & c). A key element of this initiative is lay-led self-management training whose primary aim is to facilitate the development of self-management skills rather than to provide medical information or treatment.

False negatives: exclusion errors – claimants who are at risk but who are not identified by a screening tool. They might not be provided with the help they really do need.

False positives: inclusion errors - claimants identified as being at risk by a screening tool when they are not really. They might be given an intervention they do not need, leading to deadweight losses.

Fraud (Benefit fraud): a dishonest intent to obtain financial benefits through deception – proven to a criminal standard, beyond reasonable doubt (Kitchen 2003).

Health: the World Health Organisation defines health as 'a state of complete physical, mental and social well-being and not merely the absence of disease or infirmity' (WHO 1948). More recently, WHO has stated that 'health or state of health can only be defined in terms of an individual and that person's goals and expectations' (WHO 2004) and that the 'ultimate outcome' of health is well-being and quality of life (WHO 2003).

Illness or *ill health* is implied by WHO to be anything that falls short of perfect health but WHO does not actually define illness. By extrapolation from the WHO discussion, illness is when a physical or mental condition impacts on well-being or quality of life. Alternatively, illness is 'the innately human experience of symptoms and suffering' (Kleinman 1988) or, more simply, 'the subjective feeling of being unwell' (Finkelstein & French 1993) i.e. illness is an internal, personal experience.

Illness behaviour: things that ill people say and do that express and communicate their feelings of being unwell. Sociologically, illness behaviour is 'the ways in which given symptoms may be differentially perceived, evaluated and acted (or not acted) upon by different kinds of persons and in different social situations' (Mechanic 1968). A more precise clinical definition is 'observable and potentially measurable actions and conduct that express and communicate the individual's own perception of disturbed health' (Waddell *et al* 1989).

Impairment: is 'a problem in body function or structure as a significant deviation or loss' (WHO 2001) or 'a loss, loss of use, or derangement of any body part, organ system or organ function' (AMA 2000). Impairment is generally taken to be a matter of objective evidence: 'detectable - - - by direct observation or by inference from observation' (WHO 2001). The US Social Security

Administration operationalises this as 'demonstrable by medically acceptable, clinical and laboratory diagnostic techniques'(SSA 2001). Note that impairment is not the same as the underlying disease, but is the manifestation(s) of that disease (WHO 2001).

Incapacity Benefit (IB): is the main National Insurance (NI) benefit in UK for people of working age who are unable to work because of illness or disability. Most short-term sickness is covered by Statutory Sick Pay (SSP) and the main focus of IB is on long-term incapacity once SSP finishes (although short-term, lower rate IB provides cover for shorter-term sickness for people who are not covered by SSP). IB replaced previous NI sickness and invalidity benefits from April 1995.

Incapacity for work: is reduced capacity, functioning and performance in an occupational context (and it is difficult to distinguish capacity and performance). DWP has defined (in)capacity as the extent to which the person in (un)able to carry out the physical and mental activities specified in the schedule (i.e. the functional areas covered by the Personal Capability Assessment). Capability is defined as the ability to carry out the physical and mental activities specified in the schedule. The requirement refers to 'those people whose medical condition is such that it would be unreasonable to expect them to seek or be available for work' This is an administrative definition, based on what is 'reasonable' and does not necessarily mean complete loss of capacity for all forms of work.

International Classification of Functioning (ICF) definitions (WHO 2001)

Body structures: are anatomical parts of the body such as organs, limbs and their components.

Body Functions: are the physiological and psychological functions of body systems.

Impairments: are problems in body function or structure such as a significant deviation or loss.

Activity: is the execution of a task or action by an individual.

Participation: is involvement in a life situation.

Activity Limitations: are difficulties an individual may have in executing activities. [This is equivalent to the previous definition of disability (WHO 1980), i.e. 'restricted activity' but removes the assumption that it is 'resulting from an impairment'].

Participation Restrictions: are problems an individual may experience in involvement in life situations. [This is equivalent to the previous definition of handicap (WHO 1980)].

Personal Factors: (No adequate ICF definition. See text for further discussion).

Environmental Factors: are external features of the physical, social and attitudinal world, which can have an impact on the individual's performance in a given domain.

Loss of faculty: is a UK social security term, more or less equivalent to impairment. It is an 'impairment of the proper functioning of part of the body or mind' caused by an accident or disease (*Jones v Secretary of State for Social Services* [1972] AC 944 at p1009 (HL), also reported as an appendix to R(1) 3/69). It was first introduced in 1917 as the basis of compensation in war pensions and was then used for Industrial Injuries Disablement Benefit in 1946. For IIDB, it is 'something which the Act envisages as resulting from the injury and from which, in turn, there results some disability. It may perhaps be best described as a total or partial loss of power or function of an organ of the body. Loss of faculty includes disfigurements. It is not itself a disability but is a cause, actual or potential, of one or more disabilities' (DHSS 1986). Loss of faculty was first used for anything other than injury in 1985: for Severe Disablement Allowance, it was 'any loss of power or function of an organ or part of the body which is a cause of inability to do things. A loss of faculty may be physical or mental and is taken to include disfigurement' (DHSS 1985a).

Malingering: feigning injury or illness with intent to deceive (Halligan *et al* 2003).

Medical Services doctors: Approved doctors employed full- or part-time (usually 6-8 sessions per week) by ATOS Origin Medical Services, which has a contract to provide an advice and examination service for the Department for Work and Pensions.

Medicalising: identifying or labelling a condition or behaviour as being a disorder requiring medical treatment or intervention

Models of disability (Engel 1977; Waddell 2002):

The *medical model* argues that disability is a direct consequence of disease, pathology and impairment, and management is primarily a matter of medical treatment. There is wide criticism of the medical model because it does not consider personal / psychological or social issues that influence disability.

The *social model* (UPIAS 1976, Finkelstein 1980, Oliver 1983, 1990, Barnes 1991) argues that many of the restrictions experienced by disabled people lie not in the individual's impairment but are imposed by the way society is organized for able-bodied living. Society fails to make due allowance and arrangements that would enable disabled people to fulfil the ability and potential they do retain. This includes physical settings such as lack of wheelchair access and, equally important, social attitudes. The social model often tends to underplay the role of personal/psychological factors, though the empowerment model does recognise the importance of personal responsibility (Duckworth 2001).

The *biopsychosocial model* includes biological, psychological and social dimensions and the interactions between them, and incorporates both the medical and social models (Engel 1977; Waddell 2002). Put simply, this is an individual-focused model that considers the person, their health problem, and their social context:

- Biological refers to the physical or mental health condition.

- Psychological recognises that personal and psychological factors also influence functioning and the individual must take some measure of personal responsibility for his or her behaviour.

- Social recognises the importance of the social context, pressures and constraints on behaviour and functioning.

Motive: is 'what induces a person to act, e.g. desire, fear, circumstance' (Concise English Dictionary) which raises issues of (dis)-incentives, free will and conscious choice.

Personal Capability Assessment (PCA): From April 2000, the PCA replaced the *All Work Test* to assess whether a claimant meets the requirements for Incapacity Benefit. It is the functionally based assessment used to determine if a claimant is considered to meet the threshold of incapacity for entitlement to IB. The PCA decision is informed by medical advice from an approved doctor who may conduct a medical examination of the claimant. It now focuses more on what people can do rather than on what they cannot do, and collects 'information or evidence capable of being used for assisting the person in question to obtain work or improve his prospects of obtaining it'.

Personal characteristics: include age, gender, family background, education, training and skills, work experience and history and all the issues discussed under social disadvantage.

Psychological factors: are *internal* and concern how the person thinks and feels about their health condition, disability, work and (in)capacity. They include:

a the personal experience of illness and disability
b perceptions and expectations
c attitudes and beliefs, emotions, mood, psychological distress and coping strategies
d (dis)incentives, motivation and effort.
e uncertainty

These phenomena may be expressed outwardly as ***illness behaviour.***

Rehabilitate:

Concise Oxford Dictionary (**www.askoxford.com**): '1 to restore to health or normal life by training or therapy after imprisonment, addiction or illness. - - - 3 to restore to a former condition'
Collins Dictionary (2003): '1 to help to readapt to society after illness - - -.'
Merriam Webster Dictionary (**www.m-w.com**): '2b to restore or bring to a condition of health or useful and constructive activity'
American Heritage Dictionary (**www.bartleby.com**): '1 to restore to good health or useful life, as through therapy and education'.

Rehabilitation process: a re-iterative, active, educational, problem-solving process focused on an individual's disability with the following components (Adapted slightly from Wade & Halligan 2003):

· Assessment, the identification of the nature and extent of the individual's problems and the factors relevant to their resolution including the individual's assets
· Goal setting
· Intervention, which may include either or both of:
  - Treatments, which affect the process of change
  - Support (care), which maintains the individual's life and safety
· Evaluation, to check on the effects of any intervention

Sensitivity: is the ability of a screening tool to identify those clients who will go on to long-term incapacity. It is the proportion of clients who do go on to long-term incapacity who are correctly predicted by the screening tool.

Specificity: is the ability of a screening tool to correctly identify those who will not go on to long-term incapacity. It is the proportion of clients who do return to work who are correctly predicted by the screening tool.

Severe medical conditions: have objective evidence of significant disease, pathology and physical or mental impairments: e.g. blindness, severe or progressive neurological or immune deficiency disease, active and progressive inflammatory polyarthritis, psychosis, severe learning disability, or terminal illness. These include but are not limited to ***exempt conditions*** that qualify automatically for benefits and are exempt from assessment under the DWP ***Personal Capability Assessment***.

Sickness: or, more precisely, ***the sick role*** is a social status accorded to the ill person by society, with exemption from normal social roles and carrying specific rights and responsibilities. i.e. sickness is an external, social phenomenon involving interactions between the individual, other people and society (Sigerist 1929, Parsons 1951, Mechanic 1968).

Sickness absence: work loss attributed to illness, based on (medical) certification of a (specific?) health condition.

Social disadvantage: covers a wide range of issues around poverty, discrimination and stigmatisation. It is linked to occupational status but raises broader issues of 'human (or social) capital': family background, education; training and skills; labour market opportunities including the availability, quality, pay levels and security of employment; the balance between physical and psychological demands of work and personal capabilities; control and support; financial and social status and security; social exclusion and marginalisation, life-style and behaviour that may affect health and working capacity. To a large extent, it is a matter of (relative) poverty. [Disadvantage is not really a sociological term and is not used in the sociological literature.]

Social exclusion: involves loss of social roles and reduced participation in all aspects of life, including work.

Social factors: in the broadest sense concern *external* influences or interactions with other people and society: ranging from the culture that surrounds health, sickness, disability and work; to the social constraints, pressures, costs and benefits of illness behaviour; to interactions with others at an individual level; to labour market forces and occupational factors; to economic issues.

Statutory Sick Pay (SSP): is a statutory benefit paid by UK employers for up to 28 weeks, enforced by legislation (though 90% of UK workers actually receive better pay and conditions for sickness under their contract of employment).

Symptoms: are subjective bodily or mental sensations that reach awareness and are 'bothersome' or 'of concern to that person' (Ursin 1997, Deyo *et al* 1998).

Vocational rehabilitation: the process whereby those who are ill, injured or have a disability are helped to access, maintain or return to employment or other useful occupation (BSRM 2000).

Welfare culture: is the set of ideas, values and basic principles that surround the benefits system and underpin welfare policy, the institutions of the welfare state, and the attitudes, expectations and behaviour of the various stakeholders in a given society (developed from Pfau-Effinger 2005). The term 'benefits culture' is often used incorrectly in a derogatory sense, implying conscious abuse of the benefits system and/or dependency on benefits.

FOOTNOTES

[1] The 'common good' or 'commonwealth'.

[2] 'The individual prospers best within a strong, cohesive society and such a society has to be built around a sense of mutual responsibility. Relationships with each other are not simply market based: they require social and moral principles to underpin them.' Society should be based on 'enduring values of social unity, common purpose, fairness and mutual responsibility'. 'Social justice (is about) what is just and unjust, fair and unfair, right and wrong' (Blair 1996).

[3] However, the 19th century intellectual division between individualism -v- collectivism was an over-simplification (Field 1996, 1997). Crudely, the welfare debate is still polarised between those who explain the increasing number of people on benefit by economic and labour market forces -v- those who explain the rise in dependency as being a matter of motivation, the kind of people on benefits and deep issues about their character. Both views contain an element of truth but not the whole explanation. Poverty and social disadvantage are caused *both* by economic and social structures and also by individual behaviour: both must be addressed.

[4] Beveridge (1942) described the 'five Giants on the road to reconstruction – Want, Disease, Ignorance, Squalor and Idleness'.

[5] Perhaps unlike the (long-term) unemployed who may be held - justly or unjustly - at least partly responsible for their situation.

[6] Again perhaps in contrast to unemployment.

[7] Recognising that there are even greater issues of human suffering, but it is difficult to reduce these to financial terms or for state benefits to provide financial recompense.

[8] Other options include variants on or combinations of:

- Placing responsibility for sick pay and disability pensions entirely on employers.
- A 'National Disability Income' based entirely on needs, e.g. abolition of separate 'incapacity' benefits, and covering the economic needs and costs of disability with much higher DLA benefits.
- A common 'citizen's income' covering all forms of economic inactivity, e.g. unemployment, sickness and disability, etc.
- Benefits based on a social model, presumably some form of 'compensation' for society's barriers.
- Tax Credits for people of working age, whether in or out of work.

[9] Similarly, international attempts to control disability benefit trends generally consist of:

- steps to limit or tighten access to benefits

- incentives or support to come off benefits and (return to) work

both of which require disabled people to take more personal responsibility (Kuptsch & Zeitzer 2001).

[10] Public priorities for extra government expenditure consistently rate health care (first 54%, second 28%) and education (first 28%, second 38%) far ahead of social security benefits (first 3%, second 4%, and that is mainly among recipients) (British Social Attitudes Survey 2001). Within social security, benefits for disabled people (first 20%, second 38%) come after retirement pensions (first 54%, second 22%).

[11] The disability lobby: politically active disabled people, their organisations and representatives, academics in this field and political supporters, who constitute powerful vested interests. However, they do not always speak with one voice, and may hold divergent views on particular issues.

[12] However, these authors were addressing poverty, social disadvantage and the re-distribution of wealth and said little or nothing about disability. Apart from one cryptic comment that 'adding these benefits together, sickness is now a better financial proposition for many people than health' (Titmus 1956), most of these writings seem to have taken for granted that sickness and incapacity for work are the inevitable consequence of injury or disease and automatically justify social support.

[13] This review specifically excludes social security benefits for children, those over state retirement age and measures to alleviate poverty, while fully recognizing that the highest prevalence of disability and of poverty is in the elderly, the link between disability and poverty, and the need to address childhood poverty.

[14] Some social roles may be unpaid and counted as 'economically inactive' but are nevertheless productive and important to the well-being of society, e.g. carers, mothers of young children, students, voluntary workers, etc. However, no practical mechanism for 'paying' such people has ever been developed. Whatever the social or moral arguments, the present discussion of 'wage replacement' will focus pragmatically on paid employment.

[15] We are well aware that some disabled activists would take issue with that 'conventional' view of work (Oliver & Barnes 1998, Drake 1999) but this review cannot address that philosophical and political question and is limited pragmatically to current society.

[16] This needs to be interpreted with care: 34% of people on disability and incapacity benefits say they would like to work, but on a further question only 6% say they would actually be available for work at present (Labour Force Survey Summer 2002). Alcock *et al* (2003) found that 49% of long-term sick 'would like a full-time job' but only 11% thought they had a realistic chance of getting one and only 5% were currently looking for one. Loumidis *et al* (2001b) found that 78% of people on disability and incapacity benefits did not expect to work, only 3% were actually looking for work, 7% said they wanted work but were not looking for a job, and 12% said they would need rehabilitation or training first. Grewal *et al* (2002) found that only 6% had taken any active steps to look for work in the past 4 weeks.

[17] Most GPs recognize that work can be of therapeutic benefit for both physical and psychosocial reasons. However, this view is qualified where patients work in low paid jobs of low social status, or where the jobs are considered (rightly or wrongly) to have caused or exacerbated their physical or psychological conditions (Mowlam & Lewis 2005).

[18] Interestingly, WHO does not give a precise definition of illness, perhaps reflecting difficulties with the term in the philosophical literature. The closest it comes is to state that: 'The individual defines when their state of health generates a health problem either by accessing or seeking access to the health system or by describing the issues of concern to that person' (WHO 2004). However, we would argue that seeking health care is really a separate question. The fundamental problem to the WHO focus on well-being and quality of life is that it does not clearly distinguish ill health from other forms of social disadvantage.

[19] Again, the International Classification of Diseases (ICD-10: WHO 1992-94) does not define disease, and this definition is instead based more upon the International Classification of Impairments, Disabilities and Handicaps (WHO 1980).

[20] This definition is based primarily on physical disease and is more difficult to apply to mental health conditions. Many severe mental illnesses (e.g. schizophrenia), head injuries or learning disabilities are associated with functional &/or biochemical brain changes that are properly defined as disease, or such an underlying organic basis may be directly and logically inferred from the clinical characteristics of the condition. Many less severe mental health conditions, however, are primarily subjective/behavioural complaints in which it is difficult to demonstrate any objective abnormality: these are more appropriately described as 'illness' or 'disability' (Council of Europe 2002).

[21] Some disabled people object to the term 'mental' and distinguish intellectual and psychological impairments (Oliver & Barnes 1998).

[22] '- - disability and incapacity (for) work are ill-defined and complex phenomena. Disability in particular is a slippery and expansive category: it is inherently subjective, ambiguous, fuzzy, elusive and inevitably problematic to define and measure' (Marin 2003).

[23] That is the exact WHO (1980) definition, including the parenthesis.

[24] There are pragmatic, clinical criticisms of the medical model, particularly for less severe, common health problems (Waddell 2002):

- Many patients with common health problems have little or no evidence of disease or impairment.
- There is limited correlation between disease or impairment and disability.
- It fails to consider psychosocial factors that can aggravate and perpetuate illness and disability.
- It fails to consider the physical and attitudinal social barriers that can impose restrictions on people with impairments.
- Purely medical interventions often fail to address or resolve disabilities.
- It fails to explain benefit trends.

The disability movement (Oliver 1995, Pfeiffer 1998, 2000, Hurst 2000) makes more fundamental conceptual and political criticisms of the medical model, the International Classification of Impairments, Disabilities and Handicaps (WHO 1980) and the revised International Classification of Functioning (WHO 2001):

- These assume that disability is a matter of 'sickness'. [In this review we also argue the need to distinguish sickness and disability.]
- They medicalise disability. [However, it must be recognised that many 'disabled people' are chronically ill and do need and want health care (Bury 2000).]
- They assume 'normality' as a biological rather than a social construct and create dichotomies between normal – impaired, disabled – non-disabled, and sick – healthy, which are divisive, labelling and discriminatory. [Though the ICF attempts a more universalist approach (Ustun 2000).] There are conceptual and practical difficulties defining the boundaries between these dichotomies.

- The way they discuss impairment, disability and handicap implies linear causality and fails to address social barriers, exclusion and oppression. [They certainly do not go so far as to say that disability is caused entirely be social disadvantage, as some disability activists wish. However, they do acknowledge the role of the social environment, even if not in modern ter minology or as prominently as some might wish (Bury 1998)]

- They imply that impairment and disability are static.

- The classifications have been difficult to operationalise and there are questions about their usefulness for social policy planning.

- They use offensive and handicapist language and attitudes. [The ICF attempts to use more neutral language (Ustun *et al* 2000), though some activists reject the revision because it does not move completely to a social model.]

[25] ' - - defining impairment or disability or illness or anything else for that matter is not simply a matter of language or science; it is also a matter of politics. - - - This battle is related to two political processes; exclusion and inclusion as far as disabled people and disability definitions are concerned' (Oliver 1995). See also Drake (1999).

[26] That brief description is obviously an over-simplified account of the social model. Different social model writers and academics place different emphasis on social barriers, and some disabled people themselves acknowledge the role of their impairment. Different social models have been characterised as 'materialist' (emphasising structural and institutional barriers) and 'cultural' (focusing on attitudes).

[27] Similarly, the Disability Rights Task Force Working Group on Defining Disability Discrimination (1998) defined disability 'to include the following elements:

- a physical or mental impairment

- a consequence of that impairment would be that the person would have a substantial restriction placed on his or her ability to participate in a broad range of life activities.'

[28] Emphasis as in original (Strategy Unit 2005)

[29] For example, the Disability Discrimination Act 1995 defined disability as 'a physical or mental impairment which has a substantial and long-term adverse effect on his ability to carry out normal day-to-day activities'. This has created considerable legal debate and difficulty (Stacey & Short 2000). The primary legislative definition is supplemented by three further sources: *Schedule 1* to *the DDA; the Disability Discrimination (Meaning of Disability) Regulations* 1996; and the *Guidance on Matters to be Taken into Account in Determining Questions Relating to the Definition of Disability*. Claims under the DDA have led to extensive legal argument about the interpretation and application of the definition and the medical evidence on which it should be based, which has centred on four elements. There must be:

- A physical or mental impairment

- Which has an adverse effect upon the claimant's ability to carry out day-to-day activities

- The effect must be substantial, and

- The effect must be long-term.

[30] 'The first (criticism) is that the social model ignores or is unable to deal adequately with the realities of impairment. This is based on a conceptual misunderstanding because the social

model is not about the personal experience of impairment but the collective experience of disablement' (Oliver 2004). '- - the social model is not an attempt to deal with the personal restrictions of impairment but the social barriers of disability. - - Other disabled people have criticised the social model for its assumed denial of `the pain of impairment', both physical and psychological. - - This denial of the pain of impairment has not, in reality been a denial at all. Rather it has been a pragmatic attempt to identify and address issues that can be changed through collective action rather than medical or other professional treatment' (Oliver 1995).

[31] Some advocates of the social model try to attribute every dimension of disability to society – impairment as a 'social construct', psycho-emotional 'disablism' and material/cultural barriers – (Barnes & Mercer 2004a) but that denies the reality of severe impairments and the limitations they impose (Oliver 2004). Many supporters of the social model would probably accept that even if all social barriers were removed, some people would still be unable to work because of their impairments.

[32] From its inception in 1946, IIDB provided 'disablement benefits' that were based on 'a loss of physical or mental faculty which is substantial and likely to be permanent' and which resulted in a prescribed degree of disablement (National Insurance (Industrial Injuries) Act 1944). Loss of faculty was 'something which the Act envisages as resulting from the injury and from which, in turn, there results some disability. It may perhaps be best described as a total or partial loss of power or function of an organ of the body. Loss of faculty includes disfigurements. It is not itself a disability but is a cause, actual or potential, of one or more disabilities' (DHSS 1986). 'The extent of disablement shall be assessed by reference to the disabilities incurred by the claimant as a result of the relevant loss of faculty' (National Insurance (Industrial Injuries) Act 1944). The Act made provision for Regulations to prescribe degrees of disablement corresponding to degrees of loss of faculty. Griffiths (1969) later commented that the intent was that disablement should be 'in proportion to the loss of health, strength and power to enjoy life attributable to industrial accident or prescribed industrial disease'.

The IIDB assessment process is in three logical steps. First, claimants must have a health condition that was caused by 'personal injury' in an 'industrial accident' or by one of a list of 'prescribed industrial diseases'. Second, there must be clear medical evidence that industrial accident or disease has caused loss of faculty. Third, that loss of faulty must cause 'disablement': with a threshold of 14% for receipt of benefits.

[33] Though work-related accidents have also declined and the scale of the industrial injuries scheme has been reduced, notably by changes during the 1980s and early 1990s.

[34] Under the Disability Discrimination Act 1995

- The impairment may be physical (for example, a weakening of part of the body caused through illness, by accident or congenitally) or mental (including learning disabilities and mental illnesses which are 'clinically well-recognised'). Physical impairments include sensory ones, such as those affecting sight or hearing.

- "Substantial" is not defined in the Act, but the statutory Guidance on the definition of disability explains that the requirement for an adverse effect to be substantial reflects the general understanding of "disability" as a limitation going beyond the normal differences in ability which may exist among people. A substantial effect is 'more than minor or trivial'.

- 'Long-term' means that the effects :
  - have lasted at least twelve months, or
  - are likely to last at least twelve months, or
  - are likely to last for the rest of the life of the person affected.

- An impairment affects normal day-to-day activities if it affects one of the following: mobility; manual dexterity; physical co-ordination; continence; ability to lift, carry or otherwise move everyday objects; speech, hearing or eyesight; memory or ability to concentrate, learn or understand; perception of the risk of physical danger.

[35] E.g. see the Memorandum from the Disability Rights Commission to the Joint Committee on the Draft Disability Discrimination Bill. 5 February 2004

[36] UK does not provide partial incapacity benefits. However, even partial capacity benefits still require cut-offs between different grades of incapacity.

[37] This data is from four Nordic countries, but there are similar findings from both developed and undeveloped countries (Gureje *et al* 1997, Ursin 2004), including UK (Main 1983, Wessely *et al* 1996, Gureje *et al* 1997, Unwin *et al* 1999, Sharpe & Carson 2001).

[38] This is broadly comparable to 14% of the working age population in most OECD countries (OECD 2003).

[39] Although the focus of this paper is people of working age, it should not be forgotten that two-thirds of the most severe disabilities occur in people over age 70 years (Grundy *et al* 1999).

[40] However, the oft-quoted example of Stephen Hawking may be morally illuminating, but it is too extreme to be of much general relevance. No one would 'reasonably expect' someone with such severe impairment to work or deny him social security benefits if he did not work. If Hawking's IQ had been 80 and he had no occupational training or skills, even he would never have returned to work as a labourer.

[41] Though the MISSOC (2001) survey was of adults aged 15+ and the inclusion of older people who have a higher prevalence of disability means that rate is not comparable to the working age statistics quoted throughout the present review.

[42] MISSOC (2001) found that 8% of adults in UK considered they had a disability, but for the reasons discussed in the previous footnote that is not directly comparable.

[43] 'Everyone has the right to work, to free choice of employment, to just and favourable conditions of work and to protection against unemployment' Article 23.1 Universal Declaration of Human Rights (WHO 1948).

[44] Exempt conditions now account for just under 20% of new awards of IB. See Appendix 2 for the full list of exempt conditions. In addition, claimants identified as having a severe mental health condition are exempt from filling in the questionnaire and from medical assessment.

[45] Though this is a poor term. They are only 'medically unexplained' or poorly understood in terms of the medical model and lack of explanation by underlying disease. They are entirely understandable in terms of a biopsychosocial model that allows for all of the biological, personal/psychological and social/cultural influences on health and illness (Sharpe & Carson 2001, Waddell 2002).

[46] *Ape* social policy seminar on 'The cost of vagueness' Amsterdam, The Netherlands, 8 April 2005.

[47] About 1 million UK workers report sick each week, mostly for a few day(s) only (CBI data); 700, 000 people start IB each year, but most of them were not working anyway (DWP data). 300,000 workers receive SSP at any one time: 35% of spells of sickness are over within 1 week, 55% within 2 weeks and 90% within 8 weeks; only 1% of all SSP recipients receive the full 28 weeks SSP (DWP data). This estimate is supported by the literature reviews of Burdorf *et al* (2002) and Waddell *et al* (2004).

[48] The quarter of recipients who are 'on the margins of work' i.e. who retain some contact with the labour market

[49] The remainder used various different words.

[50] Based on Scandinavian surveys by Halderson *et al* (1996) and Ursin (1997). There is a need for comparable UK studies.

[51] Detailed references to the statements listed:

- Virtually all have a genuine health condition or impairment that causes some limitations. All the evidence is that true malingering (feigning an injury or illness that does not exist) is extremely rare and recorded benefit fraud is <1% (ONS 2001, Kitchen 2003).

- Virtually all say that illness or disability affects their ability to work, and about three-quarters say it is the main reason they cannot work (Arthur *et al* 1999, Grewal *et al* 2002, Woodward *et al* 2003, Alcock *et al* 2003). However, only about a quarter say they cannot do any work at all (Alcock *et al* 2003).

- About two-thirds say they have been advised by their doctors that they *should* not work (Meager *et al* 1998, Woodward *et al* 2003, Goldestone & Douglas 2003). Health care can sometimes become a barrier rather than the solution to (return to) work (James *et al* 2002, Anema *et al* 2002, Sirvasta & Chamberlain 2005).

- 90% of new IB claimants initially expect to return to work (Green *et al* 2000), and one third to half of all IB recipients still want to work (Alcock *et al* 2003, LFS Spring 2004).

- More than half have personal circumstances and commitments that make work more difficult, e.g. child care responsibilities or caring for someone with an illness or disability (Gardiner 1997, Woodward *et al* 2003).

- Many IB recipients face multiple disadvantages and barriers to (return to) work that are significant and additive (Arthur *et al* 1999, Loumidis *et al* 2001b, Ashworth *et al* 2001, Alcock *et al* 2003, Burchardt 2003a, Dean 2003, Woodward *et al* 2003, Berthoud 2003, Grewal *et al* 2004):
  - age (about half are aged >50 years)
  - poor work history (1/3rd have already been out of work for >2 years when they start IB)
  - low skills (40% have no qualifications, 15% have basic skills problems)
  (DWP Administrative data)

- The longer someone is out of work the more distant they become from the labour market and the lower their chances of getting back into work (Waddell *et al* 2003). 75% of current recipients have been on IB > 2 years (DWP Administrative data).

- There may be lack of suitable jobs in the local labour market. There is a major problem of regional deprivation, with ten-fold variation in IB rates between the best and worst local authority areas (HMT 2003).

- Employer discrimination is still a major barrier (Sirvasta & Chamberlain 2005), especially for people with mental health conditions (Social Exclusion Unit 2004).

- Uncertainty is a key issue: about whether they will be fit to work regularly, about the risk of losing benefits or getting back on to benefits if the need arises, and about the financial consequences of coming off benefits. This is partly due to lack of information and understanding of the benefits system (Gardiner 1997, Corden & Sainsbury 2001).

- The IB regime itself 'labels' people as incapable of work, becomes a barrier to work, and reinforces other barriers (Stanley & Maxwell 2004, Howard 2004a)

  - 95% of IB recipients face at least one and 60% face 3 or more barriers to (return to) work in addition to their health condition (Woodward *et al* 2003).

[52] The medical model implies that the health condition or impairment is the primary 'cause' of disability; the social model implies that social barriers are the primary 'cause' of disability: both tend to ignore the contribution of the other and the central role of personal/psychological factors in subjective complaints.

[53] A more precise sociological definition is: 'the ways in which given symptoms may be differentially perceived, evaluated and acted (or not acted) upon by different kinds of persons and in different social situations' (Mechanic 1968). A more precise clinical definition is: 'observable and potentially measurable actions and conduct that express and communicate the individual's own perception of disturbed health' (Waddell *et al* 1989). Clinical studies, e.g. in chronic pain patients, emphasise the neurophysiological and psychological mechanisms that underpin illness behaviour (Main & Spanswick 2000, Waddell 2004b). However, see the qualifications to this in the following paragraph.

[54] These factors are variously described as obstacles or barriers: the clinical literature more often describes them as 'obstacles', the disability rights and social policy literatures as 'barriers'. Obstacles may imply they can be overcome, but barriers can also be dismantled. The question then is: overcome or dismantled by whom? Perhaps personal and rehabilitation interventions may be better able to overcome obstacles; dismantling barriers may depend more on society – which may be why different groups tend to use the different terms.

[55] Other key players – family, friends, employers and co-workers – may share and reinforce these perceptions, attitudes and beliefs.

[56] For example, during disability evaluation.

[57] See Leonard *et al* (1995) for an analysis of the complexities and limitations of the concept of 'motivation'.

[58] Life goals are the desired states or ends that people strive to obtain, maintain or avoid. There are a hierarchy of life goals from the general, idealised, self-image to specific activities, which are modified by personal and contextual factors (Sivaraman Nair 2003).

[59] Earlier welfare reformers such as Tawney (1931) and Beveridge (1942) were wholly realistic about human nature, but that got lost from the post-war consensus on social security. The influential writings of Titmuss (Abel-Smith & Titmus 1987) emphasized that the causes of social conditions 'lie in social and economic structures and not in the character or behaviour of - - - people themselves' (Deacon 1996). Indeed, for many years this largely precluded any consideration of character, behaviour or personal responsibility in the welfare debate (Phillips 1996). As a Christian socialist, Field (1996, 1997) started from the fallen state of mankind and acknowledged the

importance of 'character' and 'behaviour' and accepted the reality that 'benefits influence behaviour'. Even his critics (Field 1996) gave him credit for attempting to re-site welfare within its original moral framework.

[60] The economic model (From Waddell 2002):

- Incapacity benefit trends reflect economic pressures and incentives more than actual disability.

- Recipients of benefits are advantaged by the social security system, at a high cost to society and the taxpayer.

- Current social security trends are best overcome by adjusting the incentives and control mechanisms of the social security system.

- This model implies that social security trends are a matter of economic forces and individual choice.

The economic model is commonly applied to welfare debates on poverty and unemployment, but it is equally applicable to incapacity benefits. Normally, work is vital to the family's financial and social situation but when the bread winner is sick or disabled the incentives and controls of sick pay, social security and workers compensation benefits become equally important.

[61] Loeser *et al* (995) reviewed workers compensation studies in LBP and concluded that a 10% increase in wage replacement rates is associated with a 1-11% increase in the number of claims and a 2-11% increase in the average duration of claims. Waddell & Norlund (2000) analysed social security trends in Sweden compared with other European countries and concluded that:

- The financial level of benefits has a relatively small effect on the number of claims and the duration on benefits.

- The structure of the social security or compensation system and the availability and ease or difficulty of getting social benefits or compensation (i.e. the control mechanisms: eligibility criteria, the definition and assessment of incapacity, and the claims, adjudication and appeals procedures) have a greater impact on the number of claims and on the number and duration of benefits paid.

Gardiner (1997) reviewed empirical UK social security evidence that suggested financial incentives and benefit traps are less important than once assumed. Corden & Sainsbury (2001) found lack of awareness, low take up and limited evidence of effectiveness for the DWP financial incentives available to IB recipients at that time.

[62] There is philosophical debate about the extent of free will and individual responsibility for our actions (individualism) -v- the extent to which we are under the influence of biological, psychological and social forces (determinism) (Dennett 2003). However, many modern philosophers and politicians, the justice system, most ordinary social observation and current social security trends all suggest that most social behaviour is a matter of conscious decision and choice.

[63] Interestingly, intent comes from criminal law and does not apply in civil law, which might have been expected to be more relevant to the social security setting.

[64] Which can obviously be argued.

[65] New Labour's 'Third Way' was arguably an attempt to strike a balance between the 'Old' Labour emphasis on universal rights and the Neoconservative emphasis on individual character and responsibilities (Dwyer 1998, Lund 1999, Powell 2000).

66 'The duty of us all: to help individuals and families to realise their full potential and live a dignified life, by promoting economic independence through work, by relieving poverty where it cannot be prevented and by building a strong and cohesive society where rights are matched by responsibilities' (HM Government 1998a).

67 'Disabled people (should be) regarded as equal citizens with full rights and responsibilities. Three main dimensions are identified:
    a Economic: disabled people are seen as contributing members of society as both workers and valued customers or users.
    b Political: disabled people are recognized as empowered individuals, and voters, and a powerful interest group.
    c Moral: disabled people are seen as active citizens with all that implies in terms of rights and responsibilities' (Oliver 2004)

68 Unless serious injury or illness leaves permanent impairment that provides grounds for a disability pension

69 For example: 'Low back pain should be viewed as a chronic problem with an untidy pattern of grumbling symptoms and periods of relative freedom from pain and disability interspersed with acute episodes, exacerbations, and recurrences' (Croft *et al* 1998).

70 This is a religious and moral argument about human conduct but reaches similar conclusions to the philosophical and social argument given in the previous section.

71 Leaving aside the separate debate about conditions that may be attributed to lifestyle, e.g. smoking or alcohol-related disease (Finerman & Bennett 1995)

72 There is no good evidence on the accuracy or validity of self-certification but, in general, as assessment becomes more objective the rates and levels of reported disability fall (Labour Force Surveys vs. OPCS surveys in the same populations).

73 Most sick certificates are issued during a consultation for the purpose of seeking health care, which would have occurred anyway. Although anecdotal accounts are common (Greenhalgh 2004), it is difficult to judge how many GP consultations are for the *primary* purpose of sick certification.

74 In practice, employers also use them for company and sick pay purposes.

75 For the first six months this relates to the patient's own work – the 'own occupation test' (Social Security (Incapacity for Work) Act 1994.

76 Though this is the claimant's own account of what they were advised, which may or may not be accurate or may simply be the claimant's own opinion endorsed by or attributed to their doctor (Goldestone & Douglas 2003).

77 See Chapter 2.1 on Work and Worklessness.

78 The other, relatively rare basis for certification is if the patient working would create a risk to others, e.g. a bus driver with epilepsy.

79 Regulation and administrative changes in Sweden in 1995 attempted to focus sick certification solely on the patient's medical condition but had no lasting impact on the amount or duration of sick certification (Englund *et al* 2000, Arrelov *et al* 2003).

80 Some of the main DWP studies are Ritchie *et al* (1993), Hiscock & Ritchie (2001) and Mowlam & Lewis (2005). Key reviews include Sawney (2002) and Alexanderson & Norlund (2004)

[81] Though there is a lack of high quality scientific research on many aspects of sick certification (Alexanderson & Norlund 2004).

[82] Which cannot be accounted for by medical or socio-demographic factors.

[83] A recent survey showed that >90% of businesses think that GPs are ineffective in managing sickness absence lasting > 4 weeks, and nearly 30% feel that sick certificates can be a barrier to rehabilitation (EEF 2004a & b).

[84] Though employers are unwilling to take this on themselves and in particular are unwilling to shoulder the perceived costs, despite the costs of sickness absence and the economic business case for doing so.

[85] Based on the rights and responsibilities of the sick role and the right of society to check entitlement. This is an accepted principle and practice in occupational sick pay schemes, insurance claims and civil litigation for personal injury compensation.

[86] Though to keep this in perspective, UK has the lowest sickness absence rate in northern Europe apart from Ireland (Gimeno et al 2004).

[87] The four main disability and incapacity benefits are Incapacity Benefit, Severe Disablement Allowance, Disability Living Allowance and Income Support with disability premiums.

[88] Unless stated otherwise, all DWP statistics in this review refer to the number of 'recipients' of each benefit which for most benefits is the number of 'beneficiaries' who receive payments. However, for IB, a significant number of people who fulfil the incapacity criteria do not have full NI entitlement to the benefit so do not receive cash payment of IB but instead receive 'credits only'. These 'credits' provide access to a wide range of other financial benefits including NI contributions (and hence retirement pension in due course), other social security benefits and supplements including in particular disability premium if they fulfil the low income and means-tested criteria for IS, and relief of various charges. 39% of 'recipients' of IB now receive 'credits only'. All the other sickness and disability benefits do not have NI contribution requirements, so there are no 'credits only'.

[89] Bevan & Hayday (2001) estimated that total sickness absence costs ranged from 2-16% of a firm's annual salary bill and that the average cost of absence per employee was £465 - £2261 per annum. That would give a very much higher total cost of about £45 billion per annum.

[90] **DWP estimated benefit expenditure 2004-05** (DWP Departmental Report 2004)

Benefit	Expenditure (£billions)
Incapacity Benefit	6.76
Severe Disablement Allowance	0.72
Disability Living Allowance	8.16
Income Support (sick and disabled)	2.50
Industrial Injuries Disablement Benefit	0.76
Carer's Allowance	1.12
Total	**£20 billion**

[91] The lower estimate is based on the standard CBI figure, the higher estimate is based on Bevan & Hayday (2001), and without any allowance for the cost of ill health retirement.

92 After the first 123 weeks.

93 Though see Footnote 3.

94 Though note criticisms of the whole conceptual approach and detailed methodology of OPCS surveys by some disabled people (Abberley 1991, Barnes 1991).

95 Though that was again mainly among the elderly.

96 This wording was originally developed by Corporate Medical Group in discussions with Ministers about 1994-95 during development of the medical assessment for IB. The first published reference we have been able to find was DSS (1996).

97 The American test is highly expensive to administer in terms of scarce medical resource (much more than the current UK test).

98 See Appendix 2.

99 The insurance industry has developed similar criteria for judging ability to work (Activities of Daily Work: ADW), which complement ADL (Activities of Daily Living), and stand good comparison with the items of the PCA. The threshold for eligibility for Total and Permanent Disability is failing three of six abilities: Walking, Manual dexterity, Sitting, Responsibility and independence, Financial competence, Communication.

100 Medical Services Medical Advisers approved by the Secretary of State.

101 DWP clerical staff.

102 Pain was initially included as a 15th item but this led to 'double-counting'.

103 In line with social policy in most EU countries (OECD 2003, Prinz 2003).

104 DWP has defined (in)capacity as the extent to which the person in (un)able to carry out the physical and mental activities specified in the schedule (i.e. the functional areas covered by the Personal Capability Assessment). Capability is defined as the ability to carry out the physical and mental activities specified in the schedule.

105 Arskey et al (2002) mapped 2437 employment focused services for disabled people in Britain. Most focused on people with a particular type of impairment: 53% targeted people with learning disabilities; 46% targeted people with mental health problems. The most common services were vocational training, work placement and supported employment.

106 With widely ranging estimates from a few per cent to about half, depending on how 'access' to occupational health is defined (HSE 2002, Holland-Elliott 2004)

107 *Design for Living* by the Welsh Assembly (2005) sets out an ambitious 10-year health care delivery and public health strategy to improve the health of people in Wales. Vocational rehabilitation and several other initiatives aimed at returning people to the world of work feature prominently. This and other major ventures such as *Wales a Better Country* and *Making the Connections* stress improving Occupational Health Services. There is a concerted effort to connect with employers to address health inequalities, particularly in the South Wales Valleys and other areas of post-industrial decline where economic inactivity and morbidity are significantly higher than the national average. A well-funded programme of regeneration in the Head of the Valleys communities recognises the importance of vocational rehabilitation and job retention schemes in achieving prosperity and sustainability.

[108] Figures in late 2004 actually showed a very small reduction of 0.2% though this is not statistically significant. Although it has recently been suggested that the headline figures may be under-estimated by 5%, that is unlikely to change the trends.

[109] Though again comparisons should be made with caution because of the wide variation in benefit systems.

[110] 'Take the man redundant in his fifties. The benefits system says: get through your medical and we will treat you as early retired. Just don't ask us to do something' (Blair 1997). Unfortunately, despite improvements, that is probably equally true today.

[111] In principle these goals should be complementary, but in practice attempting to allow for every eventuality and subsequent appeals and Commissioners decisions often makes the legislation and regulations increasingly complex. Thus, there is some inevitable tension between these goals.

[112] Otherwise, there is no need to consider incapacity benefits any further.

[113] This has been discussed at various points already and will be discussed further later.

[114] From the mid-1990s, there was a sudden and nearly simultaneous assault on 'fraud' in social security systems across Europe (ISSA 1996). There was little evidence of any upsurge in fraud in so many different settings, but political fashions may be more infectious. Attacks on fraud seem tempting when other forms of cost saving are limited, and they generate less political resistance than most other policies in this highly contentious field.

[115] This does not imply that we should return to the 1979 system because, interestingly, exactly the same things were said then (NAO 1989).

[116] Given the high prevalence of symptoms in normal people, there is no need to 'invent' illness.

[117] That is lower than for any other benefits, e.g. 6% for JSA and 3.6% for IS.

[118] Though this also is an extremely complex question, with unresolved debate about the extent to which this is 'conscious' intent to deceive or due to 'unconscious' psychosocial factors (Waddell 2004a).

[119] apart from Denmark and Sweden

[120] In practice, Beveridge himself qualified this principle with additional supplements for the extra costs of long-term sickness and compensation for injuries 'sustained while serving in the national interest'.

[121] There is a third, earlier gateway to very short-term sickness absence from work for odd days or 'sickies'. This is entirely a matter of individual decision and self-certification with no access or input from medical certification or DWP. It has recently received a lot of attention as part of the debate about the 'sickness culture', but it is a separate issue that probably bears little or no relation to the longer-term sickness or disability considered in this paper. It needs to be addressed as a matter of occupational health, sickness absence management and sick pay conditions.

[122] Overall, 69% of non-medical health professionals are in favour of their profession taking on sick certification: 88% of osteopaths and chiropractors; 83% of Primary Care Nurse Practitioners; 72% of physiotherapists; but only 61% of Occupational Health Nurses and 55% of clinical psychologists (Niven 2005)

[123] 37% of non-medical health professionals stated they had no awareness of the DWP criteria for issuing advice on fitness for work or sick certificates. 52% of Clinical Psychologists and 38% of Occupational Therapists felt it could damage relationships with patients (Niven 2005).

[124] 70% of non-medical health professionals felt that taking on sick certification would result in an increased workload (Niven 2005).

[125] Despite earlier qualitative studies suggesting that GPs are not interested (Hiscock & Ritchie 2001), more recent DWP training material has been well received (by the small number of trainee and qualified GPs who participated) showing that at least some GPs are willing to enter this difficult area if it is presented properly. Effective monitoring would be likely to lead to a significant increase in take-up of training.

[126] Computerisation of certification would:

- Save GP time by mechanising a task carried out by pen and paper and essentially unchanged since 1922;

- Allow a permanent record to be kept of the advice given, required as the new GP contract makes issuing statements a responsibility of the group of practice doctors rather than individual GPs;

- Make certification records available for on-line epidemiological study (for example, to detect 'flu outbreaks and their spread);

- Allow comprehensive research into GP certification practices;

- Allow audit, re-training and re-validation of this task as for any other part of clinical practice;

- To facilitate these tasks, build an audit tool into the computerised statement issuing process so that it is easily accomplished by GPs;

- Free GPs from the constraints of the current small paper form, and allow a higher profile to be given to comments on keeping patients in work (with adjustments if necessary) rather than signing them off work entirely.

[127] e.g. showing that positive advice about work and good sick certification practice leads to faster return to work and less longer-term incapacity, while negative advice about work and too liberal sick certification leads to more longer-term worklessness and ill-health.

[128] There are other long-standing drivers in the same direction such as Pathways to Work and the Cabinet Office Review of GP bureaucracy.

[129] Access to health care is a basic human right (United Nations 1948), which is and should be distinct from the right to social security, i.e. the need for health care and entitlement to sickness and disability benefits are separate issues.

[130] When there is a high chance that he or she will be advised that there is no indication for any surgical investigation or intervention.

[131] Unless otherwise stated, DH refers to the Department of Health for England. This deals solely with England, while Wales, Scotland and Northern Ireland have their own Departments of Health.

[132] 'Employer' is used as a collective term for businesses, companies, senior management, line managers and supervisors.

[133] This was the name of a Health and Safety Executive campaign 1995-2001.

[134] Additional information can be found on the following websites: Health and Safety Executive (**www.hse.gov.uk**); Trades Union Congress (**www.tuc.org.uk**); Confederation of British Industry (**www.cbi.org.uk**); Institute of Directors (**www.iod.co.uk**); Employers Forum (**www.employers-forum.co.uk**); Federation of Small Businesses (**www.fsb.org.uk**); Chartered Institute of Personnel and Development (**www.cipd.org.uk**); Association of British Insurers (**www.abi.org.uk**); International Underwriters Association (**www.iua.co.uk**).

[135] James *et al* (2002, 2003) and NAO (2004) have reviewed current thinking and evidence on sickness absence management. The Engineering Employers Federation (EEF 2004a & b) and Nice &Thornton (2004) have surveyed current UK employer attitudes and practice on sickness absence. There are several good recent guides to sickness absence management (EEF 2004b, HSE 2004).

[136] In North America this is more commonly called 'disability management' (NIDMAR 2000), including management practices which support the coordination of work accommodations, health care and rehabilitation interventions to promote the continued safe employment of people with disabilities.

[137] Much of the evidence is not of high scientific quality: most of it is from cohort studies and there is a lack of randomized controlled trials (Krause *et al* 1998).

[138] The views of GPs or other mental health professionals involved in care of claimants with mild/moderate mental health conditions on 'whether they think there would be a substantial risk to the health of the claimant if they were found to be capable of work' (Social Security Benefits Agency 1995) is a particular anomaly that should be stopped.

[139] Better medical evidence base for benefit decisions (DWP Expert Reference Group on IB Reform 2001):

- severe medical conditions recognized more readily

- remaining capacity and potential for rehabilitation recognized more readily

- better medical advice to decision-makers.

- more cases could be decided on the basis of paper evidence

[140] The Better Medical Evidence Gathering Pilot in the Sheffield and Rotherham area during 2002 (Sainsbury *et al* 2003, Marlow & McLaughlin 2003, Sainsbury & Corden 2004)).

[141] Keeping all records reviewed, even for 3 years, could have major implications for storage, while keeping only key records would involve selection. Physical capacity might be overcome eventually be electronic storage, though that would have major resource and funding implications. It may be more practical to summarise the factual medical evidence into the Medical Adviser's report.

[142] The US Guides to the evaluation of permanent impairment (AMA 2000) emphasise that: 'Impairment should not be considered permanent until maximum medical rehabilitation has been achieved and until, in the physician's best clinical judgment, the impairment is static and well-established'.

[143] That definition of permanent is also similar to the NHS Pension Scheme Ill-health retirement benefits Statutory Provisions and Interpretation, which define permanently incapable as 'will not be able, through their medical condition, to work before the normal retirement age of the Scheme (age 60). - - - The level of proof required is the civil measure of 'on the balance of

probabilities". The Statutory Provisions and Interpretation also noted that the Scheme's medical advisers held the view that 'until all reasonable treatment options have been explored and the results evaluated, it is difficult to offer an opinion on permanence'.

[144] E.g. to include people with chronic fatigue syndrome.

[145] Though there is another heated debate about whether or not chronic fatigue syndrome, 'ME', fibromyalgia, etc. are 'well defined clinical conditions' and whether or not they have a definite biological/pathological basis (Aylward 1999, Barsky & Borus 1999, Wessely *et al* 1999).

[146] Despite certain North American attempts to define pain as an impairment to meet the demands of their compensation system (Waddell 2004a).

[147] Though the Law Commission (England) (1998) pointed out that the ICD-10 (WHO 1992-94) and DSM-IV (American Psychiatric Society 1994) classifications 'are meant to serve as guidelines to be informed by clinical judgment', should 'not be applied mechanically' and 'were not prepared for such legal purposes'.

[148] The only other possibility is the demonstration of 'marked life disruption' (Waddell 2004a). In the context of chronic pain or fatigue, this has been described as (WCBA 2004):

'determined by psychological assessment, interviews, and standardised testing, and refers to difficulty or dysfunction in the following areas:

- physical/vegetative functioning;
- affective state;
- cognitive aspects;
- vocational aspects;
- family relationships;
- social/recreational activities;
- behavior/daily activities.'

However, this is not likely to be a practical proposition for widespread use.

[149] It is common to think of the health condition as the problem and health care as the solution, but sometimes health care can become part of the problem, e.g. waiting lists for consultation or treatment can be a barrier to early return to work (James *et al* 2003; Waddell & Burton 2004b, Sirvastava & Chamberlain 2005).

[150] Incapacity is not a direct consequence of a health condition: it depends more on the relative balance between the worker's physical and mental capacity -v- the physical and mental demands of work (Feuerstein 1991; Feuerstein & Zastowny 1999).

[151] At present, Work Focused Interviews consist of some basic questions about employment history, qualifications and a basic skills screening, but do not provide enough information to identify barriers or support needs, or to develop an individualized return to work plan.

[152] Screening has two main aims (Waddell *et al* 2003):

- to identify those at risk of developing long-term incapacity, who need extra help
- for those at risk, to assess their needs and what can be done to help

Historically and conceptually, there are two different kinds of screening:

a Actuarial assessment of risk forms the historical basis of the insurance industry, which has developed sophisticated methods of identifying and weighting 'risk markers'. These data are pragmatic and *associated* with the risk, whether or not they have any causal or explanatory significance regarding the outcome or possible intervention. This is largely socio-demographic data, available in an administrative database. Actuarial science is based on complex mathematics, but in practice this produces tables of risk that are simple to use and score, and transparent.

b Clinical and psychosocial screening is more interested in how and why some people develop long-term incapacity and what can be done about it. Medicine has always been interested in predicting likely progress and outcomes, but historically that was based on isolated items of information and general clinical judgment with little scientific basis. Modern clinical screening has a stronger scientific and statistical foundation (Armitage & Berry 1994), but remains focused on clinical and psychosocial measures, clinical outcomes and return to work (which may not be quite the same as coming off benefit).

The type, timing, and accuracy of screening are linked, so screening must be directed to and designed for specific purpose(s), e.g.:

a 'administrative' screening of all claimants, largely using socio-demographic risk markers, can be used to identify those at risk of long-term incapacity, who may need more support. The main problem is how to limit the numbers and to deal with false negatives and false positives. An alternative, simpler approach is to regard all claimants who have been off work for six months to be at >50% risk of long-term incapacity (DWP administrative data) and in need of extra help. However, screening might identify some claimants at higher risk who could be offered extra help earlier.

b More detailed, individual assessment of claimants (possibly those identified as being at risk), focused on clinical, psychosocial and work-related factors, is necessary to identify barriers to return to work and to inform rehabilitation and support into work interventions.

[153] In screening, it is generally not possible to achieve > 70-80% sensitivity and specificity (Waddell *et al* 2003, Bryson & Kasparova 2003), so there are always large numbers of false positives (inclusion errors - claimants identified as being at risk when they are not really - they might be given an intervention they do not need, leading to deadweight losses) and false negatives (exclusion errors – claimants who are at risk but who are not identified by the screening tool - they might not be provided with the help they really do need).

[154] Cognitive behavioural interventions for chronic pain are designed to help patients improve their pain, disability and emotional distress by developing greater personal control and ability to undertake self-management of their condition. Despite the demonstrated efficacy of these interventions (Morley *et al* 1999, Clark 2005), some patients do not respond. The 'stages of change' model (Proschaska & DiClemente 1983, Proshaska *et al* 1991, Kerns *et al* 1997) was developed to try to explain why some patients are more or less responsive to cognitive behavioural interventions. Basically, the 'stages of change' model suggests that patients vary in their readiness to undertake an active self-management approach as an alternative to being the passive recipients of medical treatment and awaiting 'cure'. These stages are generally labeled:

1 Pre-contemplation – the stage in which people express little interest in changing their health behaviour.

2 Contemplation – the stage in which people say they are thinking about the possibility of changing their health behaviour but appear unlikely to make that change soon.

3 Preparation – the stage during which people actively consider attempts to change and are likely to do so within a month.

4 Action – the stage in which people actively work toward changing their health behaviour.

5 Maintenance – the stage in which people work to maintain changes in their health behaviour.

[155] Deadweight refers to the 'dead' or 'ineffective' element of a policy intervention: clients who receive an intervention who do not really need it or who will fail to benefit. Although the term deadweight is widely used, it is often used loosely without precise definition. It appears to be used in DWP discussions with two different meanings, which may be called (a) 'economic' and (b) 'clinical'. The 'economic' definition of deadweight comes from theory of taxation - what would have happened anyway even without the intervention. In the present context it refers to clients who receive a work-focused intervention but would have returned to work without intervention. The more 'clinical' definition of deadweight considers the success rate, the 'net gain' or 'value added' by an intervention, so clinical deadweight is all those who receive the intervention but do not benefit from it. This includes those who would have returned to work anyway (i.e. the economic deadweight) plus those who do not respond to the intervention and remain on long-term incapacity. Thus clinical deadweight also depends on the (in)effectiveness of the intervention, which introduces a completely different element (Waddell *et al* 2003).

[156] A study of social security claimants with upper limb symptoms in the Netherlands showed that 98% of occupational health doctors attributed the symptoms to work and 35% to 'disregarding pain', while 52% advised 'limited physical activity with arm'. Although these doctors' intent was to promote return to work, such perceptions and advice are probably likely to reinforce rather than reduce incapacity for work. (Paper presented at *Ape* social policy seminar, Amsterdam, The Netherlands, 8 April 2005.)

[157] The common assumption that treatment will 'cure' pathology and/or relieve symptoms, and so automatically restore function has not worked for the minority who fail to 'recover' and move on to IB. That is because (a) there is a weak correlation between symptoms and incapacity, (b) clinical outcomes are not necessarily the same as occupational outcomes c) incapacity has more to do with social and occupational issues than with health related symptoms.

[158] There is some evidence that vocational rehabilitation is more effective in an occupational setting that locates them conceptually and in practice closer to their goal (Waddell & Burton 2004b). This may raise some new and interesting questions about whether the DWP or the NHS should provide and pay for which elements of such services. That usually raises debate about which will benefit from any savings, though in truly joined-up government that should not matter!

[159] The Disability Rights Commission argues that the Access to Work scheme should be promoted more for people with common health problems, many of whom would only require minor elements of the scheme, rather than promoting it mainly for 'disabled people' (DRC 2003b). The National Employment Panel have also recommended improvements in the Access to Work scheme to make it more widely used and to improve the service to (small) employers (NEP 2005).

[160] *The Back Book* (Roland *et al* 2002) is internationally recognized to be one of the best patient educational materials available for patients with acute low back pain. It is evidence based, in line with current clinical and occupational health guidelines, and one of the few such materials that has been shown to be effective in randomized controlled trials (Waddell & Burton 2004a).

[161] Such pilot studies should be distinguished from 'pure' scientific research such as the gold standard of a randomized controlled trial (RCT): they serve a different though complementary purpose (Waddell & Burton 2004b). These are pragmatic studies in a real life situation where they must address the practicalities of implementation. It is not possible to achieve the same degree of control of the experimental intervention and setting, and the demands of scientific rigour must be adjusted accordingly. They are studies of efficacy rather than clinical effectiveness, and may reasonably inform implementation and practicalities as much as test the intervention itself. Nevertheless, when a pilot study on such a large scale achieves results of this magnitude, it is arguably even more impressive than an RCT.

[162] Though see Deacon (1998) and Walker (2003) for more thoughtful and critical academic analysis to the various proposals.

[163] There were particularly strong reactions to any possibility of any 'sick or disabled' person who met the current criteria for entitlement to incapacity or disability benefits facing any reduction in entitlement, any pressure to seek work, or any (even partial) cut in their benefits for any reason.

[164] Surely it is not true that 'someone who's had a mental breakdown' cannot ever *reasonably be expected* to work – as suggested by one mental health lobby group?

[165] Which in a welfare context is sometimes described as 'free-riding'.

[166] This is *not* paternalism (New 1999, White 2004a). Paternalism is when the state, policy makers or the benefits system makes judgments about what is best for the individual's own good, rather than leaving the individual free to decide for him or herself. However, paternalism relates to actions or behaviour that are self-regarding' i.e. that only concern the individual and do not cause any 'harm' or cost to others (Mill 1859). Claiming benefits has a direct financial cost to society and the taxpayer, so this is rather in the nature of a social contract. Moreover, the claimant has freedom of choice whether or not he or she initiates a claim for benefit.

[167] Even if there is some suspicion that they assume conditionality applies to other kinds of benefit recipients and not to themselves!

[168] Stanley *et al* (2004) then applied these tests to various conditionality policies, including those for disabled people. They concluded that the extension of work-related conditions to the receipt of IB did meet the rationale test and could be justified through the social democratic rationale of promoting equality of opportunity, by seeking to enhance disabled people's chances of moving into work. However, to fully meet the rationale test, the basic rationale and structure of IB needed to be changed. At the time they were writing (before any *Pathways* results) they considered there was no evidence that such a policy was effective, so the evidence test was not met. They concluded that the unfair side effects test imposed considerable practical challenges but that these were not insurmountable.

[169] That is supported by public opinion. 59% believe that 'cutting welfare benefits would damage too many people's lives' (British Social Attitudes Survey 2001).

[170] Collins & Rossiter (2004) then applied these tests to different conditionality policies and concluded that unemployment policy did pass their tests while family and housing policies did not. They did not consider sickness or disability.

[171] The Disability Rights Commission (Howard 2004a) have also developed a list of appraisal questions for policy makers and programme delivery.

Key questions for policy-makers:

- What are the objectives and outcomes for individuals, administrators and the public?

- Are they consistent with other policies (including the DDA)

- What behavioural change is expected and is it clear how individuals can demonstrate this?

- Does the sanction link to the condition and is it proportionate?

- Does applying the condition, and the sanction, lead to negative outcomes or hardship for individuals?

- Will incomes of those individuals rise or fall?

Key questions for programme delivery:

- Are individuals and advisers aware of the conditions and the sanctions, and how compliance is demonstrated?

- Have advisers worked to achieve compliance without using sanctions?

- Have advisers ensured individuals are aware of safeguards and rights of appeal?

- Have sanctions been applied consistently and fairly?

- Can it be shown that sanctions will not be disproportionately applied to the most vulnerable people?

[172] The Donner Commission Report is only available in the original Dutch and has never been translated into English (W de Boer, personal communication). DWP files include various descriptions and comments. The key features are summarized in Waddell *et al* (2002).

[173] Using the example of mental illness, the insurance industry approach to total and permanent disability generally consists of (P White, personal communication):

1. There is independent medical evidence (i.e. by an independent medical examination) that the claimant is suffering from a *diagnosable mental disorder*, which is not the result of their own behaviour (e.g. alcohol misuse). (Some insurance companies do not have a substance misuse exemption, but it is generally considered to be useful, not least for the claimants.)

2. There is good evidence of sufficient disability that *the claimant is not able to return to work in the foreseeable future* (this may involve attempts to return to work that have failed). For assessing functional capacity, there is good anecdotal evidence from the insurance industry that it is often more useful to have the independent examination carried out by a doctor qualified in disability assessment medicine or by a non-medical health professional such as an occupational therapist or occupational psychologist.

3. The claimant has received at least *two years of optimal medical treatment* (OMT) by a recognised medical specialist. It is surprising how many claims fail to meet this criteria. The commonest reasons for the failure of OMT are that the GP has not referred the patient, the specialist has not considered a biopsychosocial approach to rehabilitation, or a biopsychosocial rehabilitation approach has not been available in the locality where the claimant lives.

4. In effect, this usually means that *at least three years of disabling illness* are needed for a mental health or functional disorders total and permanent disability claim to be successful.